A Professional and Practitioner's Guide to Public Relations Research, Measurement, and Evaluation

A Professional and Practitioner's Guide to Public Relations Research, Measurement, and Evaluation

Third Edition

David Michaelson and Don W. Stacks

BEP BUSINESS EXPERT PRESS

A Professional and Practitioner's Guide to Public Relations Research, Measurement, and Evaluation, Third Edition

First published in 2010 by
Business Expert Press, LLC
222 East 46th Street, New York, NY 10017
www.businessexpertpress.com

ISBN-13: 978-1-63157-761-1 (paperback)
ISBN-13: 978-1-63157-762-8 (e-book)

Business Expert Press Public Relations Collection

Collection ISSN: 2157-345X (print)
Collection ISSN: 2157-3476 (electronic)

Cover and interior design by Exeter Premedia Services Private Ltd., Chennai, India

Third edition: 2017

10 9 8 7 6 5 4 3 2 1

Printed in the United States of America.

This book is dedicated to Robin Schiff and Robin Stacks—
the light of both of our lives.

Abstract

Contemporary public relations practice has developed over the last several decades from the weak third sister in the marketing, advertising, and public relations mix to a full player. To help you keep up to speed with the exciting changes and developments in communication theory and practice, this book will provide you with the necessary understanding of the problems and promises of public relations research, measurement, and evaluation. As a public relations professional, this book will act as a guide to effective use of methods, measures, and evaluation in providing grounded evidence of the success (or failure) of public relations campaigns. This outstanding contribution takes a best practices approach—one that focuses on taking the appropriate method and rigorously applying that method to collect the data that best answer the objectives of the research. It also presents an approach to public relations that focuses on establishing the profession's impact on the client's return on investment in the public relations function, whether that function be aimed at internal or external audiences using standardized measures. By the end of the book, you will understand why and how research is conducted and will be able to apply best practice standards to any research done by supply-side vendors or internal research departments.

Keywords

content analysis, evaluation, experimentation, focus groups, goals and objectives, interviewing, measurement, media analysis, nonfinancial indicators, public relations, qualitative research, quantitative research, research, research methods, return on expectation (ROE), return on investment (ROI), sampling, secondary research, social media analytics, standardized measurement, statistical analysis, survey and poll research

Contents

Preface

Seven years ago we had just completed the first edition of *A Practitioner's Guide to Public Relations Research, Measurement, and Evaluation*. In the introduction to that edition, we noted that while the technology surrounding the profession of public relations has changed dramatically over the past several decades, the core principles of the research as well as the value of effective measurement remained the same. As we noted in both the first and second editions of this book, we continue to hold to that perspective. Nonetheless, public relations research remains a dynamic field and the advances in the field over the past several years, particularly in the developments of *standardized measures* of public relations, the rise of social media and the use of online surveys led us to update our thinking about the needs of the profession. These advances include, how to measure program effectiveness, and an understanding of the dynamics for assessing the overall efficacy of public relations and corporate communication, as well as evaluating the overall research process.

This edition expands on the second edition by looking at where measurement is to be applied in the communication process and how social media analytics has helped up better understand the role and importance of advocacy in public relations.

On a personal note, we want to again recognize our enduring friendship that has continued to develop and grow during this work. Our work together has been the highlight of both of our careers and we look forward to even more collaboration over the next decade.

David Michaelson
New York, NY

Don W. Stacks
University of Miami, Miami, FL

PART I

Introduction to Public Relations Research, Measurement, and Evaluation

Part I introduces the reader to the practice of public relations and the concept of "Best Practices." Chapter 1 provides a quick glance on the history of *contemporary* public relations practice and how best practices approach makes public relations results important to a company or client. Chapter 2 presents the most current thoughts on measurement standardization and argues that for public relations to be considered a profession, it must establish standards against which its outcomes can be compared and set a basis for the function as a profession. The professional is the *strategist* who designs the public relation campaign and, in turn, must collect, assess, and evaluate data that tells him or her whether the program is on target and make corrections as needed.

Chapter 3 lays out the role of public relations as a necessary business function and establishes the groundwork for public relations research—research that focuses on business goals and objectives and the stating of such public relations goals and objectives that are measurable and indicative (can be correlated with) of business's investment in public relations through *return on investment* (ROI). It also introduces the reader to public relations' outcomes and what is labeled *return on expectations* (ROE). Finally, Chapter 4 introduces the concept of measurement, assessment, and evaluation of public relations through a coordinated campaign aimed at measuring predispositions toward behavior through attitude, belief, and value measures.

CHAPTER 1

Introduction to Research and Evaluations in Public Relations

Contemporary public relations practice has developed since the mid-20th century from the weak third sister in the marketing, advertising, and public relations mix to gain status as a full and equal player in the corporate suite. Part of that development can be traced to a change in the way public relations is practiced. The early days of public relations functions—limited to media relations and "press agentry"—have evolved to a sophisticated array of communications where public relations is no longer an afterthought, but is an integral part of the communications mix.

A central reason for this change in the perceptions of and stature of public relations in the communications world is the inclusion of research, measurement, and evaluation as a core part of the practice—tools that have been integral to the practice of marketing and advertising for decades. The purpose of this book is to provide the business reader and communications professional with the necessary and practical understanding of the problems and promises of public relations research, measurement, and evaluation—and more importantly as a guide to the effective use of methods, measures, and analysis in providing grounded evidence of the success (or failure) of public relations campaigns.

Defining Public Relations and Its Objectives

Why exactly is this profession called public relations? For many it is simply one of the three promotional areas that management uses to get its message out: marketing, advertising, and public relations. What has differentiated them in the past can be viewed in terms of (a) what a business expects it to do and (b) the kinds of outcomes it produces. In all too many eyes, public relations only includes dealing with *media relations*. That is, public relations' objective is to get coverage of the business—preferably positive—through the placement of articles and the like as endorsed by journalists.

But public relations is much more than press agentry or media relations. It is better seen as an umbrella term for any number of departments in a business or corporation that seeks to get its messages out to various publics or audiences by managing the flow of information between an *organization* and its *publics* or audiences (Grunig and Hunt 1984). *Public* is a part of a population that has been selected for study; an *audience* is a specifically targeted group within that public that has been targeted for a company's messages. What then is public relations? First and foremost, public relations serves to manage the credibility, reputation, trust, relationship, and confidence of the general public in relation to the company (Stacks 2017). As Professor Donald K. Wright noted, "Public relations is the management function that identifies, establishes, and maintains mutually beneficial relationships between an organization and the various publics on which its success or failure depends" (Wright 1990).

How is public relations practiced if it is an umbrella concept? Its practice can be defined by its function in the organization. Public relations takes on the following functions, sometimes alone and at other times as a combined function. The following list neither is complete nor is it listed by importance of function:

- Community relations
- Corporate communication
- Customer relations
- Employee relations
- Financial relations
- Governmental relations
- Media relations
- Public affairs
- Strategic communication

What then are public relations' objectives? There are three major objectives any public relations campaign seeks to accomplish. The first is to ensure that the messages get out to their intended audiences and that they are understood (*informational objective*). The second is to monitor the campaign so that benchmarks are set regarding the acceptance of messages by target audiences in terms of cognitive, affective, and behavioral attitudinal or belief acceptance or rejection or maintenance ("motivational objective"). And, the third is predicting what the target audience will actually do based on the campaign ("behavioral objective"). As Stacks (2011) points out, each objective must be met and then monitored before the next objective can be obtained. In essence, public relations is a broad scale function that encompasses the full range of communication from message development, to message delivery, receipt of message, impact on target audiences, and effect on business outcomes.

In forthcoming chapters we will introduce a number of ideas of how a public relations campaign should operate and be measured across the full range of public relations. We will look at how traditional and digital public relations campaigns experienced unintended problems due to a lack of research and how the failure to establish measurable objectives, baselines, and benchmarks limits the effectiveness of public relations. More importantly, we introduce a practical approach to public relations research that will result in better and more effective communications programs. Finally, we will move from a focus on best practices to *standards*. Best practices are sufficient conditions to research and they have been in the profession surpassed by an understanding that standards must be set that allow for evaluation against set research and measurement metrics. It is only then that results can be evaluated and transmitted to the client.

A Brief History of Public Relations Research

The formal origins of public relations research can be traced to the 1950s (*The New York Times* 1990). During that period, a company called Group Attitudes Corporation was acquired by Hill & Knowlton (*The New York Times* 1990). The primary focus of Group Attitudes Corporation was to function as a standalone yet captive arm of the parent agency. Its work included research for the Tobacco Institute (Legacy Tobacco Document

Library n.d.), as well as for other Hill & Knowlton clients. The primary focus of this research, taken from a review of several published reports, was to assess reaction to communication messages and vehicles using processes that appear similar to the research methods employed by the advertising industry during this same period. This industry model was followed over the next 25 years with the establishment of research arms at several other public relations agencies. In addition to Hill & Knowlton, the major public relations agencies that have had research departments include Burson-Marsteller (Penn Schoen Berland), Ruder Finn (Research & Forecasts), Ketchum, Weber Shandwick (KRC), Edelman (Edelman Insights), Ogilvy Public Relations, APCO, Golin Harris and Cohn & Wolfe. For the most part, the primary function of these agency-based research departments was similar to the work initially conducted by Group Attitudes Corporation. Most of these research departments were created internally, with the notable exception of Penn Schoen Berland that was acquired by WPP and later merged into Burson-Marsteller.

As early as the 1930s, methods were also being developed by advertisers and their agencies that linked exposure and persuasion measures to actual store sales. In essence, testing, measurement, analysis, and evaluation systems became an integral part of the advertising industry. These systems became so institutionalized by mid-decade that an academic journal—*The Journal of Advertising Research*—as well as an industry association—The Advertising Research Foundation—were established in 1936. Other journals followed and formal academic programs in marketing research were established at major universities throughout the United States.

During the late 1970s, it became increasingly apparent that public relations differed considerably from other communications disciplines, and advertising in particular, in its ability to be measured and evaluated. At the time, advertising testing was dominated by a variety of measurement and evaluation systems of which the *day after recall (DAR)* method, popularized by Burke Marketing Research in its work with Procter & Gamble, was one of the most common systems in use. These advertising-focused methods took on a source orientation and assumed that the message was completely controlled by the communicator (Miller and

Levine 2009; Miller and Burgoon 1974). Therefore, the ability to test message recall and message efficacy were highly controllable and, in theory, projectable as to what would occur if the advertising were actually to be placed.

With the recognition that public relations needed a different set of measures because of the unique nature of the profession, senior management at several major public relations agencies charged their research departments with the task of finding more credible and reliable methods to measure the effectiveness of public relations activities. While a number of experiments were undertaken at that time, the primary benefit derived from this experimentation was a heightened awareness of the overall *value* of measuring public relations.

This heightened awareness, along with advances in specific technologies, led to the founding of a number of research companies during the 1980s and 1990s that specialize in measuring and evaluating the *outcome* of public relations activities as well as a trade association (International Association for Measurement and Evaluation of Communication, formerly known as the Association of Media Evaluation Companies, AMEC; www.amecorg.com), the Commission on Public Relations Research and Evaluation and the Research Fellows both of which are affiliated with the Institute for Public Relations (IPR) (www.instituteforpr.org). Currently, numerous companies offer services that measure and evaluate public relations activities. These companies have traditionally focused on evaluating only the outcomes of public relations, most commonly as media or press coverage that is a direct result of media relations activities (*outputs*). Few of their staff have formal or academic research training outside of "on the job" training in content analysis and, unlike other forms of communication research, these companies typically place little emphasis on formative, programmatic or diagnostic research, or research that is used to develop communication strategies and evaluate the impact of communication activities on the target audiences.

The primary limitation of these companies is their focus on an intermediary in the public relations process—the media—rather than on the target audience(s) for these communication activities.

While the legacy of these public relations research agencies, as well as the services they provide the public relations industry, is noteworthy, for the most part they have failed to significantly advance either the science or the art of public relations measurement and evaluation because of their strong emphasis on media relations.

This lack of advancement occurred despite an insistence and commitment by the leadership of the profession that research functions as a key and essential element to the creation of effective and successful public relations programs. These industry leaders demanding the use of research in the development and evaluation of public relations programs included luminaries such as Harold Burson (Burson-Marsteller), Daniel Edelman (Edelman Worldwide), and David Finn (Ruder Finn), each of whom established dedicated research functions in their respective agencies.

The most significant commitment of the industry leadership to this nascent discipline was the founding in 1956 of the Foundation for Public Relations Research and Education (now operating as the Institute for Public Relations [IPR]) in conjunction with the Public Relations Society of America (PRSA). Over the past six decades, the Foundation has continued to emphasize the critical importance of research in the public relations process and has dedicated itself to "the science beneath the art of public relations" (Institute for Public Relations 2011). Yet even with this dedicated effort, the IPR struggles to have the public relations profession and public relations professionals recognize the importance of research and measurement as an essential element in the development of effective public relations programs. This struggle continues in spite of ongoing programs, conferences, and educational forums that focus exclusively on this agenda.

Moving Toward Excellence in Public Relations Research

While the IPR has been a continuing beacon on issues surrounding the inclusion of research in all public relations efforts, the shift toward using research to establish the foundation of public relations practice achieved its most significant support during the 1980s. In 1984, the International Association of Business Communicators (IABC) Foundation (now the IABC Research Foundation) developed a request for proposals for the landmark study of "Excellence in Public Relations and Communication Management"—a project that produced three books, many reports, and dozens of seminars for professionals on creating excellence in the practice of public relations.

In its request for proposals, the IABC Board asked for proposals for research that would demonstrate how, why, and to what extent communication contributes to the achievement of organizational objectives and how the public relations function should be organized to best achieve those objectives. The Foundation awarded a $400,000 grant to a team that included Professors James E. Grunig and Larissa Grunig of the University of Maryland and Professor David Dozier of San Diego State University.

This team, among others, produced numerous publications on excellence in public relations practice that include five major volumes: *Excellence in Public Relations and Communication Management* by James Grunig (Grunig 1992); *Manager's Guide to Excellence in Public Relations and Communication Management* by David Dozier, Larissa Grunig, and James Grunig (Dozier, Grunig, and Grunig 1995); *Excellent Public Relations and Effective Organizations: A Study of Communication Management in Three Countries* by James Grunig, Larissa Grunig, and David Dozier (Grunig, Grunig, and Dozier 2002); *Managing Public Relations* by James Grunig and Professor Todd Hunt (Grunig and Hunt 1984); and *The Future of Excellence in Public Relations and Communication Management: Challenges for the Next Generation* by Professor Elizabeth Toth (Toth 2009).

In addition, the Arthur W. Page Society underwrote one of the earliest and most business-oriented research volumes, *Using Research in Public Relations: Applications to Program Management* by Professors Glen Broom and David Dozier (Broom and Dozier 1990).

Almost 30 years later, this remains the single largest grant in this field for the development of research protocols and practices. Yet even with this effort, the inclusion of research as a basic tool in the day-to-day practice of public relations professionals remains an elusive goal.

During this period, the profession has seen growth that is best represented by the multitude of companies specializing in this area, as well as a growing academic literature in the field. Yet, even with the increased attention paid, significant variations continue to exist with the varying range of approaches to public relations measurement and evaluation.

These variations have resulted in a lack of standard measures that can be used to gauge the success of a public relations program as well as in an uneven overall quality of the research being conducted. We will cover the argument for standards and standardization of measurement and evaluation in Chapter 2.

There are likely many reasons why research in support of public relations activities failed to progress significantly over the past 60 years. These reasons cited for this lack of advancement range from a genuine lack of commitment by the profession to a lack of resources to a proprietary approach to research as a business edge to changes in the practice of public relations among others. However, there are two other areas where public relations research has failed and these are most likely the greatest contributors to its limited growth. Those failures have been due to a systematic lack of understanding and application of standards for measurement and evaluation as well as a lack of knowledge of the best practices necessary to achieve the levels of excellence required to advance the overall practice of public relations.

The Concept of Best Practices

The history of *best practices* originated in business literature during the origins of the industrial era (Taylor 1919). The concept was that, while there are multiple approaches that can be used to achieve a task or a goal, there is often a single technique, method, or process that is more effective than others in reaching an established goal. In essence, a best practice is a technique, a method, a process, or an activity, which is more effective at delivering a particular outcome than any other technique, method, process, or activity. By using best practices, projects, tasks, and activities can be accomplished more effectively and with fewer problems and complications.

There is an essential relationship between public relations research and practice. In particular, there is the relationship between evaluation and measurement and successful public relations practices. The focus of this book is on what has been labeled "best practices in public relations measurement and evaluation systems" (Michaelson and Macleod 2007). Public relations best practice entails (1) clear and well-defined research objectives, (2) rigorous research design, and (3) detailed supporting documentation. Second, is the quality and substance of the research findings that (1) demonstrate effectiveness, (2) link outputs (tactics) to outcomes, (3) develop better communication programs, (4) demonstrate an impact on business outcomes, (5) demonstrate cost effectiveness, and (6) is applicable to a broad range of activities.

As the following chart demonstrates (see Figure 1.1), there is a strong interrelationship between the organization setting communication objectives, messages sent by the organization, how those messages are received, and how the outtakes from those messages impact on the objectives goals set by the organization.

As noted in a commentary from PriceWaterhouseCoopers, "Best practices are simply the best way to perform a business process. They are the means by which leading companies achieve top performance, and they serve as goals for other companies that are striving for excellence" (www.globalbestpractices.com/Home/Document.aspx?Link=Best+practices/FAQs&Idx=BestPracticesIdx).

While the concept of best practices is often applied to the operations of a specific company, the logical extension of best practices is its application to an overall industry through the establishment of standards against which assessments can be made. The goal of this book is to present best practices as they apply to public relations research, measurement, and

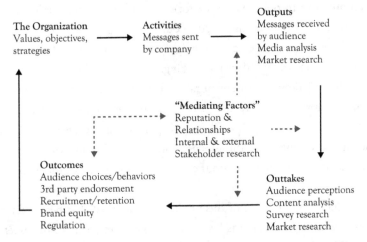

Figure 1.1 Best practices in public relations

evaluation. This presentation of these best practices is not to provide definitive answers to business problems associated with communication. Rather, these best practices are meant to be sources of creative insight for improving the application of public relations research and, in turn, improving the overall quality and effectiveness of public relations activities overall.

Before we can move to best practices, it is important to understand why we need to apply measurement to public relations activities. The role of public relations is to aid in achieving positive business outcomes. These outcomes are typically changes in attitude that impact behavior.

These attitudes are affected by communication to target audiences that contains messages which provide a motivation for audiences to take a desired action and in turn advocate for others to follow their behavior. These messages originate with the communicator and are delivered through paid, earned, shared, and owned media that is also referred to as P.E.S.O.

The challenge for most communicators is to understand where along this chain of communication challenges occur so that corrective actions can be taken which assure communication programs achieve their business objectives.

It is important to understand that applied public relations research, like all research in the business world, is a process. This process begins at a particular point as determined at the research onset and then moves from objective-to-objective with a focus on end-to-end measurement. It is a process in which findings add to our knowledge base and require us to both review prior research in the light of these findings and to use this information in strategic decision making.

Public relations measurement takes place at five distinct points where each is a critical juncture that can determine the success or failure of a communication program. These five points include creation of the message, distribution of the message, presence of the message through intermediaries, commentary on the messages and impact of the messages on behavior.

In the second edition of this book, we established that best practice public relations research was becoming the norm rather than the exception. We then advanced the notion that the profession must next look at standards against which measures of public relations performance are compared. In the next chapter we focus on three sets of standards as published in the industry-wide journal, *Public Relations Journal.* Chapter 2 discusses the communication stages that public relations activities can be evaluated against. These standards include measurement and evaluation, research ethics, and campaign effectiveness or excellence (Michaelson and Stacks 2011; Michaelson, Wright, and Stacks 2012; Bowen and Stacks 2013b).

What This Book Covers

Specifically, this book provides business readers with a basic understanding of the problems and promises of public relations research, measurement, and evaluation, while providing public relations professionals in present and future a guide to the effective use of the research methods, measures, and analytical insight that leads to meaningful evaluation in providing grounded evidence of the success (or failure) of public relations campaigns as well as for the necessary information to plan an effective campaign.

A Professional and Practitioner's Guide to Public Relations Research, Measurement, and Evaluation is divided into five broad parts broken into short chapters on:

- **Part I**: *Business and the Practice of Public Relations*
  The part covers three key areas that are essential to the creation of any effective public relations research.
  o The first is a review of basic public relations theory and how public relations activities can be tied to predicting measureable business outcomes (Chapter 1).
  o The second is a detailed analysis of the need for and standards against which public relations research can be evaluated and the application of these standards in evaluating the research and then communicating it to the client (Chapter 2).
  o The third is a detailed examination of public relations goals and objectives in light of measureable business objectives. Included in this review is a discussion of what public

relations goals and objectives can be realistically achieved
and acceptable measures for each of these basic goals and
objectives (Chapter 3).

o The fourth is a discussion of the elements of establishing
achievable public relations goals in light of overall business
objectives and then reviewing the processes for setting
communication objectives that are active, measurable, and
can be evaluated (Chapter 4).

- **Part II**: *Qualitative Methods for Effective Public Relations
Research, Measurement, and Evaluation*

  o Part II reviews the four major methodological areas that are
  commonly used in public relations research, measurement,
  and analysis. This part covers historical or secondary
  research (Chapter 5); qualitative research including
  in-depth interviews, focus groups, and participant-
  observation and quantitative research (Chapter 6); and
  content analysis (Chapter 7).

  o This part also introduces the use of baseline or benchmark,
  or both, measurements and their effective application,
  historical research methods, and how to best use secondary
  research sources as part of a complete public relations
  research program.

  o Particular emphasis is placed on content analysis as one
  of the most commonly used and misused public relations
  methodologies, as well as on quantitative methods.

- **Part III**: *Quantitative Methods for Effective Public Relations
Research Measurement and Evaluation*

  o Part III focuses on the quantitative dimension of public
  relations research, beginning with an emphasis on sampling
  (Chapter 8).

  o The application of survey research of data and data
  collection methods are reviewed in the next chapter
  (Chapter 9). Finally, a discussion of statistical reasoning
  (Chapter 10) rounds out Part III where we examine further
  understanding quantitative analysis and the concepts
  of probability and generalizing to larger audiences or

populations. Here we discuss the differences between datasets defined as "big," "large," and "small" and how the dataset reflects the goal of the research.

- **Part IV**: *Best Practices of Public Relations Research, Measurement, and Evaluation*
  - o This final part of this book looks to the future of public relations research and the specific practices that will ensure the value of research in creating effective and valuable public relations programs (Chapter 11).

Finally, Appendix B includes a bibliography of research and measurement sources, the *Dictionary of Public Relations Research and Measurement* (3rd ed.).

Taken together, each of these parts provide professionals as well as nonprofessionals with a basic understanding needed to evaluate public relations campaigns and ensure that research, measurement, and evaluation toolkits are up-to-date and complete.

CHAPTER 2

The Move Toward Standardization

This chapter is a summary of three top five peer-reviewed articles published by us with Dr. Donald K. Wright of Boston University and Dr. Shannon A. Bowen of the University of South Carolina (Michaelson and Stacks 2011; Michaelson, Wright, and Stacks 2012; Bowen and Stacks 2013b). Each article addresses a similar theme—the movement from business as usual to best practices to the standards of how we do research that is essential to the modern public relations or corporate communication function. In this move from merely counting what is sent to audiences (outputs) to examining the effects on intermediary and target audiences, we focus on outcomes that are typically described as soft rather than the hard financial indicators used by other business functions. Chapter 3 reviews and extends this business-oriented model and provides the necessary background and definitions of terms necessary to understand modern public relations. However, as demonstrated in Figure 2.1, the communication profession has moved from a focus on producing outputs to one of creating and implementing *strategies* that yield result that, in turn, can be correlated with financial data to show public relations' impact on the program or campaign.

In a sense, we've come a long way in a short period of time. In doing so, we have taken an approach to excellent public relations envisioned by Jim Grunig beyond the corporate world and into daily practice (Grunig, Grunig, and Dozier 2002).

Why Standardization?

Standardization of public relations research is the next step up from best practices. While best practices tell us *how* to best meet objectives,

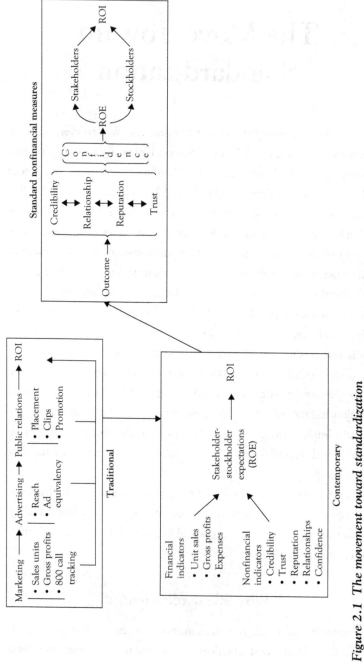

Figure 2.1 *The movement toward standardization*

standards define *what* needs to be measured. Public relations research and strategy have progressed from a rather primitive counting of outputs (the communication product: brochures, media releases, tweets, and so forth) (Stacks and Bowen 2013, 21) to a more strategic, social psychological orientation. This led Michaelson to propose the model of public relations' best practices introduced in Chapter 1 (see Figure 2.2). He defined best practices as, "A method or technique that has consistently shown results superior to those achieved with other means, and that is used as a benchmark" (Michaelson 2007; Michaelson and Macleod 2007). The model focused on how to produce the best research and had its own goals and objectives: (1) be rigorous in design, (2) be complete in measurement design and evaluation, and (3) report so that the research improves the strategic value of public relations by advancing our knowledge base.

The first question to be answered is what is a *standard*? According to the *Oxford English Dictionary*, standard is "an idea or thing used as a measure, norm, or model in comparative evaluations" (*Oxford English Dictionary* n.d.). Standards then provide *comparative evaluations* that gauge the absolute performance of programs and program elements, which, in turn, allow us to compare performance of prior and competitive programs within industry and category and relative to other industries or categories.

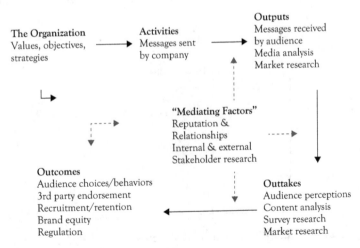

Figure 2.2 A best practices model

Source: Michaelson and Macleod (2007).

Standards are the hallmarks of *professionalism.* They provide evidence of the validity of the research process and in combination with best practices, provide rigor and reliability in measurement. This provides the public relations professional the ability to determine if specific communication goals are met (the absolute measures) and a way to identify if changes in specific measures are significant based on the performance of similar programs or campaigns (the relative measures). And, finally, standards measure progress and allow the professional to take corrective actions, if needed, to ensure communication goals and objectives are achieved (Figure 2.3)—*goals and objectives that in turn serve as the foundation for achieving business success.*

An excellent campaign or program would have multiple *measurable* objectives across the campaign. With this foundation of standardized measures, we now have the ability to effectively measure and evaluate nonfinancial data and correlate with financial data provided by other business functions. However, we must assure that business goals and objectives are parallel to our goals and objectives. For public relations, there are three standard public relations objectives. The first deals with disseminating information to target publics or audiences; this is the *informational* objective. Here we check to see if the messages were received, recalled, and understood. If a communication is not received, it has no value; if it is not recalled even if received, there is no value;

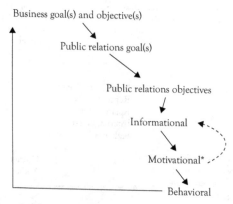

Figure 2.3 Standardizing goals and objectives

*Benchmarks not being met and informational strategies need to be reframed or refocused.
Source: Stacks (2011).

if it is received and recalled and understood, only then it has value. Each can be measured quantifiably and evaluated against expected benchmarks.

Second, does the communication do what it was strategically meant to do? This is the *motivational* objective and its focus is on *perceptions* of the message. The motivational objective consists of three components: *cognitive* (agreement, disagreement, neutrality), *affective* (emotional impact), and *connotative* (behavioral intention). If the objectives meet benchmark expectations, then the public relations function has added to business goals and objectives. Third, does the strategy actually produce intended results—expected behavior? Finally, the *behavioral objective* provides evidence that (1) the business goals and objectives are met and (2) where public relations strategy forms an important part of the larger business decision-making process. The research process represents a campaign continuum ranging from strategic development, refinement based on benchmarks once the campaign is engaged, and final outcome evaluations against an established baseline.

Research standards give the public relations professional, the corporate chief communication officer, and the public relations agency executive valuable data into strategic decisions made at what Grunig has called the managerial table by providing information that has been comparatively evaluated on those standards.

Toward a Standardization of Public Relations Research Ethics

We believe that before any research is begun, an evaluation of its ethics and the ethics of the research need to be undertaken. Shannon A. Bowen and Don W. Stacks provided an ethical standard for the public relations researcher that is based on a set of (1) principles, (2) their core values, and (3) a way to test the ethicality of a problem (Bowen and Stacks 2013a; Bowen and Stacks 2013b). It is our hope that this ethical standard will not only further professionalize the practice, but also (1) drive data collection, (2) strengthen the credibility of research reports among decision makers, and (3) increase the confidence they have in research findings. This standard should increase the legitimacy and support of public relations' role as an ethical counselor or advisor to top management.

There is a difference between *ethics* and *research ethics* in particular. First, ethics is a best practices component. As Bowen, Rawlins, and Martin noted:

> Issues managers must identify potential problems, research must be conducted, and both problems and potential solutions must be defined in an ethical manner. Therefore, *ethics* can be defined for public relations as *how we ought to decide, manage, and communicate.* (Bowen, Rawlins, and Martin 2010, 130)

Although this idea has been critiqued, many public relations professionals, as keepers of an organization's reputation, are also called upon to provide ethical guidance to their dominant coalitions (i.e., the management team) (Bowen 2008; Berger and Reber 2006; Curtin and Boynton 2001). Those dominant coalitions manage issues and support the conduct of research. Currently, *research ethics* is individualized as firms or professionals who serve to guide the research process. This approach is haphazard and leads to a lack of consistency in ethical standards across the profession. Indeed, very little ethical guidance is offered that is specific to public relations research (Stacks 2002; Stacks 2011; Stacks 2017). However, specific standards would help to unify the profession and lead to a more consistent ethical practice across all forms of data collection and analysis. Given this lack of guidance, Bowen and Stacks undertook of a study devoted to identifying the *ethics of public relations research*.

In conducting this research, they were guided by two research questions: First, "how do professional associations that deal with public relations research, both academic and professional, express codes of ethics, statements, or conduct regarding the ethical practice of research?" And, second, "if these associations have ethics guidelines, what principles or core values are espoused?"

To answer the first, they first looked at 14 public relations or corporate communication research associations related to public relations research for their published ethical codes of research. All association codes or statements were downloaded from their websites and reflect at that time the most up-to-date statements on the ethical conduct of research.[1]

They found that all 14 associations had a formal ethics statement; four of them stated codes of conduct with legal overtures. Bowen and Stacks then looked for formal *research* ethics statements, finding eight of them did state formal research ethics statements. They then looked more closely at those statements to see if they articulated one or more of five core principles identified in the ethics body of knowledge as stated by the Institute for Public Relations Measurement Commission: *intellectual honesty, fairness, dignity, disclosure,* and *respect for all involved.*

Finally, they looked for inclusion of 18 core values as identified by the Institute for Public Relations' Measurement Commission (2012). These are specific values that the ethical researcher should possess (see Table 2.1).

The number of core values found in the 14 associations ranged from 21 percent (valuing truth behind the numbers) to 86 percent (intellectual integrity). The mean percentage of all 18 core values was 58 percent. Thus, overall, the inclusion of core values across associations was barely over half. Additionally, 11 of the associations had other statements that were not analogous to the 18 core values identified here.

Table 2.1 Core ethical values*

Autonomy	Judgment
Respondent rights	Protection of proprietary data
Fairness	Public responsibility
Balance	Intellectual integrity
Duty	Good intention
Lack of bias	Reflexivity
Not using misleading data	Moral courage and objectivity
Full disclosure	
Discretion	

Source: *http://www.instituteforpr.org/research/commissions/measurement/ethics-statement/

---

[1] Two professional association websites had member-only access. Materials from those websites were gathered with the help of members, and we owe them our sincere thanks for their assistance and support.

As the results presented revealed, the ethical statement set out by the 2012 Institute for Public Relations Commission on Measurement provides a good starting point for a research ethics standard among public relations professionals:

> The duty of professionals engaged in research, measurement, and evaluation for public relations is to advance the highest ethical standards and ideals for research. All research should abide by the principles of intellectual honesty, fairness, dignity, disclosure, and respect for all stakeholders involved, namely clients (both internal and external), colleagues, research participants, the public relations profession, and the researchers themselves. (Institute for Public Relations 2012)

This statement is based on core values that are highly *deontological*, or duty based, in nature. Furthermore, it sets research ethical standards to all involved in public relations: clients, colleagues, research participants, the profession, in general, and individual researchers. Based on this evaluation, an ethical research standard was proposed:

> Research should be autonomous and abide by the principles of universalizeable and reversible duty to the truth, dignity and respect for all involved publics and stakeholders, and have a morally good will or intention to gather, analyze interpret, and report data with veracity. (Bowen and Stacks 2013a)

Toward Standardization of Measurement

In turning to standards for measurement, Michaelson and Stacks argue that such standards must take into consideration three factors: the *communication objectives* set for the problem, the *life cycle* or stage of the effort, and the *audiences* to which strategically chosen channels and messages will be created, to include intermediaries or third-party endorsers (Michaelson and Stacks 2011).

A prerequisite to any standard measure requires that we first confirm the *reliability* and *validity* of those measures. A reliable measure is one that measures consistently over time. A valid measure is one that actually measures what is intended to be measured. We can establish statistical reliability through accepted standard reliability formulas (Stacks 2017; Michaelson and Stacks 2010).[2] Validity is established in several ways or forms, usually through face validity, content validity, construct validity, and criterion-related validity. However, validity is dependent on the measure's reliability. That is, something can be reliable but not valid—a clock set earlier than the actual time may be reliable but is not a valid measure of time. *Standard measures should always include information on their reliability and validity as an ethical and transparent part of reporting.*

We can identify four standard measures of interest to public relations (see Table 2.2). Of interest in evaluating nonfinancial data during a campaign is the *outtake*, which attempts to demonstrate what audiences have understood, heeded, and responded to a communication product's call to seek further information from public relations messages prior to measuring an outcome (Stacks and Bowen 2013, 21). Outtakes often deal

Table 2.2 Standard measures

Output measures   Measurement of the number of communication products or services distributed or reaching a targeted audience, or both.
Outtake measures   Measurement of what audiences have understood or heeded or responded to a communication product's call to seek further information from public relations messages prior to measuring an outcome; audience reaction to the receipt of a communication product, including favorability of the product, recall and retention of the message embedded in the product, and whether the audience heeded or responded to a call for information or action within the message.
Outcome measures   Quantifiable changes in awareness, knowledge, attitude, opinion, and behavior levels that occur as a result of a public relations program or campaign; an effect, consequence, or impact of a set or program of communication activities or products, and may be either short-term (immediate) or long-term.
Intermediary measures   Quantifiable measures of messages provided by third-party endorsers or advocates.

---

[2] For continuous measures the Coefficient Alpha is used, for categorical measures the KR-20 is used. In content analysis, there are a number of reliability statistics available—Scott's pi index, Holsti's coefficient, Cohen's Kappa.

with audience's reaction to the message, including *favorability* toward, *recall accuracy*, and *retention* of that message. It also measures whether the audience is planning to respond to a call for information or action. The outtake is also examined when using intermediary measurement where key messages are assessed for *inclusion, tone,* and *accuracy*.

The outcome measures the *quantifiable* changes in *awareness, knowledge, attitude, opinion,* and *behavioral intent* that occur as a result of a public relations program or campaign (Stacks and Bowen 2013, 21). It is an effect, consequence, or impact of a set or program actions, and may be either short-term (immediate) or long-term. Both standard measures of outtakes and outcomes should be employed in assessing target audiences or targeted third-party endorsers.

Nonfinancial measures gather perceived or attitudinal data (Stacks and Bowen 2013, 19). Target audience measures are basically defined into five standard types, reflecting how they meet the requirements of informative, motivational, and behavioral objectives (see Table 2.3). The first are measures of *awareness and recall*. The second are measures of brand, product, service, issues, or topic *knowledge*. Both measures focus on gathering objective knowledge (i.e., are stakeholders aware of and recall accurately the message as intended, and how much do they actually know about the object of interest?). *Interest and relationship* measures focus on attitudes toward the object and its relationship to the respondent in terms of peers, family, community, and so forth. *Preference* measures focus behavioral intentions toward the object, whether they intend to purchase or support the object. And, finally, *advocacy* measures, which focus on behavioral intentions—aim to measure the likeliness that they will advocate for the object.

B.A.S.I.C. is a life-cycle approach to measuring *communication* objectives (see Figure 2.4). It argues that we need to take into account where on the life cycle the audience is—are they aware? If so, can we advance their knowledge, sustain the relevance of the outcome, initiate action, and create advocacy? As you might expect, these communication objectives clearly reflect informational (*awareness*), motivational (*knowledge, relevance, action*), and behavioral (*advocacy*) objectives.

These communications are aimed at target publics and more specific audiences, as defined by combined *demographic, psychographic, lifestyles,*

Table 2.3 Target audience measures

Awareness or recall   Thinking back to what you have just (*read, observed, reviewed, or saw*), place an X in the boxes if you remember (*reading, observing, reviewing, or seeing*) about any of the following (*brands, products, services, issues, or topics*).
Knowledge   Based on everything you have read, seen, or heard, how believable is the information you just saw about the (*brand, product, service, issue, or topic*)? By believable we mean that you are confident that what you are (*seeing, reading, hearing, or observing*) is truthful and credible.
Interest or relationship   Based on what you know of this brand, product, service, issue, or topic, how much interest do you have with it? How does this brand, product, service, issue, or topic relate to you, your friends, family, and community?
Preference or intent   Based on everything you have (*seen, read, heard, or observed*) about this (*brand, product, service, issue, topic*), how likely you are to (*purchase, try, or support*) this (*brand, product, service, issue, topic*). Would you say you are "very likely," "somewhat likely," "neither likely nor unlikely," "somewhat unlikely" or "very unlikely" to (*purchase, try, or support*) this (*brand, product, service, issue, or topic*)?
Advocacy   Statements such as: I will recommend this (*brand, product, service, issue, or topic*) to my friends and relatives. People like me can benefit from this (*brand, product, service, issue, or topic*).   I like to tell people about (*brands, products, services, issues, or topics*) that work well for me. Word-of-mouth is the best way to learn about (*brands, products, services, issues, or topics*). User reviews on websites are valuable sources of information about (*brands, products, services, issues, or topics*).

netgraphics,[3] characteristics. Intermediaries are also included and represent targeted *outtake* audiences—the media and third party endorsers who often serve an *intervening* audience role. Finally, in today's world the social media must be evaluated as a key channel for delivering messages to relational peers, opinion leaders, and advocates through blogs, tweets, and YouTube® communications.

Intermediary measures (see Table 2.4) focus on what is contained in third-party or advocate *messages*. Do the messages contain the basic facts or key points? Are there misstatements or erroneous information? And, is there an absence of basic facts or omission of some or all the facts? The methodology typically employed is content analysis.

---

[3] A netgraphic identifies how an audience approaches and uses the social media.

- B.A.S.I.C. communication objectives for public relations efforts:

  – Build awareness

  – Advance knowledge

  – Sustain relevance

  – Initiate action

  – Create advocacy

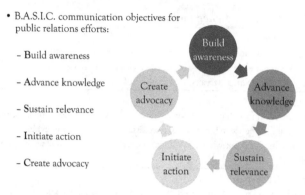

Figure 2.4 Communication objectives

Table 2.4 Intermediary measures

Three specific measures:
The presence of basic facts in the third-party or intermediary story or message.
The presence of misstatements or erroneous information.
The absence or omission of basic facts that should be included in a complete story.

Presenting Standardized Measurement

While these standards are the basis for valid and reliable measurement, there is also the additional need to collect and present this data so that the measured results provide meaningful insights that positively impact campaign and program performance.

In a 2016 presentation on strategic standardization in public relations, Stacks points out that standardization goes beyond the data and also includes the presentation of that data (Stacks 2016). In that presentation, he identifies seven data and analytical standards that need to be incorporated in communication measurement:

- Collecting data across the entire campaign timeline
- Describing and interpreting the data
- Using descriptive statistics to reported as percentages, proportions, means, medians, standard deviations, and other generally accepted forms of data presentation
- Applying inferential statistics to interpret descriptive data for changes over time and to detect trends
- Establishing baselines to establish campaign success

- Creating datasets that are clear and provide the information needed to make decisions
- Testing differences in the data with a high level of statistical confidence (95th confidence level) so the insights are reliable.

As noted in Chapter 1, collecting data across the entire campaign timeline or "end-to-end measurement" is essential in order to identify at which stage a communication program is meeting or failing to meet its goals. Only through this type of measurement can a public relations professional effectively manage a program or campaign.

Our 2011 article provides more detail and numerous examples of how to create standard public relations measures. These details are provided and discussed in Chapter 4. Before we turn to the third area where the profession is moving toward standards, we need to underline that *if you have not measured you cannot evaluate; if you measure and that measurement is not reliable or valid, then your evaluation will not be reliable or valid.*

Toward a Standard Model of Program Excellence

Over the past two decades, a significant literature has developed that examines those factors most influential in creating effective public relations. The most prominent publications in this literature are the research on *excellence in the practice of public relations* authored by James Grunig, Larissa Grunig, and David Dozier (Grunig, Grunig, and Dozier 2002; Dozier, Grunig, and Grunig 1995; Grunig and Grunig 2006). That research broke new ground in reliably identifying factors that allow public relations professionals to increase their effectiveness in meeting communication goals and objectives for their organizations.

While the work that defined excellence in public relations has been significant and influential on the practice of public relations, unintended gaps exist. These gaps limit the overall utility of the work in assisting public relations professionals in achieving overall excellence in practice. The gap that is most noteworthy is the lack of a specific definition of what determines excellence on the actual outputs, outtakes, and outcomes of public relations professionals—specifically public relations programs, campaigns, and activities. This is not intended to diminish the importance of the work by Grunig, Grunig, and Dozier. Rather, its intent is to build on that research and to create a unified theory of what constitutes *the full scope of excellence* in the profession (Michaelson, Wright, and Stacks 2012).

So, how can the public relations function or agency establish the actual impact of a campaign? It does so by:

- First, following the *established standards of measurement and research as stated earlier and in later chapters in this volume* (Michaelson and Stacks 2011)
- Second, *defining excellence*
- And, third, *effectively evaluating excellence.*

The questions then become (1) what is excellence; (2) how can it be evaluated; and (3) what standards should the public relations profession establish to create a *metric for program or campaign excellence?*

The quest for excellence began over 20 years ago when Grunig and colleagues first examined what they felt were companies that practiced "excellence in communication." Based on a survey of corporate communication practices across industries and international boundaries, they reported that companies practiced excellence in communications if seven factors were practiced (see Table 2.5).

Table 2.5 The concept of communication excellence

The *excellence in public relations* project
Report said organizations practiced excellence in communication if: • Senior management team was committed to communication excellence • Chief communication officer reported directly to the CEO • Company was committed to tell the truth and prove it with action • PR and communication was more preventive than reactive • PR efforts began with research, followed by strategic planning, followed by the communication (or action) stage and always included an evaluation of communication effectiveness • Company was committed to conducting communication research that focused upon outcomes and not just outputs • Company was committed to education, training, and development of its public relations and communication professionals

Source: Grunig 1992; Grunig, Grunig, and Dozier 2002.

There are as listed in Table 2.6 other criteria for defining companies that are excellent communicators. In other words, we followed along the lines advanced earlier regarding standards of research ethics and measurement.

It is our contention that companies which demonstrate excellence in communication have learned three things over the phases of public relations campaigns or activities (see Figure 2.5). First, they understand that in the programming of a campaign during the *developmental phase*, the issue is first examined from its location on the communication life cycle. They set the public relations function's goals and objectives parallel to the business's goals and objectives and establish a baseline against which to evaluate planning plan over time. And they create three sets of measureable objectives with targeted benchmarks.

Second, during the *refinement phase* they actively measure objectives quantitatively relative to expected benchmarks and phases within

Table 2.6 Other factors defining communication excellence

Judging criteria of major public relations awards
Secondary research such as generally accepted practices (GAP) surveys such as the Annenberg series
Examinations of what various organizations are doing in terms of: • Setting objectives • Research and planning • Identifying target audiences • Evaluating communications excellence • Establishing ROI measures for public relations and communication efforts • Developing some general understanding about the contributions of public relations and communication to the business bottom line

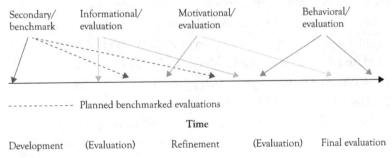

Figure 2.5 The research continuum

that campaign. They then alter or change tactics based on these benchmarks, and continually scan the environment for unexpected events or actions.

Finally, they correlate nonfinancial outcomes (i.e., behavioral intentions) to business function financial outcomes as measureable return on investment (ROI) for its return on expectations (ROE) planning (these concepts are covered in detail in the next chapter).

> *Excellence*, then, can be defined and evaluated as the public relations function *adopting standards of research that focus on the relationship between the company's and the public relations' goals and the establishing of mutually supportive measurable objectives with targeted benchmarks that are measured and evaluated against baseline and expected nonfinancial outcomes, and correlating those findings with the data obtained by other functions' financial outcomes so that they may be entered into whatever company decision-making strategies are employed (e.g., Six Sigma, Balanced Scorecard).* (Michaelson, Wright, and Stacks 2012)

The Excellence Pyramid

Once excellence has been defined in a potentially measurable way, it must be evaluated. Evaluation, we argue, is best conducted against a model that sets the standards for effective, very effective, and excellent activities.

An effective campaign meets the basic needs and is considered successful but does not advance because it fails to measure up to the requirements of the stage. If it can meet the standards of the next stage, that is, intermediate, it is evaluated as very effective. And, if it reaches the third and final stage—*advanced*—it is evaluated excellent. The model, then, takes the form of a three-level pyramid (see Figure 2.6), similar to Maslow's *Hierarchy of Needs* and Herzburg's *Two-Factor Hygienic Model of Motivation* (Maslow 1970; Herzberg 1966; Herzberg 1968; Herzberg, Mausner, and Snydermann 1959). We turn now to an examination of what constitutes each level.

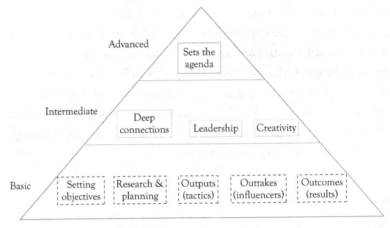

Figure 2.6 The Excellence Pyramid

Level 1: Basic

As shown in Figure 2.6, the model suggested for campaign programming excellence begins at the *basic* level. It includes the five components discussed earlier when laying out the argument for measurement standards whereby the campaign can demonstrate that it:

1. Set public relations goals and objectives relevant to the business goals and objectives.
2. Conducted research and planned the campaign based on that research.
3. Produced outputs that effectively reached target audiences.
4. Measured outtakes to determine that the campaign was on phase and target.
5. And, produced nonfinancial outcomes (results) that could be correlated to other business functions financial outcomes.

Each component has criteria that must be met to ensure that a campaign will do what it is supposed to. It is binary outcome—either it was carried out and carried out correctly or it was either neglected or carried out incorrectly. Furthermore, the components are addressed sequentially, from left to right. Each is *essential* to the next to ensure campaign success and demonstrate an impact on business goals and objectives. Finally, these components are objective and evaluated as to whether they have met a particular standard and are either present or not present in a campaign. If the standard components are found in each of the five categories, the programming can be evaluated as demonstrating basic effectiveness, that is, it was successful but did not really advance company, brand, or whatever goal was being attempted. To do so requires that the campaign meet three criteria at the intermediate level.

Level 2: Intermediate

Once the essential components have been satisfied, the company or agency may move to evaluating the programming at the second, that is, *intermediate level*. Unlike the basic level, which is objectively measured, the intermediate level is more subjective and must be evaluated on some scalar measure, one that includes a midpoint for uncertainty (Stacks 2017; Stacks and Michaelson 2010). As shown, the second level consists of three factors:

1. *Deep connections to target audiences*: Planning that achieves an intermediate level of excellence builds a bond or *relationship* between the campaign and audiences through motivational objective messaging strategies.
2. *Global leadership support and engagement*: Planning that achieves an intermediate level of excellence is *supported by senior management* and is *aligned across the company, product, or brand's environment*; and they have *internal support at the highest level*. This puts the communication function, as Grunig et al., argue at the "management table."
3. *Creativity and innovation* is demonstrated when a unique approach to the problem, product, brand, or issue is taken. Since the communication function is responsible for messaging strategy across the board, it makes sense that intermediate excellent programming will be *original in approach, inventive in distribution* through the best communicational channels, and *innovative and efficient* in its execution. Creativity sets campaign planning apart from competing campaigns and often results in further enhancing the communication function's credibility within senior management.

All three factors come into play when there are buy-ins by the corporate management team that yields supportive commentary and criticism on potential tactical outputs. Furthermore, at this level, overall campaign planning clearly involves business or corporate strategy with the communication function fully integrated into the larger campaign.

Level 3: Advanced

Indication of excellence is found at the highest, advanced level of campaign outcome. Here, *public relations sets the agenda for target audiences on key messages*. That agenda should be extended to a larger environment through advocacy or word-of-mouth and other diagonal, grapevine forms of message transmission—blogs, tweets, Facebook mentions, and so forth. This extension is critical in *establishing a two-way symmetrical dialogue between company and target audience(s)* in a strategic long-term plan linked to company, product, brand, or issue goals. Advanced planning also *demonstrates leadership* not only in internal planning but also impacts on the profession as well. It becomes the *standard benchmark against which others establish levels of excellence*—that is, it is timeless in strategy, tactics, and demonstrable measured results that clearly show a connection to overall business goals and objectives.

Summary and Conclusion

Based on our discussion of ethnical, measurement, and outcome standards, we believe that we can come to several conclusions.

1. Public relations has arrived at a stage of professionalism that demands certain standards of research.
2. Standards for ethical research, including principles and core values, can be identified, taught, and evaluated, thus increasing our professionalism.
3. Measurement standards are necessary for comparative evaluation against not only competitors but also to produce results that can be factored into a company's decision-making strategies, therefore, increasing public relations' impact on business strategy.

4. Excellent research and measurement must take an end-to-end approach to prove its effectiveness and usefulness to the client.
5. Public relations excellence can be defined and evaluated.
6. Several standardizing models and tests have been identified and proposed that should be the focus of continuing research.

Finally, we conclude with the notion that as a young profession, our profession has extended its reach across time, distance, and culture. Continued discussion of standards and best practices of research ethics, measurement and evaluation, and planning excellence can only enhance and strengthen our profession.

Chapter 3 builds on these research standards and turn our focus to how research helps the public relations professional make a case that he or she has contributed to a client's or company's success.

CHAPTER 3

The Business of Public Relations

In Chapters 1 and 2 we introduced the concept of best practices and standardization through the history of public relations research. In this chapter we introduce and discuss the role of public relations as it relates to the larger goals and objectives of the organization. Public relations' impact on an organization's *return on investment* (ROI) is a fairly new concept. As the profession has turned from a tactical role to the strategic management of communication, the profession has had to continually wrestle with having to prove its worth. As part of the promotional mix of communication, public relations works in conjunction with advertising and marketing as an integral tool. Typically, the promotional component (advertising, marketing, or public relations) most likely to meet an organization's communications needs and objectives takes the lead in creating programs and setting the communication agenda (Caywood 1997; Harris 1993, 1998; Schutz, Tannenbaum, and Lauterborn 1998). Up to the last decade that lead almost always has fallen to marketing. Consequently, between the last decade of the 20th and first decade of the 21st centuries, significant proportions of public relations activities, other than media relations, were expected to help support product marketing. Today, however, that role and the move toward truly integrated communications have put public relations—and corporate communication more specifically—at a different and more substantive level in organizations, as noted in the Arthur W. Page Society's seminal monograph, *The Authentic Enterprise* (Arthur W. Page Society 2009). That role is to support the overall business objectives of the organization.

Establishing the Public Relations Campaign

On the basis of this discussion it should be clear that a public relations approach to any business goal or objective necessarily incorporates research as a cornerstone in the development, refinement, and evaluation of any campaign that supports organizational objectives. Boston University Professor Donald K. Wright has gone so far as to state that "if you don't have research on the front end and evaluation on the back end, it isn't PR" (Wright 1990). Wright stresses the role of research and theory in public relations. Wright (1990) states that there are four basic assumptions to public relations research in daily practice, assumptions that reflect a best practices approach to public relations research:

1. The decision-making process is basically the same in all organizations [businesses].
2. All communication [programming and] research should
   a. Set objectives;
   b. Determine a strategy that establishes those objectives; and
   c. Implement tactics that bring those strategies to life.
3. All campaign research can be divided into three general phases:
   a. Development (initial research helping to establish goals and objectives);
   b. Refinement (continuous evaluation on expected benchmarks once the campaign is initiated and changed as deemed necessary to meet campaign goals and objectives); and
   c. Evaluation (a final review of the campaign aimed at establishing success or failure for not only business but also public relations goals and objectives).
4. Communication research is behavior-driven and knowledge (theory)-based.

The final assumption drives home the challenge of public relations research as a mediating factor—that public relations programming and its measurement and evaluation strive to impact on stake and stockholder behavior through the management of message-based programming that impacts on awareness, interest, attitudes, and then intended behavior that supports organizational objectives. On the basis of these assumptions, it should be clear that public relations that follows best practices and standards as introduced earlier in this book does the necessary background or competitive analyses that will help drive the public relations effort. It is during the developmental phase or stage that goals and objectives are created that support the business's goals and objectives.

It is important to understand that public relations efforts— sometimes referred to as actions, programs, or campaigns—can and should be evaluated against this standard. This was introduced in Chapter 2 as looking at effectiveness as excellence. Briefly, the basic or proponent needs of the Excellence Pyramid (see pages 29–32) are focused on goals and objectives, research, and tactics, persuasion, and outcome. Without stated measureable goals and objectives, there is no way to evaluate the data gathered during a campaign to make claims of success. This, together, with the appropriate research methods employed during the campaign, the employment of standardized measures of effectiveness data, and the statistical assessment of those data, we cannot *evaluate during and after the effort*. We turn now to public relations goals and objectives.

Understanding Goals and Objectives

It is important to understand that goals and objectives are different in several important ways. A goal is a *projected* outcome that is desired (Stacks and Bowen 2013). Hence, a goal might be to sell or lease X number of automobiles resulting in company profit or to reduce absenteeism to increase profits or to get more positive media attention to a product.

Goals are expectations and fairly open as to results. An objective, on the other hand, is "an explicit statement [or statements] that support[s] a communication strategy" (Stacks and Bowen 2013, 20). In all too many cases, public relations campaigns suffer because they confuse goals with objectives, leading to inabilities to demonstrate impact or influence on business goals and objectives.

Public relations objectives are no different from marketing and advertising objectives in one critical sense—the need for establishing a

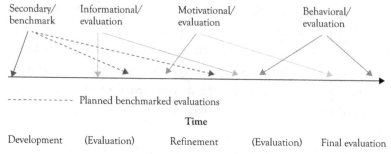

Figure 3.1 Planned benchmarking

Source: Used with permission of Don W. Stacks and Guilford Press.

campaign baseline for the necessary conditions needed to achieve business goals with benchmarks that need to be stressed in every instance. Quite simply, without a starting point or baseline research results, public relations cannot demonstrate campaign success or failure and in turn business success or failure. Furthermore, without projected benchmarks it is difficult to demonstrate how strategy and tactics impact on campaign goals. Unfortunately, most public relations campaigns today fail to establish the beginning baseline and set expected benchmarks throughout the campaign. As related to Wright's assumptions first introduced in Chapter 2, Figure 3.1 demonstrates the relationship between the baseline benchmark, planned benchmarks, and continuous testing of the campaign (Wright 1990). Best practice campaign management would set multiple planned benchmarks to establish campaign effectiveness and allow for revision of objectives, if necessary in order to assure success.

Stating the Objectives

All research and evaluation planning should end with formal statements of the campaign's objectives. This is a standard that not all campaigns rise to. These objectives need to be related to the overall business goals and objectives and can be more specific, relating to specific outcomes during the campaign for which the public relations portion is being conducted. In general, the objective takes the form of a "to" statement: To do something that by such a date is expected to result in an outcome. Hence, a business objective might be, "To gain a percent market share by the end of third quarter sales through enhanced communication programs." The business goal would be to increase market share.

From a best practices approach, the objective should have been written with a benchmark for comparison or against the initial campaign baseline. Hence, a better objective would have been:

> *To increase market share from 7 percent [baseline] to 10 percent by the end of third quarter sales through enhanced communication programs.*

The enhanced communication programs could then be further defined in terms of public relations, advertising, and marketing goals and objectives.

Public Relations Objectives

To better comprehend what public relations objectives are, it is important to understand the three basic functions that public relations does in any business campaign. According to Stacks (2011), all public relations activities fulfill three basic functions:

- First, the public relations function is to get necessary information out to the appropriate audience. An audience that behaves without understanding why it did so cannot be expected to do so again; hence, an important function is to ensure that the information necessary for any intended action is out and has been understood, this is stated as an *informational objective*. This information can include general awareness of a product service or issue as well as detailed knowledge.
- Second, once it has been established that the information has been (a) received and (b) understood, then the information's effect must be measured and evaluated—whether attitudes, beliefs, values, or both have been shaped, changed, or reinforced. This is stated as a *motivational objective*.

- And, third, once it has been verified that the information
  has been received, understood, and has had an impact on
  the audience, the campaign has influenced the audience to
  intended action such as a stated intent to purchase. This is
  stated as a *behavioral objective.*

The relationship between the three objective types should be clear. If the information is not reaching the target audiences, then the campaign's media relations strategy has not done what it was expected to do and research into the media channels employed reexamined. If that information has been received but not understood, then research must establish why—as Michaelson and Griffin (2009) did when they examined MetLife news stories and found systematic reporting problems confusing the target audience—and corrective action taken to put the campaign back on track. (This study is examined in more detail in the Chapter 7 on content analysis; it is the first study to measure reporting errors by the media and suggest remedial action to reduce them.) Once the information has been received and understood, then the audience must be evaluated to establish effect or impact. If the campaign is to change attitudes toward a product, is it actually doing so? If so, has that change been what was planned? If not, the message strategy must be reexamined. The informational and motivational objectives lead to the final public relations objective—the campaign outcome is such that audience intends to behave as expected—and the public relations campaign has contributed to business objectives and goals.

Stating Public Relations Research Objectives

From a measurement and evaluation point of view, most public relations objectives fall woefully short of being precise enough to establish what kinds of research methods are required. Obviously, the type of research being conducted will differ in terms of cost. In-depth interviews are more expensive than surveys, for instance, in terms of understanding how audiences will or have responded to a campaign. Also, the measurement and evaluation of the campaign is influenced by the public relations tactics being employed. Future chapters explore the various methods public relations researchers employ to measure outcomes. In this section, we examine the *research secondary objectives* associated with public relations objectives. For each public relations objective there should be *at least* one research objective. These research objectives determine which research methods are to be employed, when they are to be employed, and the expected outcome (Stacks 2017). If the informational objective is "to increase auto purchasers knowledge of the 2015 models from 2014 [baseline] through increased use of employee blogging [tactic] by nine percent [informational outcome]," the research objective should state how and when measurement and evaluation is to take place. Thus, a public relations research objective might be:

> *To gather data from social media users [audience] who intend to purchase a new auto on their understanding of new models [continuing informational outcome] to ascertain if intended purchasing has increased from benchmark [behavioral outcome]. The most appropriate way to collect this data is through an Internet-based web survey [method] three times during the first and second quarters of 2017 [time frame].*

Other methods employed might include conducting focus groups of audience members, content analyses of reactions to employee blogs, tracking website requests for more information, and so forth. What the research objective does is to specify methods.

Public Relations Role as Defined at the Managerial Level

Public relations historically has focused primarily on media relations—getting the message out. It was not until the last quarter of a century that the focus of public relations has shifted to the strategic value it provides on the organization's ROI. This change, from a strictly media-relations perspective to one that includes a broader strategic management perspective, can be seen in how public relations' *outputs*—communication materials that are produced to support the corporation—have changed over the years (Stacks 2017). Figure 3.2 shows the early relationships between

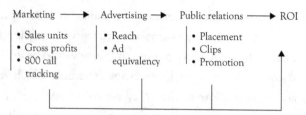

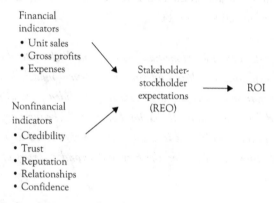

Figure 3.2 *Traditional perspectives on the relationships between marketing, advertising, and public relations*

Source: Used with permission of Don W. Stacks and Guilford Press.

Figure 3.3 *Contemporary thought on the relationships between marketing, advertising, and public relations*

Source: Used with permission of Don W. Stacks and Guilford Press.

marketing, advertising, and public relations. Here we can see that in traditional practice, marketing drives advertising, which in turn drives public relations.

Influence, starting with marketing, originates at the far left. Why? Because marketing provides hard data on what it drives toward the investment put into it; advertising provides numeric data based on circulation figures that reflect awareness, interest, and intent to purchase—data that may be of questionable use, but backed by considerable secondary data on *potential* purchasers of a product or service (Stacks 2017). On the other hand, public relations provided little numeric data beyond the number of press materials sent out and the number of articles that contain information from those press materials.

When using a strategic management approach, however, contemporary public relations assumes a different role, one that divides promotional communication (e.g., marketing, advertising, and public relations) *outcomes* into two classes of *indicators*, financial and nonfinancial (see Figure 3.3).

Understanding Nonfinancial Indicators

Since nonfinancial indicators are not "hard," how are they measured? Basically all nonfinancial indicators are subjective and exist in the minds of the public or target audience a client seeks to influence. To demonstrate impact, a nonfinancial indicator—often referred to as *key performance indicator* (KPI)—must show how it relates to a business goal or objective. That is, in the mixed-marketing model, for example, how does the public relations effort impact on awareness, knowledge, interest, and intent to purchase? In an employee relations effort, how does managerial relationship affect employee morale or absenteeism?

The nonfinancial indicators that have demonstrated public relations value and impact are *perceptual.* They are social and psychological in nature and, as such, must be approached using subjective, yet reliable and valid measurement. Yet even though they are perceptual, they clearly indicate an impact on the financial indicators and need to be treated in much the same way. Thus, a public relations objective should find a way to demonstrate how the output is communicated to those who may influence the intended public or target audience to do something. This is done through specification of an *outtake*, a specified evaluation of a product or company or idea by an opinion leader (Stacks and Bowen 2013, 21). As noted earlier, an opinion leader—a stock analyst, political analyst, politician, or editorial endorsement—can change a target audience's perceptions of whatever it is that the opinion leader opines on. As noted in Figure 3.4, the variables the public relations professional can use via some messaging strategy have demonstrated influence on opinion leaders. Indeed, the public relations goal may be to improve client reputation through influencing—persuading—opinion leader reporting on that client.

Financial indicators traditionally include marketing and advertising outcomes, while public relations nonfinancial indicators deal with

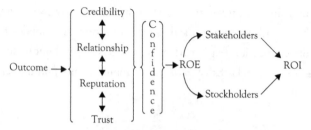

Figure 3.4 A strategic communication management model of public relations' influence on ROI

Source: Used with permission of Don W. Stacks and Guilford Press.

outcomes—defined as the "data gathered that do not include 'hard' data such as sales, profits, attendance; data that are social in nature and reflect attitudinal variables such as credibility, relationships, reputation, trust, and confidence"—that can be demonstrated to impact an organization's social and financial goals and objectives (Stacks and Bowen 2013, 19). While financial indicators deal with hard-core data, nonfinancial indicators deal with social data—perceptions, attitudes, and beliefs that have demonstrated impact on what public relations refers to as "third-party endorsers" (Michaelson and Stacks 2007). Figure 3.2 also noted that the outcomes of interest from a promotional approach are mediated by the expectations of stake or stockholders, but from the public relations perspective those expectations can be manipulated via carefully selected messages aimed at influential audience members (e.g., editors, analysts, or any opinion leaders).

These relationships for the nonfinancial indicators have been further conceptualized by Stacks (2011) as a working model of the relationships between and within the nonfinancial variables as demonstrated in Figure 2.4. This represents a strategic model of communication management that can be parsed out to establish how much each variable contributes to the final ROI. As Stacks notes, these indicators can be written as a mathematical formula:

$$\text{Outcome} = \beta \pm [C_{\text{redibility}} \pm R_{\text{elationship}} \pm R_{\text{eputation}} \pm T_{\text{rust}}] \pm C_{\text{onfidence}} + \text{error}$$

In this formula, β is the starting point [in a promotional campaign] that is in turn influenced by credibility, relationship, reputation, and trust and then further modified by audience confidence. That confidence can be in the product, service, or even the overall organization and has an overall tolerance that can be described as error. This model allows the professional to classify specific outcomes as functions of the nonfinancial indicators that can be used to *predict* outcomes and provide guidance in communication decisions (see Chapter 9, Statistical Analysis).

Understand the Relationship to Financial Indicators

This model is not independent of the financial indicators, but works in conjunction with them, especially when public relations is approached from a mixed-marketing model (Weiner 2007). In the mixed-marketing model, public relations efforts are focused on providing data that correlate directly to sales and have taken the form of approximated advertising indicators. These indicators—reach and circulation, for instance—try to establish the value of *placed* public relations activities when compared to the actual paid value of an advertisement. The problem with such indicators is that they do not reflect value but reflect costs associated with placement. While advertisers can specify where their material is placed in the various media (the more prominent the greater the cost), public relations placements cannot be guaranteed. In fact, the Commissions on Public Relations Measurement and Evaluation no longer accepts pseudo advertising as representing true public relations value, while attempting to identify better measures of impact on ROI.

The Challenge of Establishing Public Relations Effect on ROI

The challenge for public relations is to establish a relationship between financial indicators and the nonfinancial indicators that also influence a business's bottom line that is now more than simply financial and has added social responsibility and ecology (e.g., the "triple bottom line"). For instance, how does a company's relationship with its customer's impact on sales performance? How does reputation impact on stock prices? What happens when a trusted company does something bad? Are green companies more socially responsible and profitable? A recent Edelman

"Goodpurpose" study reported by *PR Week* "found that found 61 percent of consumers worldwide have purchased a brand that supports a good cause even if it wasn't the cheapest brand," which demonstrates the impact of social responsibility as a public relations outcome (PR Week 2009).

The correlation between a financial indicator and a nonfinancial indicator is the first step. A second step is to show over time how the nonfinancial indicators influence company outcome. We know, for instance, that it only takes one bad analyst report on a publicly-traded company to drop stock prices. Furthermore, we know that consumer confidence in a company can drive sales, stock prices, and other business outcomes. And, third, we need to look at these relationships based on how they have influenced business goals and objectives from a set point in time—a benchmark against which comparisons can be made and strategic decisions made.

Finally, the public relations effort should be viewed in terms of the traditional outcome model associated with promotional communication and, in particular, where it currently is in the communication life cycle as discussed with B.A.S.I.C. in Chapter 2. That is, each phase of the public relations campaign must clearly understand what part of the campaign it is being employed in and the campaign's strategy associated with it. For instance, is the campaign to introduce a new brand, in which case its goal is most likely to establish brand awareness? If awareness is not a goal, then perhaps it is increasing interest and understanding of the brand. If awareness and interest and understanding are present, then perhaps the campaign is to create desire for the brand. If awareness, interest, understanding, and desire are present then perhaps the campaign's goal is to influence adoption of the brand.

These goals can then be stated more precisely by looking at what nonfinancial variables are most relevant for the brand over a campaign. Attitudinal outcomes such as increased homophily or authority might be part of the campaign's strategy in a new brand introduction (Stacks and Michaelson 2009) or reputation variables such as social responsibility and company familiarity (Carroll 2006) might be used to influence intentions to purchase. In the end, however, the public relations outcomes must have a demonstrated correlation to business outcome; that is, ROE must demonstrate impact on ROI.

Summary

This chapter introduced the reader to the relationships public relations has to business goals and objectives. It has established that the public relations effort does not exist in a vacuum but works closely with business goals and objectives, whether they be financial or nonfinancial. By now readers should have a basic understanding of outputs, outtakes, and outcomes and how they relate to the public relations effort. Furthermore, they should understand the importance of setting realistic and measurable objectives.

The next chapter examines the major research methods employed by public relations to gather the information (data) necessary to evaluate the public relations effort. The section begins with the gathering of existing information through historical and secondary data. It then examines the use of content analysis—perhaps the most common of the methods used by public relations researchers. Following content analysis, qualitative methods are explored—in-depth interviews, focus groups, and participant observation. The last two chapters focus on the quantitative gathering of data through an understanding of sampling and then survey and poll methodology.

CHAPTER 4

Measuring Public Relations Outcomes

Previous chapters noted the need for public relations professionals' understanding and ability to measure the outcomes they hope to achieve in their campaign programming. This is not a new topic, yet it has taken on tremendous interest over the past 25 years as the profession sought to be able to demonstrate effectiveness. Public relations measurement, as noted in Chapter 3, often deals with what academics would call mediating or intermediary variables—things that will impact on the final business outcome but are not necessarily financial in nature. Organizational, brand, or product credibility is one of those variables; something that cannot be seen but can be measured and verified as a valid and reliable *predictor* of final outcome, which for public relations is increasingly focusing on nonfinancial indicators. Furthermore, since the beginning of the 21st century, scholars and professionals have pushed for a standardization of measures used to create scalar measures to ensure equivalency of data and produce comparative analyses (Michaelson and Stacks 2011). This chapter introduces the readers to measurement and evaluation from a social scientific perspective, one that allows the public relations professional to create reliable and valid measures of nonfinancial indicators (see Chapter 3). The chapter differentiates between hard financial indicators and soft nonfinancial indicators. As discussed previously, nonfinancial indicators include, but are not limited to, measures of confidence, credibility, relationship, reputation, trust, and indicators of awareness, interest and understanding, desire, and intent to adopt (Stacks and Carroll 2004).

Fundamentals of Data and Measurement

What does it mean when someone says that they are measuring something? Does it mean that what is being measured is observable? Does it establish differences or similarities between objects of measurement? Is it something that comes naturally? Is it done to create data that can be used to establish relationships between things? Finally, does it mean anything in particular? All of these are questions that measurement researchers ask daily when they try to create, use, or evaluate measures for any use. Public relations measurement researchers are no different, except that they have entered the process a little later than their promotional communication colleagues.

So, what does it mean when we say we are measuring something? It means that we are establishing a ruler that allows for comparisons and interpretations of "data" obtained from those measures (Stacks 2017). For instance, in the physical world, measurement is fairly straight forward; we often use inches, centimeters, yards, meters, miles, and so forth to measure linear distance (although it is unclear from this whether we are talking of horizontal or vertical distance). What we have established, however, is a *metric*—"[a] numeric value associated with campaign research demonstrating statistically whether outtake or, outcome, or both objectives are being reached" (Stacks and Bowen 2013)—that can be used to describe something; distance or height in this case. However, in the social world we also measure things that are not as observable, but are "potentially observable"—credibility, reputation, trust to name but a few things. Based on our created nonfinancial measures we can then make decisions as to whether something is longer or shorter, higher in credibility, or lower in trust when compared against something else.

However, notice that the interpretation of the measurement is usually less precise than the measure itself. Measurement interpretation often says something is heavier than something else—and in many instances this can be done with different measures, pounds of personal weight as compared to stones of personal weight. While measurement is more precise and can be tested for its reliability and validity, interpretation is, well, determined with words.

Measurement as a Public Relations Tool

In its simplest form, measurement is an observation. From a business perspective, measurement is most often used to track financially related variables. These variables include number of units produced, stock prices, gross and net profits, and so forth. Their measurement is quite precise since the data are hard, that is, they are directly observable and can be counted. Marketing can tell how many products are sold per 1-800-phone call-in, can calculate the cost per call across a number of other hard data points—number of hours staff put in, returns, and so forth (see Chapter 3). Human resources can provide a breakdown of cost per unit by employee and employee costs (wages and benefits, for instance).

From a public relations perspective, measurement is less precise because the data are soft. Soft data are not easily observed, which is one reason why investment in public relations measurement has suffered. Instead of focusing on the mediating variables that affect business outcome, public relations *counted* simple indicators of distribution. As such the "clip book" measured success in the number of releases sent out and picked up in the media (numbers), we could count the number of "likes" on Facebook and the number of "Tweets" mentioning a client or brand, the story's placement in the media (could be measured as above or below the fold, page number, presence, or absence of an accompanying photograph), or related to the equivalent cost of comparable advertising (a measure that the Commission on Public Relations Measurement and Evaluation has deemed inappropriate and misleading but many still use) (Commission on Public Relations Measurement and Evaluation 2009). Importantly, since the mid-1990s measurement has become important to public relations because public relations theory and strategy driven by that theory, driven hard by public relations academics and some professionals, who have backgrounds in anthropology, communication, psychology, and sociology, have argued hard for the mediating impact of public relations and demanded that public relations measurement begin to focus of nonfinancial variables on bottom-line results. This is not to say that simple counts are invalid; they are just one of a number of measurement tools the professional can use to demonstrate effectiveness, but they are not as precise or do they provide the data required to demonstrate impact on bottom lines.

Once it is established that reliable and valid nonfinancial measures can be created, their effectiveness during and after the campaign as related to the financial indicators can be assessed. What this provides the public relations professional is a way to actually establish campaign impact against planned benchmarks, compare public relations effectiveness as related to ancillary marketing and advertising indicators, and at campaign's end demonstrate impact on final return on investment within the public relations department and the general business as a whole. Stated in terms of public relations effectiveness, measurement is an integral function of the Excellence Pyramid's basic or proponent level (see pp. 29–32) (Michaelson, Wright, and Stacks 2012).

So, what exactly should public relations measurement be concerned with? Where there is hard data based on financially related measures, they should be gathered, interpreted, and evaluated. Where there is soft data based on nonfinancially related measures, those measures should be created or, if available from academic or business sources, adapted, gathered, interpreted, and evaluated. In the end, both sets of data—financial and nonfinancial—should be used to assess impact on public relations and general business goals and objectives. Nonfinancial measures are related to particular public or audiences' awareness, knowledge, values, beliefs, attitudes, and intended actions—variables that from the social sciences we know impact the decision making (Stacks and Salwen 2009; Botan and Hazelton 2006).

Data and Measurement

Measurement is *a systematic process of observing and recording of those observations as data* (Stacks 2011, 45). Stated differently, it is "a way of giving an activity a precise dimension, generally by comparison to some standard; usually done in a quantifiable or numerical manner" (Stacks and Bowen 2013, 18). Data *are the observations themselves* that are used for comparative or descriptive purposes (Stacks and Bowen 2013, 8). As noted earlier, financial and nonfinancial data are different; while financial data can be actually counted, nonfinancial data must be collected as reflecting an individual's values, beliefs, and attitudes. The collection of data differs then in that nonfinancial data come from measurement developed to assess an individual's opinions that reflect their inner thinking processes. This is covered in a later section, but for now the basics of data need to be addressed.

Basically, data can be defined as existing in four distinctly different forms or levels. Furthermore, these levels are systematically linked by how they are defined. How the particular data are defined influences how they are interpreted and ultimately evaluated. The definitional process begins by establishing whether the data are based on categories (*categorical-level data*) or along a continuum (*continuous-level data*). Furthermore, in terms of evaluation, data that are defined as continuous are generally more powerful (they provide more information about the observations in terms of being able to calculate the mean, standard deviation, and variance of observations) than data that are categorical, which can only be reported as simple counts, percentages of category, or simple proportions. Hence, we have two types of data that can be subdivided each into two levels.

Categorical Data

At the categorical level we have *nominal-level data*, data that are defined by simply systematically naming the observations but making no assessment beyond the names. For instance, there are many different ways that public relations measurement is practiced. Distinguishing between corporate and agency, for instance, is measurement of public relations practice that simply distinguishes between two of many different practice units. The measure says nothing about which is more important, which is more effective, which is more representative, or which even has more professionals practicing in the area. Traditional public relations measurement dealing with the number of press releases picked up by the media would produce nominal-level data, the measure would tell us how many releases were picked up in various papers, but not the quality of the release or whether the stories were accurate.

As noted earlier, nominal measurement's role is to simply differentiate between subcategories of some outcome variable. For instance, a public relations campaign may want to get a simple indication of an attributed message source's credibility or of several potential attributed sources. The simplest and probably most direct measure would be to ask people whether they thought the sources were credible: "In your opinion, is so-and-so a believable source? Yes or No." Similarly, one of your authors in conducting public relations gubernatorial candidates in the late 1970s asked survey respondents "Who is the governor of Alabama?" and then checked off the names reported. Each name was equal to other names; hence, the measurement was nominal. Finally, intent to purchase or recommend purchase is often measured via a simple "Do you intend to purchase or recommend stock in company X? Yes or No."

If we define our measurement system as more than simply distinguishing by assessing some relative quality—larger or smaller, expensive or cheap, taller or shorter—the measurement system produces *ordinal-level data*, data that order the observations systematically based on some criteria clearly defined in advance. Thus, we could measure public relations units by the number of clients they had or by their net income or by the number of employees each had (large, medium, small). The measurement creates an ordered set of data that differ on some preassigned quality. Of importance to ordinal-level data analysis is that there is no overlap between categories. For instance, age is a variable that is difficult to get survey responses to when respondents are asked, "What is your age in years?" People often refuse or will stretch their responses from the truth. The same is true of income questions. Ordinal measurement provides a way around both problems by establishing a systematic system: Age may be under 18; 19 to 25; 26 to 50; 51 to 65; and over 65 and income may be under $10,000; $11,000 to $20,000; $21,000 to $50,000; and over $50,000. Note that the categories are not equal, or are they intended to be; instead they represent an ordered number of categories that meet some measurement criteria (could be based on previous research or could be from an analysis of census data).

Ordinal-level measurement is often called *forced choice* measurement because respondents must choose a category or be placed in a nonresponsive category by the researcher. Hence, an ordinal measure of credibility would take the form of naming a source and asking a respondent whether she was very believable, believable, or not believable. Should the respondent not make a decision, he would be placed in a refused to answer (RTA) category. An ordinal measure of awareness might be phrased, "How aware are you of the current governor of Alabama? Very aware, aware, not aware." For the intent to purchase measure, an ordinal measure might be stated as, "Company X is offering stock at $xx.xx, how sure are you about purchasing this stock? Will definitely purchase, may purchase, may not purchase, definitely will not purchase." For both the final examples, refusal to answer for whatever reason would result in the respondent being placed in the RTA category.

Continuous Data

Continuous-level data are found on a continuum and how that continuum is defined dictates what type of data they are. Continuous data that exist within an interval on the continuum are called *interval-level data* because it does not matter where in that interval the observation is within the interval; it is measured as being that interval. It does not matter where in the interval the observation is, just that it is observed as the interval. Hence, the difference between the numbers 1, 2, and 3 are exactly one unit from each (1 is one unit from 2; 3 is two units from 1 and one unit from 2). This will become more important a little later, but for now think of age as the variable being measured. Upon a birthday you are one year older, even though you may only be one day older than you were the day before. If thinking in terms of money, five dollars is an interval measure. A majority of public relations measures produce interval-level data (Stacks 2011).

Public relations use of interval-level measures, as will be expanded on shortly, has been limited, primarily because the profession has employed a marketing approach to measurement that forces respondents to make a definite choice regarding the measurement object. Interval-level measurement requires that the perceived distance between points on the continuum appear to be equal, hence the forced choice does not allow for a respondent to be unsure or uncertain or undecided. An interval measure would add an arbitrary mid-point among the categories allowing respondents to be uncertain and would make RTA a truly nonresponsive choice.

Hence, our interval measures for the earlier examples would allow for uncertainty. For our credibility measure the responses would be, "very believable, believable, neither believable nor not believable, not believable, very not believable." In the same manner, awareness responses would be, "very aware, aware, neither aware nor unaware, unaware, not aware," and the intent responses would be, "will definitely purchase, may purchase, may or may not purchase, may not purchase, definitely will not purchase." Measures that produce data that can be found anywhere on a continuum that has a true zero (0) point are called *ratio-level data.* Most hard financial data are interval in nature: units produced, employee work hours, and gross or net income in dollars and cents. Furthermore, since there is a true zero point (interval data may have a zero point, but it is arbitrary just where it exists along a continuum), the measure can further be defined in terms of absolute difference from zero; hence, it can be used to measure profit and loss.

The use of ratio-level measures in public relations is found even less than interval measures. A ratio measure would ask respondents to make a decision based on where on a continuum they would fall regarding the object of measure. For instance, we might ask, "On a scale of 0 to 100, where 0 is the complete absence of credibility and 100 is completely credible, where would we place X." The same would be done for awareness and intent.

Continuous-level data are found in nonfinancial measures, but primarily at the interval-level. Public relations has not required the precision of ratio measures for a number of reasons, but primarily because the measurement of psychological indicators, of which credibility, confidence, relationship, reputation, and trust are commonly used measures do not require that much precision. They measure what a person thinks, but such measures have been correlated to actual behavior and find high correlations between what is expressed (opinion) and what is done. Ratio-level measures are also more difficult to administer and require sophisticated statistical knowledge to interpret and evaluate. Furthermore, as evidenced by the thermometer example, which many would consider to be a ratio measure, the zero point (where water freezes) is arbitrary—either 0°C or 32°F. The actual ratio-level measure would be in Kelvin, where 0 K is equal to –237.59°C or –459.67°F.

Such precision is not required in most public relations measurement systems.

Datasets

Before moving on to creating and using measurement, we need to talk a little more about the data itself. As defined earlier, data are observations. Those observations are defined as "variables" that have been operationalized into quantitative metrics that "define" the observations in a systematic and verifiable way. A number of variables and observations are placed in a dataset—a structured or unstructured formation that often takes the form of a spreadsheet, such as Excel (or as we will discuss later, as a SPSS data file). How the dataset is structured and how large it is determines if it is one of the three types of datasets: small, large, or big.

Small Data

The dataset that most of us think about when we conduct research is a relationship between specific variables and specific observations that is structured. In small data, variables are analyzed as if they are the only ones in the research. Small data are used primarily to test assumptions, answer specific research questions, or test hypotheses. It rarely has more than 1,000 observations and limits itself to only those variables that the researcher feels are important.

Large Data

Large data are a structured dataset, but it has many more variables and observations than does a small dataset. Large datasets commonly have over 1,000 or more observations and may include as many variables as the researcher believes may be active in the target audience. Large data are used primarily to establish norms against which specific subpopulation findings are tested. Large data are most likely to be "field" data or data from studies that involve "real world" condition. By contrast, small data are more likely to be derived from "experimental" studies that take place in controlled environments. Each, as we will discuss in later chapters, has its own advantages and disadvantages.

Big Data

The current fad today is to focus on "Big Data." Big data are a huge dataset or multiple datasets with many, many variables and thousands or more observations. Much of these data come from data "warehouses" from which the data have been inputted and then analyzed. What makes big data unique is that the dataset is *unstructured*. Unstructured datasets provide analyses by allowing the computer program computing the analyses to create relationships among variables according to a particular algorithm (a formula).

One of the most common uses of big data is to identify audience or stakeholder segments that have an impact on or can influence outcomes. A *segment* is a particular part of the dataset that describes customers, brands, and so forth by some differentiation system. For example, segments may be demographic, they may be social-economic, or they may be psychographic. Understanding the unique relationships the variables have with each other allows researchers to set priorities or proportions of audiences for each variable.

Distinguishing big data can be done by looking at what has been called the "seven Vs": volume, velocity, variety, veracity, variability, visualization, and value. Volume refers to the size of the dataset and is usually referenced in terms of bytes of data; big datasets typically are described in terms of petabytes (one quadrillion bytes of data). Velocity deals with the speed at which the data are "captured," often from online data streams. Variety means that you are not limited to quantifying your data into numbers (e.g., male=1; female=2); you can actually use anything for data: GPS coordinates, text, logos, and so forth. Veracity focuses on the trust you place in your data, especially if you are using artificial intelligence (AI) programs to create relationships and new variables from those relationships. Visualization refers on how you take humongous datasets and demonstrate the relationships visually as the data coming in may be so varied and fast that it is difficult to make sense of them at any one given time. Finally, value refers to what you plan on doing with the data—it may be that you are testing a strategy or theory about segments of your target audience; in so doing you are defining what you expect to find.

Each of these Vs gives big data an advantage in a fast-moving and Internet-interrelated world. Careful consideration must be taken when deciding (a) what kind of data you are using, (b) what types of data you will be analyzing, and (c) whether the data analysis is historical (i.e., you collect the data and analyze them later) or relational (i.e., you analyze the data as they create new variables from current variables and observations in real time).

Big data are here to stay and computers that have the speed and memory are being developed as faster and more powerful every year. You may never use big data, but you should understand what it can and cannot do for you.

Creating and Using Measurement Systems

To better understand measurement and evaluation, let's try something. In the left margin of this page, put the total number of words contained on the page as a ratio measure. (Why is it ratio? Because it could range from zero—no words—to the actual count you get.) Now count the number of sentences on the page and put that in left margin as an interval measure. (Why interval? A single word could be a sentence if it has punctuation, although there might be no sentences, there are words on this page.) Now count the number of long, medium, and short sentences as an ordinal measure and put it in the left margin. (Why ordinal? Because you will have to come up with a rationale for what constitutes a long, a medium, and a short sentence—say long would be more than 10 words; medium between 9 and 4 words; short less than 4 words.) Finally, count the number of nouns and then pronouns on the page and put it in the left margin.

Please turn back to Page 56 and reread that page and then come back to this page. Now run your counts again and put what you observe in the right margin for each measurement level. Did you get the same results? If so, your counting is reliable and probably valid. If you did not get the same results (similar doesn't count), you've just met two of measurement's problems: reliability and validity. We will return to both in a while, but for now think back on what you did the second time that might have created what we will call measurement error.

Basically, all measurement has some error in it. The job of good measurement is to keep that error as small as possible. This is done in several ways, from diligently creating a measurement system that can be employed by different people at different times that comes up with the same results each time and person to carefully looking at how that system is described or operationalized.

Measuring Public Relations Outcomes

Based on what has been discussed thus far, it should be clear that public relations outcomes that have direct impact on business goals and objectives are nonfinancial in nature. What this means is that public relations serves as a mediating or influencing factor on the final outcome of any campaign and its programming (outputs aimed at specific opinion leaders or influencers who will then serve as "third-party endorsers" or advocates of the campaign messages). These mediating factors are not something that are readily apparent, they are *potentially* observable. What this means is that public relations measures focus on the perceptions that publics and target audiences have of a business, company, brand, individual member, or whatever.

The problem with mediating variables is that they cannot be *directly* measured. Unlike financial-like data such as profits and losses, employee hours, number of products produced, public relations variables exist in the *minds* of those individuals to whom the public relations effort is being targeted. Thus, public relations measurement seeks to understand *perceptions* of the measurement object's qualities—perceptions of product or company credibility, reputation, trust, and the perceived relationship and confidence in that relationship those individuals have with the object of measurement.

So, how does a public relations researcher measure something he or she cannot see? The answer is to do it as any social scientist would. Since the early 1900s, social scientists have measured with varying degrees of reliability and validity internal thoughts or perceptions (Thurstone and Chave 1929; Likert 1932; Dillard and Pfau 2002). What we know from this body of research is that behaviors can be inferred from people's expressions about something. That is, we know that behaviors are influenced by awareness, knowledge, attitudes, beliefs, values, and intents. The problem is that all reside in our mind and although we can observe brain functioning through different forms of activity, we obviously do not have a way to peer into the deep recesses of the mind where awareness, knowledge, attitudes, beliefs, values, and intents reside. What social scientists do is to correlate actual behavior with intended behavior—actual behavior being the action taken by an individual and intended behavior being the expressed course of action an individual *says* he will do. What an individual says he will do is defined as his *opinion* on some future or past action. We know from anthropological, communication, psychological, and sociological studies that opinions are the expression of *attitudes*, which are defined as predispositions to act in some way. Attitudes in turn are based on *belief systems*, which are more primitive and allow for fairly simple internal processing. Beliefs are formed based on value systems, which are so basic that most people do not actually think about unless threatened (Dillard and Pfau 2002).

Thus, public relations researchers focus on creating measures that reflect the inner feelings and thoughts of their public or targeted audiences. Creating such measures requires an understanding of culture and language. Culture because it tends to create our value systems. Language because people express their cognitive and affective responses to something through whatever language is spoken and behavioral intentions because we can express intent. Furthermore, if measured carefully—which means that the measures are (a) measuring what we think they are measuring (are valid) and (b) do so time and again (are reliable)—they have been demonstrated to reflect actual behavior up to 60 percent of the time (Miller 2002), which occurs much higher than would be expected from chance alone.

So, public relations researchers assess outcomes based on systems of measurement that will *predict* behavior. The problem comes in determining whether those measures are valid and reliable. With financial indicators—much like count words on a page—the researcher can count and recount until he or she is certain that the number is correct. This is not possible with social and nonfinancial measures as there are a multitude of things that may be operating at different times when measuring them. Add to this the real problem of businesses creating and then not sharing measures due to the proprietary nature of business in general, and it becomes clear that there are many nonfinancial measures and that their creation and validation may not be open to all (hence public relations researchers often have to rely on academics to create basic instruments and then adapt them to the specific problem).

The problem, then, is creating reliable and valid measures of variables that will mediate the intended and then actual behavior of a public or target audience. Social scientists do this by creating attitudinal or belief *scales*, measures that collect data by asking questions, or making statements that respondents answer or react to. Notice that the plural form is used here—questions and statements. When someone responds to a single statement or answers a single question (an *item*), the research cannot be certain that the response is reliable. Its reliability cannot be judged, validity cannot be established.

Measuring and Validating Nonfinancial, Social Variables

There are many measures found in the social sciences literature that could be adapted to public relations. However, unlike academic research that can take months if not years to conduct, public relations professionals are rarely allowed much time to prepare and substantiate their measurement efforts. The rise of public relations research and measurement firms— some standalone and some as part of larger, multifunctional public relations agencies—has provided some movement toward the greater use of measurement. But with the proprietary nature of many of these measures, they are not often shared with other professionals. Reports are written and presented of findings employing these measures, but the actual measures and how they are computed, weighted, or assessed rarely find their way into print. Therefore, it is incumbent on the public relations professional to understand the basics of measuring social and nonfinancial variables. An informed client, after all, is the best client and being able to participate in establishing a measurement system—even if done so quickly to collect data on ongoing programs—should provide a better and more targeted measure.

Creating Nonfinancial or Social Measures

As far back as the early 19th century, social scientists have been creating measures of human behavior and measures that predict those behaviors. The earliest of those social scientists created what amounts to measures that assess attitudes, beliefs, and values. They do so through the use of language—that is, they understood that measures are dependent on the language people use to communicate and that not all languages have common meanings or phrases that are even similar to other languages. These measures are called *measurement scales* and are composed of *items*—statements or bipolar wording groups—that when added and averaged provide the outcome measure of interest. Since public relations measurement is often done through polls and surveys or through carefully constructed questionnaires, only three of the many approaches to attitude measurement are actually found.

Equal Appearing Interval Scale. The oldest measurement system was developed by Thurstone and Chave in 1929 (Thurstone and Chave 1929). In this system an attitude or belief object was measured by what they called "equal appearing intervals." The intervals were actually numeric values of statements created and tested to range from one end of the attitudinal continuum to the other. Hence, items were created and tested on a large sample of people from the population to be measured. Hundreds of statements about the attitude object were created and participants asked to put each into one of 11 piles, from very unfavorable to very favorable for instance, and then the statement's average was computed and its range of assigned favorableness was examined. From this analysis of hundreds of statements, a large number were determined to be valid and reliable items in a larger scale. A total of 50 to 60 of the items could then be given to participants who then simply indicated which they agreed with which were then summed and divided by the number they agree with to create a score.

The advantage to Thurstone and Chave's measure is that the measure has validity for a large number of people based on pre-established values. Postadministration reliability should be high because of all the work done to prepare the scale items. The disadvantage comes from the amount of time it takes to create and validate the measure—something even more daunting in today's social networking media.

Likert-Like Measures. In 1932 Rensis Likert reported on a different attitude measure that has become a staple of public relations measurement (Likert 1932). Likert's system employed an odd-numbered response set to a simple statement to which respondents selected which response category best represented their feelings on the attitude object. Likert argued that with multiple statements focusing on the same attitude object that an "equal appearing interval" measure could be created that was reliable and valid. Where Likert differed from Thurstone and Chave was the creation of a midpoint between positive and negative responses. Furthermore, he stressed the need for each category to be a direct opposite of its linguistic partner. For instance, in the classic Likert-like scale, the opposites of "strongly agree" and "agree" are "disagree" and "strongly disagree." The midpoint is "neither agree nor disagree." However, the categories could just as easily be "excellent" and "good," which would be opposed by "bad" and "terrible." The problem comes with calling the attitude object "terrible"—something that most clients would prefer not knowing.

To become truly interval-level data, however, Likert argued that there must be multiple statements, at least two or three, and that they should be stated as degrees of opposition. For instance, the statement "I love brand X" would be opposed by "I hate brand X" and a middle-ground statement would be "I like brand X." These would then be randomly placed with other items and presented to a respondent in a paper and pencil measure. If the respondent agreed with the first statement, he or she should disagree with the second and be somewhere in the middle of the third statement. This provides a sort of internal reliability that can be observed just through paper and pencil markings.

Likert-type measures have the advantage that they can be created quite quickly and have demonstrated consistent reliability if created systematically following the validation steps discussed earlier. There are problems with languages other than English in terms of direct translation; the traditional strongly agree to strongly disagree category system does not work in Spanish or in Semitic languages such as Hebrew.

Semantic Differential Measures. Finally, in 1957, Charles Osgood, George Suci, and Percy Tannenbaum produced a different measurement system that relied not on categories but on a true continuum as bounded by bipolar words or phrases, which they labeled the "semantic differential" (Osgood, Suci, and Tannenbaum 1957). Their work built on that of Thurstone and Chave and Likert and was a carefully conducted measurement program that identified a number of bipolar adjectives that were demonstrated to be valid and reliable measures of attitude. In particular, they found that a series of items could measure an attitude's cognitive, affective, and activity (behavioral) dimensions. The format of the measure, however, has limited its use. The measure consists of lines of items bipolar terms whose terms have been randomly reversed to require that each be carefully read. For instance, one of the dimensions regularly employed included in the activity dimension uses three items: active–passive, sharp–dull, and fast–slow. Each would be separated by an odd number of spaces on the continuum between each and the respondent would read each and place a mark on the continuum where her perception of an attitude object was:

Brand X

Active ____:____:____:____:____:____:____ Passive
Sharp ____:____:____:____:____:____:____ Dull
Slow ____:____:____:____:____:____:____ Fast

When used with paper and pencil responses, the semantic differential is a reliable measure of any attitude object or even a position stated as a sentence (e.g., "Health care should be universal for all Americans."). It is important that the visual nature of measure be maintained, a problem with many web-based survey programs and it is almost impossible to use in a person-to-person interview or telephone survey.

Establishing Scale Reliability and Validity

As noted earlier in this chapter, measurement reliability and validity are major concerns when constructing a measurement system or instrument. Reliability means that what you are measuring will be measured the same way each time. Validity means that you are actually measuring what you say you are measuring. Interestingly, to establish validity, you must first establish reliability—a measure that is not reliable is never valid (Stacks 2017).

Reliability. A clock that is set five minutes fast and an alarm set for 7:00 in the morning should go off at 7:00 each morning if it is reliable. But the question then becomes, is it actually a valid measure of time? Obviously, the clock is reliable but is it 7:00 when the alarm goes off or is it actually 6:55, and how much "error" are you willing to accept. Furthermore, are you certain after only one "test" that the alarm will go off on time later? We first looked at this a few pages ago, when we talked about the problem with one-item measures. A response to a single "testing" can never establish reliability—the behavior (marking as with a pencil or physically observing a behavior) could be random or could be a clear observation of what happened); *the problem is that we do not know and what we do not know we cannot explain.* Hence, we need repeated observations stated in different ways to really ascertain a measure's reliability.

We also know that unlike the hard sciences or in measures that do not involve humans (such as learning psychology's white mice studies), humans due to the nature of their ability to construct abstraction rarely are 100 percent reliable over time. Thus, what measurement attempts to do is to establish what is considered a reliability index that runs from 0.00 (completely unreliable) to 1.00 (completely reliable). This index is expressed in what we know about—systematic error or known variance among measurement participants—and what we do not know—random error or unknown variance among measurement participants—in measurement, stated as systematic error divided by random error. Furthermore, if we take the reliability finding, square it, and then subtract it from 1.00 we have an index of what we know and what we do not know about a measurement's reliability. Thus, if a measure is reported to have a reliability of 0.90, we find that 81 percent of the variance in responding to the measure is known or systematic error ("good" error, we can explain it) and 19 percent of the variance is still random error ("bad" error, we cannot explain it). So, even a measure that is 90 percent reliable is almost 20 percent unreliable. Ninety-five percent is a commonly used standard in public relations research. However, Stacks suggests that 90 percent or better reliability is excellent, 80 to 90 percent reliability is good, and that anything below 80 percent requires that the measure be approached with caution (Stacks 2017).

Validity. Validity—whether we are measuring what we think we are measuring—is more than a philosophical concern. If we think we are measuring reputation but instead are measuring something else, then all the results—the *hard* data obtained from which to correlate other, financial indicators—will be worthless. In academia, where time and *subjects* (students who typically gain course credit for participating in a measure's creation and validation) are plentiful, a measure is created in four basic steps, each addressing validity first and second, then reliability comes back in at step three and finally step four provides indicators of actual usefulness.

The first step in any measurement system is to do the necessary secondary research to understand just exactly what it is that is to be measured. This *due diligence* step produces *face validity*, or validity based on the measurement researcher's knowledge of the area and of other extant measures. The measure at this step is only as valid as the amount of research time put into secondary research (to include studying about measurement—*psychometrics*) and the researcher's own credibility. Once the researcher has completed a large set of *potential* items she turns to the second step for what is called content validity. Step two requires that others who have knowledge in the attitude object examine each item to ensure that the items do indeed relate to what the researcher thinks she is going to measure. Furthermore, because individual researchers often do not see where conflicts or contradictions may occur, this panel of *experts* can point out where items are poorly stated—they may not relate to the attitude object or they may be *double-barreled*—have two or more possible meanings so that responses to the item are never fully understood; they usually are words or phrases joined by "and," "but," or "or." Once the researcher has examined the item pool and the evaluation of the expert panel, she may turn to step three.

Step three examines the measure for its construct validity. *Construct validity* deals with how respondents actually see the entire measurement scale. People evaluate attitude objects on three dimensions: what they think of them (*cognitive*); how they react to them (*affective*); and how they plan on acting toward them (*connotative* or sometimes labeled as "behavioral"). Step three requires that the items left from step two be randomized and given to a fairly large number of respondents. The measurement scale is then coded into a computer and the results from the scale's items then submitted to statistical testing to ascertain if the measure "falls out" the same way as the researcher intended.[1] If so, and at this phase of step three, the items that are kept in the scale can be submitted to reliability analysis. If the reliabilities are 0.80 or better (0.70 if the measure will be tested again), the fourth step is analyzed to see if the measure actually is measuring outcomes similar to what should be expected. For instance, if the scale is measuring credibility, how does it correlate to different measures? If there is an event that is being evaluated, do known groups respond the same way as expected—for instance die-hard Republicans reporting Sara Palin's credibility is high, while moderate Republicans or Democrats reporting her credibility low. Comparison provides the fourth step of validity—*criterion-related validity*.

Reliability and Validity. As noted, there is a relationship between a measure's reliability and its validity. Obviously, a measure that is not reliable will never be valid; however, a valid measure may not be reliable due to problems with the measure's wording or other factors that may reduce reliability, such as testing situations, participant language abilities, and so forth.

Extant Measures

How does a public relations professional deal with the 24/7 nature of his job from a measurement perspective, especially with more pressure being placed on him to "demonstrate ROI?" There are hundreds of social

---

[1] This is done through a statistical test called Factor Analysis. Although way beyond the scope of this volume, Factor Analysis takes the items in a scale and tests to see how they are related to each other. A "factor" or "dimension" emerges from the correlations that have been "stretched" to ensure maximum relationship and for other items that appear to be close to be truly within that dimension. There are two types of Factor Analysis—the one that would be used if creating a new measure is called Exploratory Factor Analysis (EFA). The second, which analyses the factor structure of an extant measure, is called Confirmatory Factor Analysis (CFA). Regardless of whether being created or whether an existing measure is used, Factor Analysis should be conducted on participant responses to the measure. EFA and CFA is not reliability analysis, although many people will confuse one for the other.

variable measures in the academic literature. Indeed, Delbert Miller's *Handbook* provides multiple measures used in the social sciences, provides background on their development, and reliability and validity information (Miller 2002). In communication, where nonfinancial indicators relating to credibility, relationship, reputation, and trust abound, two books are excellent sources for measurement scales that can be adapted to whatever the current problem is (Rubin, Rubin, and Haridakisk 2010; Rubin, Palmgreen, and Sypher 1994). Finally, scholarly journals often publish the scales and items employed in published articles and if not the authors can be contacted to provide the scales employed in their studies.

There are two sets of standard measures. First, there are *intermediary measures*. These measures focus on three specific things that are found in outtakes:

1. Whether the presence of basic facts are actually found in third-party advocacy or in stories and messages published or aired in the social and traditional media.
2. The presence of misstatements or erroneous information in such messages and stories.
3. The absence or omission of basic facts that should be included in a complete story.

Additional intermediary measures can include topics from the outtakes, the presence of spokespersons as well as the overall sentiment or tone about the subject of the article or online posting.

These measures typically employ content analysis and the data are nominal—included or not included—or ordinal—positive, neutral, negative—in nature as found in the stories and messages obtained through the social or traditional media.

Second, there are *target audience measures*, which take the form of outtake and outcome measures. There are six outcome areas: awareness, knowledge, interest, relationship, preference or intent, and advocacy. These measures have become the standard against which other measures can be evaluated (Michaelson and Stacks 2011) and appears in Appendix A of this book. Each measure describes how the data are to be collected and offers prototype questions and responses categories.

Case: The Multiplier Studies

As a case in point, and one that demonstrates combining academic researchers and professional measurement researchers often produce superior results. We will look at three studies that sought to test the long-held assumption that public relations produced X-times more outcome than advertising—or a first test of the *multiplier effect* (Stacks and Michaelson 2004; Michaelson and Stacks 2007; Stacks and Michaelson 2009). This case was chosen because your authors conducted it and can explain why certain measures were created and the outcomes. The theoretical rationale and study design are available in *Public Relations Journal*; we will focus on the measurement questions and outcomes.

The first study asked a limited number of students to respond to either an advertisement or print editorial copy for one of three products (bottled water, bandage, and flu medication) across four media (print editorial, print advertisement, radio advertisement, web page advertisement) and then evaluate that product as to its credibility (believability) and intent to purchase via a paper-and-pencil self-administered test. These variables were defined initially as traditional business-type forced choice measures, except that a middle point was added ("neither good nor bad") and respondents who failed to complete an item where coded as RTA. Analyses found no differences across media for any of the three products or against a group who received no stimulus and only the evaluative measures. However, due to the nature of the one-item "measures," we could not be certain if the findings were due to the fact that there was no multiplier effect or respondents marking behavior was unreliable. Furthermore, the study's employment of multiple attitude objects or brands may have impacted on the outcomes of interest. Discussion of the study at the 2004 Measurement Summit also pointed out problems with self-administered measures, student populations, and a small number of participants.

Therefore, approaching the revised study as if it were a project for a client (and a client actually came forth and funded the follow-up studies but wished to remain anonymous), we rethought the study from both design and measurement perspectives. The new study differed significantly from what we now called the "pilot study." First, by looking at it as a best practices campaign, we created a new product brand—one that would not have any history or baggage attached to it and one that fit into a series of other brands in similar product lines: Zip Chips, a health snack. However, we wondered, what outcomes would demonstrate a public relations multiplier effect over advertising for a product with no history. A review of marketing and social science literature focused our attention on several outcome nonfinancial variables: credibility, homophily (degree of similarity on an attitude or behavior, brand knowledge), and image as mediating factors that would predict intent to purchase.

Credibility was further defined as brand authoritativeness and character. Each submeasure was defined by multiple items responded to on a Likert-type strongly agree to strongly disagree continuum. The credibility statements for authority employed were:

- The product has been presented honestly.
- Based on what I know of it, this product is very good.
- This product is very consumer unfriendly.
- Based on what I know of it, I find this product quite pleasant to use.
- This product is awful.

The statements for character were:

- Based on what I know of it, this product is an excellent choice for me.
- This product is a value for its price.
- I think this product is very reliable.

The homophily statements were adapted from a measure developed by McCroskey, Richmond, and Daly (1975) known as the Perceived Homophily Measure. Homophily measures the degree of similarity between people on an attitude and in our case was adapted to provide measures of attitudinal and behavioral similarity. All items were responded to on a Likert-type strongly agree to strongly disagree continuum. Attitudinal homophily was measured on the following items:

- This product is something that is like me.
- People who buy this product are very much like me.
- I would purchase this product because it reflects my lifestyle.

Behavioral homophily was measured on the following items:

- This product is used by people in my economic class.
- This product reflects my social background.
- People who use this product are culturally similar to me.

In addition, participants were asked to compare their knowledge and awareness of the Zip Chip brand against other chip brands. Finally, they were asked a series of questions assessing their knowledge of the brand, how the brand compared to other brands in the same product class, and their intent to purchase Zip Chips.

Three hundred fifty-one shoppers located in six malls in major cities representative of the 48 contiguous United States were randomly selected to participate. All were first screened for age and newspaper readership (the editorial and ad were limited to print media) and were exposed to either the advertisement, the editorial as would have been seen in *The New York Times*, or to a control group who received only the measurement instrument. Instead of reading a testing packet, all participants were interviewed about their attitudes toward Zip Chips by trained interviewers *in situ*. The data were then coded and statistically analyzed. The first analyses were to establish the psychometric validity of the measures and then their reliabilities. The results found the measurement scales to possess the expected dimensions and with good or better reliabilities.

The results found no major differences across the study, with the exception of the homophily outcomes, which were significantly higher for those reading the public relations copy than those who saw the advertisement. Furthermore, an analysis of the "don't know" responses to the outcome measures found that those who were exposed to the public relations copy were less unsure of themselves than those exposed to the advertisement copy.

This study was presented in several venues and published on the Institute for Public Relations website. Discussion focused not on the measures, but on the single stimulus presentation. Therefore, a follow-up study using the same outcome measures, but with the advertisement and the print editorial imbedded in a full-page *The New York Times* spread was shown to 651 nationwide at the same 6 malls. The findings were similar, but of more importance from a measurement perspective; the nonfinancial outcome measures were found both reliable and valid.

This case demonstrates that public relations outcomes can be measured and that those measuring instruments or scales can be created quite quickly. Furthermore, the basic steps in establishing their validity and reliability can be completed quickly, but only if the measurement researcher has a good understanding of the outcome variables and how they might be adapted to a measurement program within a campaign. The next chapter introduces the concept of secondary research and analysis as a method that helps inform the measurement, assessment, and evaluation process.

Summary

This chapter has taken the reader through the process of creating reliable and valid measures of nonfinancial indicators. It began by setting the stage for public relations measurement that correlates to business outcomes. After a short discussion of the types of variables public relations can measure, it focused on setting up those measures as four different levels of data and what each level added to our ability to establish public relations impact on final return on investment. The chapter then focuses on different kinds of measures appropriate for public relations nonfinancial measurement and ended with a measurement case.

Understanding both the kind and type of data being used is important when reporting research findings. Each of the measurement metrics discussed (and demonstrated in Appendix A) provides important advantages and disadvantages. These may take into consideration how the scale items are presented, the actual reliability of measures employed, and how validity has been established. When asked, the researcher should be able to respond to any question with a solid interpretation of why the measures were used, how they were created, and how reliability and validity were established.

PART II

Qualitative Methods for Effective Public Relations Research, Measurement, and Evaluation

Part II introduces the reader to the gathering of information from a *qualitative or historical perspective*. This perspective is typically employed when the researcher seeks to understand in detail a problem and has no concern with generalizing those findings to a larger audience or population. The part begins with where all research starts, regardless of methodologies employed—with what has been researched and reported in the past or *secondary research*. Building upon what has been found through secondary research, which will help in firming up public relations goals and objectives in relation to the larger business goals and objectives, three particular tools of qualitative methodology are explored—*interview*, *focus group*, and *participant observation* methodologies. The part ends with an understanding of *content analysis* methodology for traditional and social media, a qualitative tool that serves to bridge the qualitative from the quantitative.

CHAPTER 5

Secondary Research

All research methods begin with the gathering of information or data available on a given topic or problem. This gathering of information is called *secondary research* and although extremely important, it may be the most overlooked of the public relations research methodologies available to professionals (Stacks 2013). Why? First, part of being overlooked may stem from the 24 by 7 nature of public relations—seldom it would seem do public relations professionals have the necessary lead time to conduct a *systematic* secondary research on some topic. Second, a great many public relations professionals have little academic coursework in public relations, and a great many have never attempted a research methods course (the perception is that public relations is focused primarily on getting the message out, not evaluating its impact—a perception that by now should be understood as wrong and backward). And, finally, public relations only recently began to try and connect public relations programming to business goals and objectives.

We noted in Chapters 1 and 2 that any public relations activity—campaign or program—can be evaluated via the Excellence Pyramid (see pp. 29–33). At the most basic level public relations goals and objectives must be stated. The basis for these goals and objectives can be found in an understanding of what has been done in the past by others, to include the company or firm itself. Secondary research then is the first step in an activity and, furthermore, it helps the researcher decide on research methodologies, methods, analytical tools, assessments, and evaluation. Basically, *effective research requires some form of secondary research*.

Interestingly, if one were to look at public relations budgets as compared to its advertising and marketing counterparts, very little money by comparison is provided for research and most of that is allocated to the actual collection of campaign data (Jeffries 2006; Lindenmann 2001).

This, then, begs the question: What do we know about a given topic and where can we gather existing information or data on a particular outcome variable of interest—and how can we do it as cheaply as possible? The answer: Use existing information and data available from the client or from within the organization or from public documentation found in a variety of places. This is not to say that this data will be free, but it will be less expensive than if gathered by one of the methodologies in the following chapters and it certainly will drive the questions asked when collecting data from other methodologies.

Understanding Secondary Research

Secondary research, as defined in the *Dictionary of Public Relations Measurement and Research* (third ed.) is "[a]n informal research methodology that examines extant data in order to draw conclusions; a systematic reanalysis of a vast array of existing data; often used in benchmarking and benchmark studies" (Stacks and Bowen 2013). Stated differently, it is the gathering and analyzing of information and data that have already been published in some manner or reside in personal libraries. Secondary research, then, takes a second look at information and data relevant to a particular goal or objective (Brody and Stone 1989). This information often leads to the creation of personal libraries that contain source material that the public relations professional—or any professional for that matter—will go back to time and time again. Perhaps this volume will become part of the reader's personal library.

What constitutes a library? Materials found in libraries are generally classified into five categories: books, periodicals (newspapers, magazines, professional journals, academic journals), unpublished papers, videos or films, and databases. At one time all would be physically present in the library. However, in today's libraries, with the exception of books (and this is changing as more and more books—like this one—are being published as electronic copy), a great majority of the rest are now filed away electronically. Historically, the library was a physical location; today that library can be physically located but accessible to researchers through the Internet or it may reside on special websites.

Case Studies as a Special Category

Case studies, which can take on any of the five information sources, are an important element of the public relations library. According to Stacks, public relations case studies can take two forms, historical or strategic (grounded) (Stacks 2011, 157–71). The most common case study found is the historical case. The *historical case* presents a campaign or a research program in a linear fashion, from beginning to end. It assesses what the problem was, the background research, the objectives set, the communication plan put into place, and the evaluation of that plan. The *strategic case study* focuses on strategy and is modeled after case studies found in business. It provides a case history but does not provide a complete history; instead, it asks the reader to make strategic decisions and then produces what is often called a teaching note that evaluates what was done and why it worked or did not. There is a push in the profession for more strategic case studies as public relations professionals are being asked more and more for strategic input into business decisions. Four places to look for public relations case studies from both the historical or strategic approaches are found on the Arthur W. Page Society, Institute for Public Relations, International Public Relations Research Conference, and the Public Relations Society of America websites.

Secondary research requires that the researchers have access to it. Although this may sound obvious, many people do not know where to start when they begin to study a problem or are given an objective. Sources of information have an important part in the research program, are located in many places, come in at least three types, have their own validity and reliability, and can be analyzed qualitatively *and* quantitatively. In this chapter we examine each of these not only as part of the methodology, but also as a way of setting up which methodologies need to be run when collecting data.

Planning on Conducting Research

Although it seems self-evident, planning to conduct research is often an overlooked part of the research program. As noted in Chapter 3, the developmental stage of a campaign requires considerable research to define goals and objectives, establish outcomes relevant to those goals and objectives, understand what has been done previously to inform the decision-making process, and choose the appropriate methodologies and analytical approaches. Secondary research is also a vital methodology for choosing measurement systems.

Perhaps one of the most important tasks completed in the development phase of a research program is the stating of questions that will be answered and inform the active research. What secondary research does is provide the researcher with the information necessary to answer four questions relevant to *all* research programs. These questions are typically considered in order, as one informs the next; however, each may be singularly important in a research program. We will quickly review the four questions: questions of definition, questions of fact, questions of value, and questions of policy (Hocking, Stacks, and McDermott 2003; Stacks 2017).

Questions of Definition

Since the concern of public relations is to establish that the outcomes of a campaign have met targeted objectives and that these outcomes also correlate to business objectives, it is important that the outcomes are evaluated by data from valid and reliable measures. As noted in Chapter 3, the cornerstone of measurement, especially measurement that focuses on nonfinancial indicators of success or failure, is heavily dependent on definition. How the outcome variables are defined creates the base for all future research—whether that research focuses on methods or measurement. For instance, what is trust in relation to the public relations campaign? Is it the outcome variable (hence it is affected by strategies that target credibility, confidence, reputation, and relationship) or is it one of the variables that public relations focuses on to change perceptions about the product of the campaign? Furthermore, there are numerous definitions of trust, just as there are for other nonfinancial indicator variables; some are already defined (termed *reportative*, such as those found in the *Dictionary of Public Relations Research and Measurement* [see Appendix B] or *Communication Research Measures: A Sourcebook*) and yet others are defined or "stipulated to" in relation to the campaign. Thus, trust may be defined differently than commonly defined as reflected in the needs of the campaign. Secondary research helps to establish which definitions are relevant to the campaign and which need to be stipulated to as different as found in other campaigns or cases found in the literature.

Questions of Fact

Questions of fact follow from definition and seek to establish whether the outcome variables do indeed exist. For financial or physical variables, answering a question of fact is quite easy—observe whether the variable exists. For nonfinancial or social variables, the question is not as straightforward or easy to answer. Nonfinancial variables are indicators that by definition cannot be seen. They can be inferred through measurement of attitudes and beliefs, but their correlation to actual behavior is never 100 percent. Hence, measurement enters into the answer—and measurement instrument or scale reliability and validity are paramount. If you have a reliable and valid measure of the *concept* of trust and it correlates well with other demonstrated measures, then you have answered the question of fact. Secondary research provides a history of measures and their reliability and validity, as well as cases from previous campaigns to evaluate for effectiveness in measuring what is intended to measure.

Questions of Value

Not all research is factually oriented. Sometimes a researcher is interested in how well or good or sufficient an outcome is. This involves answering what has been called a qualitative question, where the value of something is being evaluated. It may be that the research is interested less in the number of responses but the quality of the responses; what has been left out of a news release, not what was in it; the quality of the relationship between important opinion leaders and a product or a company. Questions of value answer such questions and secondary research provides the researcher with an understanding of the communication's value based on previous campaigns and cases.

Questions of Policy

What happens when a campaign is kicked off? What can the researcher find that indicate strategies were appropriate for the problem or client? Questions of policy answers the "should" question—should the measurement scale been adapted because of audience differences not identified in the developmental stage? Should a different data-gathering methodology have been employed? Should a different sampling technique have been used? Should there have been more planned assessment of tactics as the campaign developed? Answers to questions like these are found in being able to look back and evaluate previous research through cases histories and other campaigns. Questions of policy are not typically answered until after the campaign is over and a complete campaign evaluation undertaken; however, secondary research can help answer such questions in advance of the campaign and at its developmental stage.

Baselines and Benchmarks

It should be clear that secondary research is required when developing the research program supporting a public relations campaign. What secondary research ultimately provides the researcher are three things. First, it can often be used to establish a baseline—quantitative data that exists at the beginning of a campaign and is used to measure effectiveness at the end of that campaign. Second, it ultimately provides the researcher is a benchmark—defined as "[a] planned KPI [key performance indictor] testing whether a campaign is on target and phase against baseline expectations" (Stacks and Bowen 2013, 3)—or series of benchmarks for later comparison during the campaign based on informational, motivational, and behavioral objectives—quantitative measurement that gauge whether that campaign is on schedule and is meeting expectations. Third, it can serve as a foundation for developing strategies and messaging based on these benchmarks.

Secondary research also serves as feedback for later assessment during the campaign—what methodologies should be used, how many times should data be gathered, what policies should be in place if analysis indicates that objectives are not being met. Too few public relations campaigns actually set benchmarks and then test against even though such testing provides a continuous evaluation of a campaign from kickoff to completion. Furthermore, many public relations campaigns cannot address the question of effectiveness because they fail to establish initial benchmarks against which to compare at campaign's end.

Information Types

What types of information does secondary research seek? In general, there are three types of information that differ in terms of their authenticity and reliability. They differ by the source of the information. *Primary sources* of information are the actual documents, journal articles, books, news reports, videos, and so forth as actually produced or printed. There is no question as to interpretation as they come from the individual or organization that created it. Sometimes primary sources are not available for any of a number of reasons and we have to rely on *secondary sources*, or reports of the primary source through the eyes of someone else. Without access to the primary source, the researcher has to ensure that what the secondary source is reporting is what was actually in the primary source. This is often done through cross-referencing several secondary sources, ensuring that the reporting is at least reliable and also providing evidence of any bias in the secondary reporting. Finally, there are *tertiary sources*, which are reports of the secondary source. There are times even with today's Internet accessibility to many information sources that primary and secondary sources are simply not available. The primary and secondary sources may be confidential reports, may be in restricted access sites, or may simply no longer exist and the researcher is left with a report of a report of a report.

Clearly, the goal of anyone conducting secondary research is to gain access to the primary sources. When primary sources are not available, secondary sources should be approached with caution and tested for reliability of reporting. Tertiary sources should be examined but rarely used; however, they may provide new avenues to a problem or a help if working through definitional problems.

Information Sources

Where does a researcher turn when searching for information while conducting secondary research? Traditionally, the answer to that question was easy and clear-cut: the library, or actually libraries. Today, the researcher has a myriad of sources to select from and access to more sources than ever before—both print and online. This creates great opportunity but also is fraught with problems, mainly an ability to establish the reliability and validity of that information. Let's compare a traditional source for beginning secondary research when little is known about the campaign object: an encyclopedia such as the *Encyclopedia Britannica* and the online encyclopedia, *Wikipedia*. Both are accessible electronically. While *Britannica* is truly peer-reviewed (has editors who review the entries for factual errors), the other allows for users to add new entries or edit older entries. *Wikipedia's* advantages of being updated as events change are offset by entries that have been added to promote a particular point of view or are truly wrong. As Marcia DiStaso noted, the problem is that with *Wikipedia* the researcher cannot gauge the accuracy or intent of the entry (DiStaso 2013).

Traditional Sources

The traditional source for secondary research is the physical library, of which there are two major types, public and private. *Public libraries* are found in almost every city and town in the United States, are open to all, and are the repository of books, magazines, and newspapers (local, national, and sometimes international). There are also public libraries that are not open to all and are found on university and college campuses. These libraries are generally reserved for faculty and students and other researchers who are given access for serious research; they are generally research-oriented, but often contain many of the same books, magazines, and newspapers the public library does. In addition, they may have special collections associated only with that particular school library.

Private libraries severely restrict access to their holdings. Private universities and colleges often have large holdings but permission is required by the general public to access them. Still, they are more accessible than other private libraries, such as professional association, corporate, or personal libraries. Trade association libraries often contain excellent reports and data on a particular sector of the economy and are generally available with little difficulty, but mainly for paid members. Organizational or corporate libraries are much more difficult to access and access may even be limited within the company to specific people. Many contain confidential reports and sensitive data that the organization does not want to be made public. Public relations professionals who work for companies should have access to corporate libraries and those working with agencies also should have access to information relevant to the problem they have been hired to work on. The final library is the personal library. As the name suggests, this is the library of an individual and is usually specific to that individual's interests. Most academics have their own libraries of books and academic and professional journals that help them with their research. All professionals should build their own working library from which to refer to as they gain expertise in particular areas or for general source material (this book, as would others in the series, should be in a personal library).

The preceding discussion should not leave an impression that libraries are no different than they were in Middle Ages. The modern library is a true repository of information and almost all libraries are highly interconnected via the Internet so that public access is available without actually ever setting foot in a physical library. What makes the traditional library important, however, is that someone has made decisions on what information will be available and checked it out for reliability and validity. Libraries, whether public or private, offer access to the contemporary source of information: the Internet.

Contemporary Sources

The Internet has opened secondary research up, giving researchers unparalleled access to information of all types and sources of information. This access, however, does not mean that all sources are valid or reliable. As more and more reputable groups put their information on the Internet, validity and reliability concerns should diminish. Most of what researchers find on the Internet initially comes from search engines and search engine optimization (SEO) and search engine marketing (SEM) have become hot topics. SEO deals with getting Internet searches to websites via search engines through unpaid searches; SEM deals with paid Internet searches (http://en.wikipedia.org/wiki/Search_engine_optimization). Regardless of which path a researcher chooses, working with search engines is no different than using the Dewey Decimal System in the 20th century.

Search Engines

Using a search engine takes some thought. A simple search engine query using Google found millions of possible search results using the phrase, "public relations." This did not include "PR" as an acronym, which would have yielded even more results. Using a search engine first requires that the researcher has in her mind exactly what she is looking for—meaning that she has carefully defined what she is seeking. Second, it is possible to refine the search using what are called *Boolean operators*, terms that help to limit or expand searches. Phrases such as "and," "or," "not," or "else" help the search engine to expand or reduce the search. Although not Boolean operators specifically, the use of quotation marks also serves to provide input to the search engine, thus further refining the search. Thus, using "public" and "relations" would yield many more than 100,000 sites; furthermore, some search engines allow the searching for specific terms within so many words of each other. For instance, searching for all references to George Walker Bush, knowing they may be "George W. Bush" or "George Bush" helps to refine the search. Third, the results that come up on the computer screen are not always listed by relevance, importance, or even number of times accessed. Companies can pay to have their websites listed early as advertisers. Knowing this and how Boolean operators operate make the search more efficient.

Although there are many search engines available, some are more known than others but some are more central to the secondary research process in that they may be more specialized. For instance, using Bing, Google, or any other search engine is like using a dictionary or encyclopedia. Factiva and LexisNexis are more media-oriented search engines, as are the search engines associated with major newspapers, such as the *New York Times*, *Wall Street Journal*, and *Washington Post* to name but a few national newspapers with search engines that allow researchers to access articles from what used to be physical news morgues. If you want to search for case studies in public relations, advertising, or marketing, you can access Warc (www.warc.com), a case study website. More specific search engines, those searching for medical terms or advice, might include WebMD. Legal questions and findings can be found in Westlaw or Lexis if the researcher has access to it. And finally, anyone wanting to get search for U.S. government information can use LexisNexis or at least two U.S. governmental sites, archives.gov or gpoaccess.gov.

Finally, given the popularity of the social media—blogs and tweets— search engines have been developed for social media communication. Three top-line search engines are socialmention, whostalkin, and toprank-blog, with more being developed by public relations agencies' research departments. This provides access to online discussions including Twitter and other social media platforms. We will discuss this in greater detail in Chapter 7—Content Analysis.

Databases

Where have search engines come from? Years ago when you wanted to search online for something you went to a database, such as the 1970s HUMRO, which provided one- or two-line notations for mainly unpublished documents that were searched via a series of key words, such as Shakespeare or Abraham Lincoln. Public-relations-specific databases that have developed into powerful websites include the previously mentioned LexisNexis, PR Newswire, Businesswire, Cison, and ABI or Confirm.

Assessing Source Reliability and Validity

As noted, much of today's information can be found on the Internet. While Internet content has made access to information easier than ever, it has also made establishing that information's reliability and validity more difficult to ascertain. Secondary researchers should always be wary of information that comes from the Internet, especially where the website sponsor is not known, is not listed, or has no contact information listed. Assuming that the information has been found and that it appears that the information comes from a credible source, then secondary researchers establish its validity and reliability in three subjective ways: content, authority, and through established critical standards (Stacks 2017; Stacks 2002). Assessing *content* focuses on answering the following questions positively:

1. Does the content deal with what you need?
2. Does the content match with what you already know?

Assessing *authority* focuses on answering the following questions:

1. Who actually wrote the material? What is his or her credibility in the area?
2. Has the material been subjected to editing, fact checking for accuracy, or been submitted to a panel of judges for review prior to publishing?
3. Is the source of the information clearly stated and contact information provided?

Assessing by *critical standards* is more difficult and comes after the information has been read. McCormick suggests the following five questions be answered (McCormick 1985):

1. Are the main points and issues clearly identified?
2. Are the underlying assumptions or arguments generally acceptable?
3. Is evidence presented adequate, evaluated clearly, and supportive of the conclusions?
4. Is there bias and is that bias addressed?
5. Is it well written, edited, or both?

A second way to assess secondary sources that include data, such as found in professional associations or governmental sources, is to actually conduct statistical tests on that data. As Hocking, Stacks, and McDermott (2003) point out, there are statistical techniques that can be run on summarized or aggregated data and, if the actual datasets are available, researchers can run confirmatory tests on the data and compare results to that published and interpreted.

Secondary Research in Measurement and Evaluation

As noted in Chapters 2 and 3 and earlier in this chapter, secondary research is particularly important in creating measurement instruments to assess nonfinancial outcomes, collecting data to check against benchmarks, and evaluating communication program success. From a best-practices approach, secondary research is essential in carrying out and evaluating a communication program or campaign. It begins with an ability to understand past experiences of clients and products, critically evaluate similar programs through case studies, find information that can be used as benchmarks or if not available to go into the field to collect that information. Best practice secondary research also dictates what type of data (qualitative or quantitative or both) is to be collected and how. Furthermore, it establishes expectations of outcomes along the campaign timeline that can be tested against or sets critical benchmarks for testing. Finally, secondary research provides the research program the necessary background against which to conduct final evaluations and to identify and correlate against other business objectives, including advertising and marketing.

Secondary Research Case

Media Assessment of Saudi Arabia's Reputation and Foreign Perceptions Between September 1, 2007 and November 9, 2007[1]

As part of opening up the Kingdom of Saudi Arabia to the outside world, the Saudis admitted a large number of journalists to cover the Saudi-hosted 2007 Organization of Petroleum Exporting Countries (OPEC) summit in Riyadh. The Saudi Ministry of Foreign Affairs wanted an international perspective on what the journalists might cover and simultaneously what effect OPEC's recent oil price rises had on OPEC's reputation and from that prepare anticipatory pointers to how the media agenda might play out.

A research company was engaged to conduct secondary research on OPEC, of the Kingdom of Saudi Arabia, and worldwide perceptions of

---

[1] This case was originally carried out by Echo Research, Inc., under the direction of Dr. David Michaelson. Used with permission of Echo Research.

both. This secondary research was necessary to prepare the research team to establish current perceptions of OPEC and Saudi Arabia, as well as to identify regions of the world, types of media to follow, and potential coding problems. It also sought to identify key opinion leaders and leading analyst companies. The goal was to present the Saudis with strategic recommendations for media relationships and key messaging strategies. The study's objectives were to be able to identify foreign journalist key concerns, areas where the Saudis and OPEC could expect questions and potential story areas relating to not only oil, but also stories driven by outside perceptions of Saudi culture.

The study analyzed 584 stories obtained from the general media and social media citizen-blogs from the United States, United Kingdom, France, Germany, Spain, Italy, and China—most of the leading economic powers and countries with major interests in OPEC and Saudi oil. This required that the coding of media extracts be done in multiple languages, which added a complication in terms of understanding what words, phrases, or utterances meant. An analysis of secondary data suggested that several areas would be examined, to first include perceptions of Saudi business, society and government, human rights abuses, and terrorism sponsorship. The second examined perceptions of OPEC and included oil supply and oil-based economics and concerns about Middle East stability. In addition, a large dictionary of terminology across languages was set up for coder training.

Based on the secondary research the study produced a number of findings and suggestions. The report found a number of assets and liabilities as found through media lens, identified what it labeled "big, bad issues" that journalists would arrive with and that could drive coverage, to include fringe stories, stories not related to oil but societal differences and potential misunderstandings based on such factors of treatment women to the freedom of the press. The study also assessed OPEC from opinion leader analysis and analyst reports, yielding 12 key factors cited for the increase in oil prices.

The study also identified clusters of journalists and their reporting on key issues for both Saudi Arabia and OPEC. The clusters were defined by topic and message tone (positive, negative, neutral).

Finally, based on the secondary research's pointing to areas and the actual findings, suggestions as to recommendations were made as to key messaging strategies and to strategic media management recommendations.

Secondary research played a key role in this study by establishing expectations for events, key messaging strategies, and media recommendations. Through a thorough search of existing literature and media stories the research firm was well prepared to conduct the actual gathering of data and subsequent media analysis.

Evaluation and Interpretation

Advertising campaigns spend large amounts of time looking at secondary data as a way to establish baselines for an advertising campaign. Part and parcel of this activity is to better understand what people like and dislike. A second feature of secondary analysis, however, is to identify the potential viewers by such normative features as demographics, psychographics, life style, social media use, and other more esoteric analyses. As noted in this chapter, secondary research is an important element in all developmental phases of a campaign. Clients often balk at having secondary research conducted, often believing that it is the agency or firm's responsibility before submitting a response to a request for proposal (RFP, see Pritchard and Smith 2015). The researcher's responsibility, however, is to point out that much of the data required in the developmental phase can be found elsewhere and where that data cannot be found, primary research will be necessary—an expensive addition to the research timeline in terms of costs and time.

Summary

All public relations practice should begin with secondary research. Best practice requires that as complete as possible secondary research be accomplished. Many times, however, secondary research or the review of existing data is overlooked as a major research methodology. Past public relations practices, which did not set baselines or benchmarks against which to test for success or failure of the public relations efforts may have made secondary research seem an afterthought. The 24 by 7 nature of *reactive* public relations—of tidying up or fixing a crisis—may also figure into the historical lack of secondary research. It should be noted that advertising and marketing programs make secondary research an essential part of their research programs. Contemporary public relations from a strategic or *proactive* approach requires that professionals have an understanding of previous research, competitors, and expected business goals and objectives and continually add to their personal or corporate or agency libraries secondary materials that can be easily accessed. Contemporary public relations has made this a necessary requirement rather than a sufficient requirement for best practices.

CHAPTER 6

Qualitative Research Methodologies

Research can take place in a wide variety of forms, and each of these forms offers unique benefits that can be used to shape and evaluate public relations programs. One of the most basic forms of research is called *qualitative research*. For purposes of describing qualitative research, its applications, and its limitations, it is important to understand what qualitative research is.

The Dictionary of Public Relations Measurement and Research defines qualitative research as "research that seeks in-depth understanding of particular cases and issues, rather than generalizable statistical information, through probing, open-ended methods such as depth interviews, focus groups and ethnographic observation" (Stacks and Bowen 2013, 25). Qualitative research differs substantially from quantitative research where the research "produces generalizable findings by collecting and analyzing data in objective ways, such as experiments and closed-ended, forced-choice questionnaires of sufficiently large samples ... relies heavily on statistical and numerical measures" (Stacks and Bowen 2013, 25).

In essence, qualitative research examines opinions and ideas in depth using the language of a small sample of individuals to explain their representative thoughts, ideas, and reactions to concepts. While this form of research demonstrates the depth and complexity of ideas, it is limited in demonstrating how widely ideas are held among a stakeholder group or a broader population; in other words, its findings are not meant to be generalized beyond the small number of individuals sampled.

The specific value of qualitative research is its ability to provide three key benefits that are not available through other forms of research:

- An understanding of issues in the language and perspective of the stakeholder being studied.
- Clarification of the findings of quantitative research.
- An ability to probe issues to understand the underlying reasons why consumers or others feel the way they do about a particular subject or product.

Language and Perspective of the Stakeholder

One of the challenges in conducting almost all forms of research is being able to understand the meaning and intent of the group being studied. This is a classic issue that has confounded social scientists across most disciplines. The work of the anthropologist Clifford Geertz is probably the best example of the *value* of qualitative research. In his 1976 monograph, Geertz argues that in order to truly understand the issues and intentions of the persons or subject under study, it is essential to step outside the perspective of the researcher and to attempt to understand the issues or questions from the perspective of and in the language of the observed (Geertz 1976). This is the central value of qualitative research.

In this form of research, the intent is to present the perspective and consciousness of the observed subjects in conjunction with their own explanation (Michaelson 1979, 140). This explanation and understanding serves as the foundation for preparing questionnaires and other structured research instruments that speak to the respondent of the survey in his or her own language. By using this approach, respondents fully comprehend the question and the intent of the question. In turn, they are able to provide useful and detailed responses with minimal misunderstanding or ambiguity. This procedure increases the validity and reliability of the overall study (see Chapter 4).

Clarification of Quantitative Findings and Probing of Issues

One of the primary functions of qualitative research is to assist in the development of larger scale, quantitative research (see Part III). While this is one of widest uses for qualitative research, there are other applications that can play an essential role in public relations research.

A key attribute of qualitative research is its inherent *flexibility*. The researcher in working *with* the study participant is free to explore ideas and concepts that would otherwise be eliminated if a formal and structured questionnaire was used. That is, qualitative approaches also allow the respondent in the study to raise issues, questions, and observations with the researcher that normally would not be taken into account if the responses were limited to responding to a standard set of response categories that are shared among everyone participating in the survey. In essence, rather than collecting data, *qualitative research is an iterative process that functions as a dialog between the observed and the observer.*

This flexibility is particularly useful when the researcher needs to understand the underlying issues behind an attitude or a behavior being observed. The central question the researcher is asking at the juncture is "why?": "Why did you buy that product rather than another?," "Why did you vote for that candidate?," or "Why do you like one product more than another?"

The answer to these questions can be used to determine those benefits that influence or modify behavior and can also be used to create communications that are more effective in reaching their goals.

The Application of Qualitative Research

However, understanding the application of qualitative research only addresses half the question. It is equally important to understand each of the three qualitative research data collection methods as each has different applications and each provides unique benefits to the researcher.

The remainder of this chapter reviews three popular and widely used forms of qualitative research found in public relations:

- *In-depth interviews:* An informal research method in which an individual interviews another in a one-on-one situation.
- *Focus groups:* An informal research method that uses a group approach to gain an in-depth understanding of a client, object, or product.

- *Participant observation:* An informal research method where the researcher takes an active role in the life of an organization or community, observes and records interactions, and then analyzes those interactions.

The challenge for the public relations researcher is to know which form of qualitative research to use in order to achieve the information objectives for the study. These objectives can include exploratory research to identify issues, pilot studies to explore language and aid in the development of quantitative or structured data collection instruments, confirmatory research used to further explain the "whys" behind quantitative findings, as well as research that can stand on its own.

The Common Elements of All Forms of Qualitative Research

Regardless of the specific method of data collection, each of the three basic forms of qualitative research has common elements that need to be put in place. These common elements include the following:

- Defining the objectives for the study.
- What are the decisions that need to be made?
- What is the information needed to make that decision?
- Who is the best source for this information?
- Identifying the types of respondents or stakeholders who will be included in the study.
- What characteristics or attributes do they have in common?
- What products do they use?
- What are their shared attitudes or behaviors?
- Obtaining lists or other sample sources that can be used to identify specific individuals who meet the criteria to qualify as respondents for the study and possibly be included as participants.
- Preparing data collection instruments or interview guides that will assist the interviewer in conducting interviews that are consistent across the entire sample and ensure the information objectives for the study are met.

- Conducting the interviews in a manner that will assure open and honest responses.
- Analyzing the interviews in order to reach clear conclusions and recommendations that address the information objectives for the study.

Sample Sources

Although Chapter 8 addresses sampling in detail, it is important to understand that the sources for the samples to be included in qualitative research study can vary widely. These sources can be as simple as a list of employees of a company or as complex as individuals who share an unusual preference as well an attitude or behavior about or toward a product or a service. Furthermore, those chosen for the sample need not be selected at random; qualitative researchers have an advantage in that they may target specific individuals due to their status, importance, or other characteristics.

Types of lists that can be used include registered users of products, specialized directories, subscription lists, and warranty lists. These lists are available from list brokers and focus group facilities, as well as from clients who may have collected this information for other purposes. The information required for these lists includes the name of the individual being recruited and contact information, as well as any information that may be relevant in the decision to ask for their cooperation in the study.

Recruiting Respondents for Study Participation

Recruiting respondents for a study can be accomplished in a variety of different manners that are as diverse as the types of respondents who are likely to participate in this type of research. For example, executive interviews are often arranged through a client or third-party that not only has knowledge of the project but also has a direct relationship with the potential respondent. In these circumstances, the respondent knows the purpose of the research and has a direct stake in the outcome. However, the typical qualitative research project requires a more complex process in order to assure the objectives of the study are met.

In many qualitative research projects, respondents are not selected for *who* they are. Rather they are included in the study for *what* they do or prefer, *where* they may live, *when* they do things, or *why* they might engage in specific activities. The process for identifying these potential respondents is called *screening*. Typically, the screening process is based on a questionnaire. The questionnaire asks a series of questions that are designed to ensure that the participants in a qualitative study exactly match the specifications for the project. This ensures that the objectives for the study are met.

The typical screening questionnaire usually takes less than five minutes to administer and can ask about product use or ownership, personal demographic or household characteristics, intended behaviors, attitudes, or preferences. In many instances, the questions are written in a manner that will mask the intent or focus of the study so that respondents participating in the project are unaware of the actual intent or focus of the study. For example, if the focus of the study is about wristwatches, it is likely the respondents for the project will also be asked about other product uses as part of the screening process (e.g., rings, necklaces, earrings). This procedure is followed so that respondents do not have preconceived attitudes or biases based on their prior knowledge. It also helps to assure that respondents provide honest responses during the actual interview.

In addition to these screening items, the questionnaire also includes detailed information about when and where the interview will take place and what, if any compensation that may be provided in exchange for their cooperation. These incentives are typically only used for consumer or general public research and some limited business-to-business applications. For consumers or the general public, a fee is often offered. Senior executives, physicians, or other hard-to-reach audiences may be offered incentive payments as high as several hundred dollars in exchange for their cooperation and assistance. Incentives or other gifts, however, are inappropriate for qualitative research among employees or among those that have a direct interest in the outcome of the research.

Discussion or Interview Guide

Once the respondents of study participants are recruited for participation in the research, it is essential to make sure that the data collection matches the objectives of the research, which should reflect the business objectives of the internal or external client, and that the interviews are conducted *consistently*. However, since the questions are typically open-ended in qualitative research, it becomes more challenging to design than structured data collection instruments such as a questionnaire. Structured questionnaires are commonly designed around specific questions that have a predefined set of potential answers. These answer categories can be as simple as yes or no or can be as complex as scaled questions that ask the degree to which someone agrees or disagrees with a concept or an idea (see Chapter 3).[1] Qualitative research, however, requires a much more flexible approach that allows the interviewer *and* the study participant opportunities to expand upon their questions and answers, as well as explore concepts and ideas that may arise in the course of the interview.

The process that is used in this type of interview is called *open-ended interviewing*. An open-ended interview asks questions such as the following:

- Please describe how you use the product or service.
- What do you think of the candidate?

These questions are often supplemented with probes that get at the underlying reasons behind why a position is held. *Probes* typically include follow-up questions such as the following:

- Why do you feel that way?
- Would you give me an example?
- Can you elaborate on that idea?
- Could you explain that further or give more detail?
- I'm not sure I understand what you're saying.
- Is there anything else that will help me to understand?

The interview typically starts with a broad, general discussion on a topic that leads into questions that become increasing specific. This

---

[1] A typical scale may be "strongly agree," "somewhat agree," "neither agree nor disagree," "somewhat disagree," or "strongly disagree."

approach will introduce the topic of the interview to the respondents who start by typically commenting on their more general attitudes or experiences. This stage of the interview is designed to set the context of how respondents use a product or service or understand a situation. This context is used to set the stage for the remainder of the interview that asks more specific questions.

It is also important to note that it is the responsibility of the interviewer to fully disclose why the research is taking place and how the findings will be used. This discussion does not have to be specific nor does the client or the sponsoring organization need to be identified. A typical explanation could include: "This study is been done to understand consumer reaction to a new product. The findings of the study will be used to help develop a better advertisement."

Respondents also need to be assured that their responses are confidential and anonymous; that is, their names will not be associated with the findings or their responses be reported in ways that could potentially identify them—something that is extremely important to get responses that are genuine to the matters under study and aids the study by allowing respondents to be candid and open in their responses. If the session is being recorded, it is also essential to disclose this to the study participants and to let them know that the recording will only be used to aid the research team in the analysis.

These are the common elements of each of the three basic forms of qualitative research. It is the role of the researcher to determine which of these three types of interviewing methods is the most appropriate form of data collection for the study at hand (see Table 6.1).

Table 6.1 Comparing the three forms of qualitative research

Benefit	In-depth interviews	Focus groups	Participant observation
Involvement of challenging or difficult to reach respondents	✓		
Ability to ask in-depth questions	✓	✓	✓
Interaction and exchange of ideas		✓	
Concept testing	✓	✓	
Understanding actual product, service, or activity use			✓

In-Depth Interviews

The in-depth interview is the most researcher-controlled of the qualitative methods. These interviews are generally conducted one-on-one and the researcher has more control over respondent answers to questions than in the other two qualitative methods.

When to Use In-Depth Interviews

In-depth interviews are most effective when it is necessary to interview study respondents who fall into one of the following different categories:

- Senior level or difficult-to-reach individuals who are unlikely to have flexible schedules and are therefore unlikely to be willing or able to participate in a group study.
- When respondents or study participants are widely geographically dispersed.
- When comments or input from another study participant or even being in the same room with another participant would influence or inhibit candid or honest responses.
- If it is necessary to recreate an environment where the respondent is exposed to concepts and ideas in a natural setting such as reading a magazine or watching television.

The process for conducting the research follows the qualitative research guidelines that cover sampling, recruiting, and the types of questions asked, as well as the general research principles of defining the stakeholders or respondents for the research, determining what information is needed and soliciting the cooperation of the respondents asked to participate in the research.

Focus Groups

The focus group, often called a *controlled group discussion*, removes some control over the research session. In the focus group a moderator, sometimes the researcher himself or herself asks predetermined questions to a group of recruited individuals and exercises control through nonverbal eye contact or direct questions to specific members once a dialogue within the focus group has been achieved, typically drawing out reticent participants or probing for more or different responses.

When to Use Focus Groups

The greatest value of focus groups is having stakeholders with a shared or common background or interest exchange ideas on a product, service, or activity. The broad objective of this type of research is to have the group explore the diversity of opinion on a topic and to provide feedback on concepts and ideas that take into account that diversity.

One of the most common applications of focus groups is to test communication programs. These programs can range from simple copy tests where respondents are exposed to advertising or press materials and are asked to determine what they learned as well as how effective the materials are in communicating intended ideas. Other applications can include exploration of attitudes to assist in creating structured surveys, clarification of survey findings, and reactions to events or spokespersons. In each instance however, the groups are exploring how respondents feel on a topic, why they hold that opinion, and how their opinions differ or converge from their peers.

Participant Recruitment

Most focus groups are recruited through professional services that specialize in this type of service. These recruiters rely on structured screener questionnaire discussed earlier. Screeners can cover a wide variety of topics and are typically masked so the purpose or the actual topic of the focus group is not revealed in advance to the respondents. This precaution is taken so that respondents provide "top-of-mind responses." These responses are generally considered to be more open and honest since they are not preconditioned, responses that the respondent believes the moderator or other observers want to hear.

The typical screener will initially ask about product, service, or activity use and may include specific questions about brands used or considered. Attitudinal questions may also be asked in addition to the product, service, or activity behavior questions. These questions are often supplemented with demographic questions that can be used to create the desired profile of the group. For example, in some instances it is preferable to have an even mix of men and women in a group session. In other instances, men and women might be in separate groups, particularly if it is perceived that gender plays a role in shaping opinions. This separation is done to encourage open dialogue among peers, as well as provide groups that are easier to compare and contrast. Other types of demographic considerations around which groups may be organized are age (younger and older), education, or even marital status. The final section of the screener is an invitation to attend the group.

The invitation provides a brief description of a general topic, when and where the group will take place, and the compensation the respondent might expect to receive for participation. As noted earlier, this compensation can range from as little as $40 to as much as several hundred dollars depending on the type of respondent and the location or city where the groups take place.

Discussion Guide

The discussion or interview guide for a focus group follows the same structure that is used for an individual in-depth interview. The only difference that needs to be considered is group dynamics. Questions should be structured to encourage dialogue *between* participants in the focus group, as well as uncover the diversity of opinion on a topic. These types of questions may include: "What are other people's opinions on this topic?" "Why do you feel differently about that?" or "Are there any other ways of thinking about this?"

Probing questions also need to be included that encourage this type of interchange. These probes can include questions such as: "Why do you feel that way?," "How did you reach that conclusion?," or "What motivated you to make that decision?" These types of questions get at the foundations of the issues by looking at motivations and rationales that can be used to understand behaviors and preferences. This understanding is often used to develop the core messages and language of effective communication programs.

Moderator

Group interviewing requires very specific skills that differ considerably from those required for individual in-depth interviews. Consequently, it strongly recommended that any research project requiring focus groups considers a professionally trained and experienced individual who has specific expertise with this type of data collection method. However, the selection of a moderator often requires much more than experience with group interviews. Careful consideration also needs to be given to their experience with the topic or product category, the objectives of the research, and the nature of the respondents participating in the group interview.

An example where a moderator with a specific category skills or background would be considered is for a pharmaceutical product targeted to older women. In this instance, it is important for the moderator to be conversant on pharmaceutical products, as well as being able to communicate to the respondents in open manner that encourages frank discussion and interchange. In this instance, it is highly likely that a middle- to more senior-aged female moderator would be the best choice for conducting the interviews.

Interviewing Room

The location of the focus group needs careful consideration. In general, the following need to be considered when deciding on a location and arrange of a focus group room.

- The room should be a conference or seminar room with a large table that seats 10 interview participants, as well the moderator. Preferably, the seating in the room should be arranged as shown in Figure 6.1.
- Name cards with names should be available for each participant. These can be prepared with card stock and markers.
- Recording equipment should be available. A stationary compact video camera that can be mounted on a tripod works

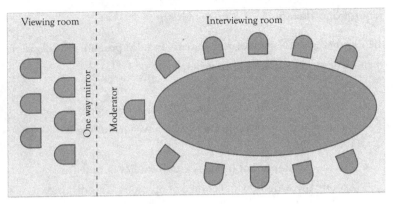

Figure 6.1 Focus group room arrangement

very well. The tripod would be placed behind and above the moderator or behind the viewing mirror in order to get a full view of the participants. Table-level omni-dimensional microphones will help insure better sound quality, but this is not a necessity.

- Assuming a mirrored viewing room is not available, and if a second room is available nearby or next door, you may want to have a video monitor available so observers can watch the groups live.

- Beverages or light snacks should be available as focus group sessions can last up to two hours and this will help increase participation in the groups.

In some instances, focus groups may be conducted online or by telephone. However, the preferred method remains the in person or live focus group. This allows for direct observation of nonverbal behavior, gives the moderator an opportunity to easily identify quiet or reluctant participants, and to encourage active participation in the group and allows for direct interaction between respondents. In instances such as employee focus groups where the presence of senior managers may inhibit free discussion, questions that would normally be asked in person are sent to participants in advance and are returned summarized and used as discussion starting stimuli with no attribution of specific respondents.

General Specifications for a Focus Group

The number and diversity of respondents is an important consideration when planning a focus group. In general:

- Groups are most productive with 8 to 10 respondents participating. You should try to avoid over-recruiting if possible.
- Diversity is important in focus group studies in order to explore the widest possible range of opinions. This diversity may include age, gender, or various types of product use. However, in order to aid in the analysis, you may want to organize groups so they are homogeneous. This will encourage shared opinions as well as a willingness to be open. An example where this is important is on sensitive personal issues such as financial issues or sexuality.
- If multiple groups are scheduled for a single time period, the groups should be scheduled with a break of 15 to 30 minutes between sessions. This will allow the moderator to collect his or her thoughts and prepare for the next session.

An important consideration is the number of groups scheduled for a given study. Generally, two or more groups should be scheduled if funding allows. This allows the researcher to establish if responses, although subjective, are similar between the two groups and helps in the final evaluation of the focus group study. When homogeneous groups are planned, say on sex—male-only and female-only groups—researchers can establish not only the reliability of group responses, but also differences between the groups.

Participant Observation

Participant observation offers researchers the least amount of control over collecting data. Concerns about participant observation as a method arise when people are unobtrusively observed going about their daily activities, which is one form of participant observation often found in academic settings (Hocking, Stacks, and McDermott 2003). The form suggested in this volume differs in that the observation is not unobtrusive, but instead takes place within environments wherein the respondents actually live, work, or socialize, or both.

When to Use Participant Observation

Participant observation is a research method borrowed from cultural anthropology. In this method, also sometimes referred to as *ethnography*, "the researcher takes an active role in the life of an organization or community, observes and records interactions, and then analyzes those interactions" (Stacks and Bowen 2013, 22). The data collection method tries to understand how individuals and groups function in their natural settings.

Consequently, the most appropriate use of this method is to gain an understanding of how individuals and groups actually use or interact with a product, service, or activity and how that product, service, and activity fits into their day-to-day lives.

This type of research has been applied to a wide variety of settings and applications including consumer products, as well as to corporations in order to gain an understanding of how individuals interact with products, their environment, and each other.

The Interview

Unlike other forms of qualitative research, there is less structure and the questions are flexible to reflect that each participant in the study lives or works in a different environment. The interviewer spends a considerable portion of the interview observing how the product, service, or activity is engaged or interacted with and questions are asked about what the respondent is doing. Instead, the questions focus on why they choose to engage in specific interactions and how they became involved.

Like other forms of qualitative research, these interviews and observations are often recorded using both audio and video equipment. Video recording becomes particularly important since significant portions of the data collection are observation rather than the interrogative forms used in other forms of qualitative research.

One of the primary features of the participant observation interview is that the data collection period is often long and very open-ended. Observations can be as short as a few minutes or can often extend for days, depending on the nature of the observation, the type of respondent, and the overall objectives of the research. Consequently, participant observations typically rely on a very limited number of interviews, using sample sizes that are considerably smaller than other forms of qualitative research. In many instances, this type of study may consist of no more than a handful of independent observations.

The Interviewer

The skills required for participant observation research differ considerably from those used in other forms of qualitative research. It is important for the researcher to take note of the product use as well as the interactions with the overall environment. Questions are used to supplement these observations and often have to be developed during the course of the interview.

Case Study: Assessing Employee Attitudes Toward Change After Coming Out of Chapter 11 Bankruptcy in the Energy Sector

What happens to employee attitudes toward senior management after new management takes a formerly regulated company out of bankruptcy and instills a new vision and mission? This question was asked by a large energy company in the late 1990s. Research into the company revealed that it was a poorly run but large company dominated by one geographic region and a company that focused primarily on the delivery of energy products to business and residential customers. The company went bankrupt just prior to the energy deregulation legislation of the 1980s and was brought out of bankruptcy by a young CEO in the mid-1990s under an umbrella structure of central administration and 16 other energy-related subsidiaries ranging from energy development to transportation to delivery.

After about five years from bankruptcy, the senior vice president for human resources, in conjunction with the CEO, requested an outside set of consultants to provide an assessment of employee perceptions of the company's new mission and vision, which stressed the safe, reliable delivery of inexpensive energy. To meet this new company vision and mission, employees were asked to work harder and more efficiently. The consultants, after conducting as much secondary research as possible about the company and the new energy industry and having conducted several earlier studies on the company's media coverage and employee perceptions of communication tools, created a questionnaire and conducted a random survey of employees weighted to represent the 16 subsidiaries and umbrella organization that yielded slightly more than 400 responses that were in line with subsidiary and umbrella employee percentages of the total population. The findings delivered rather bleak news— new employees reported low morale and poor communication, older employees felt betrayed and that newer employees did not understand the industry; all employees felt that in spite of a large new home office building, replete with all the computerized bells and whistles available at that time that senior management was going to sell them out.

The survey, while instructive could not answer the "how well," "how much value," or "why" questions that seemed to plague responses. Furthermore, the consultants had not been able to interview senior management, with the exception being the human resources and communication senior vice presidents who were now responsible for the study (the CEO removed himself from the study, asking only for a final report), subsidiary leadership, or union leaders. It was agreed that the consultants would take the survey results and conduct a series of focus groups among the subsidiaries and the umbrella office. Because of costs, a limited number of focus groups were run (14 in seven locations) and only two-hour groups per physical area were conducted. Within each focus group respondents were invited to participate such that all levels of the organization were represented among the 10 to 12 participants—from fuel truck operators to vice presidents and the proportion of males to females was calculated based on data provided by human resources and all participants were guaranteed confidentiality and anonymity. In only one group was there a problem with a senior manager as a respondent and he removed himself from the focus group at break time.

The results confirmed the survey findings and more. Since the survey had been conducted, the CEO, who used to frequently travel between subsidiaries and when in the home office would walk the hallways to discuss business and other things with employees, had locked himself in his glass-walled office and had increased the number of administrative assistants, resulting in reduced personal visibility while still working in what the umbrella company employees called the *glass office*. Furthermore, the CEO's profile had risen across the energy industry while he had reduced contact with employees. Employees were consistent across all focus groups, in their perceptions and attitudes, that the vision and mission, while something to strive for was not where the time and money were being put. Indeed, one group had done further investigation into the CEO's background and noted that he stayed on average five years with a company he brought out of bankruptcy before selling it and moving on.

The focus groups provided a vast amount of additional information that could have been used to increase internal communication and a number of suggestions from the focus groups on how to better meet the company's new vision and mission statements. The report was written and submitted. Approximately a year later, the company was bought out by another energy company.

Limitations of Qualitative Research

Qualitative research has unique benefits that are unavailable from other forms of data collection. It is flexible and adaptable. It gets at underlying issues. It probes for the "whys" behind the "whats." However, even with these benefits, qualitative research is not appropriate in every instance.

The four primary limitations are that qualitative research is (1) costly, (2) time consuming or labor intensive, (3) cannot be used to reliable measure or determine the extent to which attitudes, opinions, or behaviors are held or engaged in by a particular population, and (4) do not provide a reliable basis for measuring the impact of a communication program.

The costs of qualitative in-depth interviews can often exceed $1,000 per interview when preparation time and analysis time are taken into consideration. Focus groups are also costly with expense often ranging from $6,000 to $10,000 per group depending the types of respondents and the locations of the groups. Added to the fact that data collection can take a considerable amount of time to complete, the overall number of interviews included in qualitative research is often quite limited. This makes it difficult to extrapolate the results to a broader population. However, when used in combination with surveys, qualitative research is a powerful tool for effective and useful communication research.

Evaluation and Interpretation

Qualitative research is a costly yet important method to have in your toolbox. Many clients believe that qualitative research is less expensive than quantitative research, but they are looking at it wrong. In reality, qualitative research limits your interpretation of results; it also takes much longer to conduct and analyze. What qualitative data gives you is a better, in-depth understanding of problem being researched. To get this, however, it gives up any chance to generalize to a larger population. It is an important method to really understand what motivates people, how third-party endorsers think, and a sometimes needed developmental strategy to better understand a problem or perception of some event, brand, or service. Costs aside, conducting qualitative research allows the researcher to better interpret quantitative findings, especially when those findings are ambiguous or counter to expectations.

CHAPTER 7

Content Analysis

Content analysis is one of the most commonly used and at the same time misused public relations measurement and evaluation tools. Because it is often considered the most basic form of public relations measurement, content analysis is frequently seen as a less effective and less reliable form of public relations measurement and evaluation. However, when properly used, content analysis can be critical in evaluating overall communication effectiveness and function to help plan more effective public relations and media relations strategies.

This chapter explores several key aspects of content analysis, starting with a basic understanding of the nine types of traditional public relations content analysis that are commonly used and explores alternative approaches that can be used in conjunction with other forms of research including web or social media analytics. Thus, content analysis is an essential tool in an overall public relations measurement and evaluation toolkit.

Understanding the Basics of Traditional Content Analysis

Before we look at the specific forms of content analysis, we need to first examine the basic steps anyone using any of these nine types of traditional analysis must take. While content analysis appears to be a very basic and straightforward research method, it is more complicated than it seems and must be approached in a systematic manner that requires the researcher to make informed decisions at each step of the research process.

Determining the Analytic Framework

As with any sound research method, the researcher should begin by examining what has been done before by conducting, at least informally, a secondary or historical review of similar studies or cases. This provides the researcher with information that is necessary to establish what will be evaluated as part of the content analysis. This includes (1) which messages, (2) the priorities of those messages, (3) how to classify and count the messages or parts, and (4) how to establish whether the coding was reliable and the competitive framework for the analysis. This analysis is compiled into a document often referred to as a *code sheet* that lists all the issues and messages as well as competitors that are included as part of the overall study.

For a more complete review of the analytical framework, see the *Primer of Public Relations Research* (Stacks 2017).

Selecting the Message Pool

If the content analysis is conducted on all messages that are obtainable in a given set of articles then the message pool or population results in a *census* of all messages. However, in many instances obtaining all messages is not practical as many of these messages are not directly relevant to the business issues that are at hand. Consequently, it is common practice and some type of selective sampling of these messages must be completed. These messages can be determined in two manners. The first is through a review of a sample of articles to determine which messages or issues are common across the articles. The second approach is to determine these messages *a priori*, that is, independently of what is actually written. These messages used in the analysis are those that are typically important to the recipient of the study. Practically, the message selection is a hybrid approach that actually uses both of these methods in an iterative combination of hypothesis testing and evaluation in order to obtain a final list.

Establishing the Unit of Analysis

Once your message pool has been established, content analysis requires that what is being analyzed must be defined. This is called establishing the unit(s) of analysis. The unit of analysis can take on several forms—and often more than one is established for analysis. The unit of analysis defines what is being analyzed and is generally found in one of the two classes (Holsti 1969). *Manifest* units of analysis are *what can be seen*: words, pictures, names, spatial calculations, and so forth. *Latent* units of analysis are *what must be inferred* from the content: accuracy, tone, and indicators of liking, violence, and so forth. The unit of analysis is carefully defined and then pretested to ensure that coders (those who will actually review each message and decide how the unit of analysis is to be interpreted) are evaluating the same content the same way.

Establishing Category Systems

Once the unit of analysis has been defined and tested, the next step is to create a category system. The category system is where you will place your units of analysis as they are evaluated. This is often referred to as coding, but actually what is coded is dependent on the category system created. There are several rules to establishing categories.

First, the *categories must reflect the purpose of the research*. That is, if our study is on company X's reputation, then categories should include reputational units of analysis, so a category on auto racing would not reflect the purpose (unless the company had an affiliation with racing).

Second, *the categories must be exhaustive*. The content must be put in a category, it cannot be left out. This leaves the ubiquitous category, "other" as a catch-up. Best practiced content analysis always pretests the category system on randomly selected content before conducting a full-fledged analysis to ensure the categories are exhaustive. As a rule of thumb, when the other category reaches 10 percent, the category system should be reexamined. At times events may occur that require a new category to be added. Theoretically, the content should be recoded taking into account the new category, but in practice a note is made and then the other categories are compared before and after this point in time.

Third, *categories must be independent of each other*—that is, something cannot be put in one because it is not in another, the content must fit by definition, although as noted previously, sometimes events force new categories. At the beginning of a content analysis, for instance, at one time you could categorize football and basketball positions by player jersey number. Today a point guard could wear the number 50 or 1; the same is true in football, where almost all linemen had jerseys between 50 and 70 but now some wear between 80 and 90.

Finally, *all categories must represent one classification system.* As noted earlier, categorizing professional athletes by jersey number for each playing position (i.e., linemen in the 60s and 70s, quarterbacks between 10 and 19, wide receivers between 20 and 29), while problematic today is a valid classification system. If the content analysis were to have a second system, say jersey color, then confusion might occur and the classification system might yield error in placing content in the correct category. This can affect the validity and reliability of the analysis (see Chapter 4).

Coding

This step should be the easiest, once the unit(s) of analysis and category system has been put into place. Coding requires that someone trained in the content make decisions as to which categories the content goes. Coders should be carefully trained to (1) understand the unit of analysis being coded and (2) place that content in the appropriate category. All coders (ranging from one to several) should have practiced coding the data until minimal coding errors are obtained.

Establishing Coding Reliability

Coding reliability tells the research how much error in coding judgment occurs. While 100 percent coding reliability is the goal, there is *always* some coding error. During coder training, reliability estimates of coding should be conducted until coders are in agreement at least 90 percent of the time (Stacks 2017). After the coding has been completed, a final reliability should be run using either Holsti's reliability coefficient or Scott's *pi* statistic (Holsti 1969; Scott 1955). Holsti's coefficient is a general reliability estimate and is quite easy to hand calculate, while Scott's *pi* is much more difficult to compute but is much more conservative. Most computerized content analysis programs now include both.

Approaches to Traditional Content Analysis

Content analysis takes many different forms, with each form measuring and evaluating very different aspects of a public or media relations program or campaign. Overall, there are nine distinct types of content analysis commonly used in public relations, with many methods being combined into unified or composite analyses. The nine types of content analysis can be further divided into three general categories base on what is actually coded, they include the following:

- No message evaluation
  - o Clip counting
  - o Circulation and readership analysis
  - o Advertising value equivalence (AVE)
- Manifest message evaluation
  - o Simple content analysis
  - o Message analysis
- Latent message evaluation
  - o Tonality analysis
  - o Prominence analysis
  - o Quality of coverage
  - o Competitive analysis

As a first step in reviewing the application of content analysis in public relations measurement and evaluation, we will review how each of these nine types of analysis are typically applied in public relations.

No Message Evaluation

There are three basic approaches to content analysis in public relations that do not deal with message evaluation—clip counting, circulation and readability analyses, and advertising value equivalency.

Clip Counting

This is the most basic—and perhaps most antiquated—form of content analysis used in public relations. With this system, relevant articles or posts are collected and typically sorted chronologically or by date. The analysis generally consists of a summary listing the publications and dates of publication as well as the total article count. Typically, these clips are bound together in chronological volumes. One of the most common analyses used in combination with clip counting is the "thud factor" or the overall volume of noise generated when the book of bound press clips hits or thuds against a table or other flat surface.

The analysis contains no insights, discussion of or interpretation of the coverage and is dependent on the recipient of the report to draw judgments about the actual content. These judgments are generally qualitative, usually based on reading a handful of articles, articles that may or may not typify the actual coverage a media relations effort actually received.

Circulation and Readership Analysis

The next level of content analysis builds upon clip counting by adding information about each article that is gathered from secondary data sources. At present time, these sources typically include BurrelleLuce (provides press-clipping services that also include circulation information and other third-party information about the article), Nielsen Research (provides television audience measurement and related services that are used to determine audience size and composition for broadcast and cable programming), Arbitron (a media and marketing research firm that is used to measure audiences for radio and for other media services), Scarborough (a provider of readership information for local and national newspapers), Audit Bureau of Circulations (ABC, a third-party organization that audits and certifies the circulation of print publications), Experian Simmons or GFK MRI (formerly known as Mediamark Research) (National surveys of consumers that measure consumer purchases as well as consumer media habits. These surveys are commonly used as tools for planning media purchases by advertisers). Numerous sources also exist for volumes of social media stories and posts including Radian6, Sysomos, and Sprout Social.

The specific types of information added to a clip counting analysis may include circulation of the publication or number of printed or hard copies distributed, total readership or the total number of actual readers (circulation multiplied by average number of readers for each copy or visits to a particular website), demographic profiles of the readership of each publication or site (e.g., age, gender, income, education), and possibly even product use, attitudinal, lifestyle, or psychographic information.

A common approach with this type of analysis is to present a total circulation, total readership, or total viewership that is the total number of copies distributed or the total number of individuals who are likely to have read a given copy or a posting. Total readership is also referred to as "pass along" or gross readership.

However, these approaches can be further modified to only include qualified readers—those readers who are of specific interest to the evaluator—who are part of the target audience for the publication, regional analyses, and other subsets. An example of a qualified reader is a particular gender or age group to whom a public relations program is directed (e.g., men 18–34 years old, college graduates, military officers, etc.). Actual analysis of the content of the articles, however, is not part of this study.

Advertising Value Equivalence (AVE)

AVE is an estimate of the cost of purchase of advertising that has an equivalent size and location in a given publication on a specific day. These estimates are typically based on information provided by Standard Rate and Data Service (SRDS), which is a database of media rates and information that is used by advertising agencies. This approach is discredited by many public relations practitioners as well as by leading researchers, primarily based on the assumption used in many advertising value analyses that a public relations placement is worth more than or is a multiple of an equivalent advertisement in its overall impact or effect. Recently published work, however, demonstrates that advertising and public relations are likely to be equally effective at communicating similar messages (Stacks and Michaelson 2009). While there are some applications where AVEs may have some limited utility, this approach is generally considered flawed (Jeffries-Fox 2003) and has been discredited by all leading research organizations dealing with public relations measurement.[1]

As in the analysis of circulation or readership, actual analysis of the content of the articles is not included in this type of study.

Manifest Message Evaluation

Manifest message evaluation takes two forms, simple content analysis and message analysis.

Simple Content Analysis

This is a simple or basic analysis that classifies or codes what is written into categories that can in turn be statistically analyzed. The categories or codes are developed by a close textual analysis of a small sample of randomly selected articles, often as few as 10 percent. The remaining articles are analyzed based on the presence of these codes. Each article is read to determine the presence of specific pieces of information that is classified according to the codes. Information from the codes is then entered into a database to determine the frequency of codes or classifications of information.

Because this approach is based on the presence of specific codes or categories, this method accurately represents only what is actually written. Intended messages or specific items of information that are not included in the codes or do not appear in the articles are not included in the analysis. This method also does not draw inferences about the accuracy or desirability of the information that is included in the articles.

Coding is commonly done using readers who have been specifically trained to perform this task. This approach is limited by the potential fallibility and inconsistency of the readers responsible for the coding. To address

---

[1] Advertising value equivalence (AVE) was formally discredited by the public relations profession in 2010 in a document called the Barcelona Principles. For a fuller discussion of the Barcelona Principles refer to The International Association for Measurement and Evaluation of Communication (AMEC) website: www. amecorg.com.

this challenge, many organizations coding or classifying the content of news articles limit the number of readers to just a handful. This use of a limited number of readers assures consistency and, in turn, results in a higher degree of *intercoder reliability* or "the extent to which the different judges tend to assign exactly the same rating to each object" (Tinsley and Weiss 2000).

In the past few years, computerized systems have been developed to address these issues. However, these systems tend to be inflexible and often miss articles or misclassify the results. While significant advances have been made in this area, the most accurate coding is still conducted using human readers.

Message Analysis

Message analysis differs from simple or basic content analysis by centering the analysis on the presence of intended messages in articles. Key messages are developed based on communication objectives (see Chapters 1 and 2). These communication objectives are translated into codes that become the basis of the analysis. Articles are coded by the presence of key messages included in each article. The analytic process is similar to a simple content analysis where the codes from each article are entered into a database for statistical analysis. Message analysis, however, is still limited in its overall scope since it only includes the presence or absence of specific messages. Accuracy and completeness of messages is not part of the overall analysis.

Latent Message Evaluation

Latent message evaluation currently takes on four forms and is the direction that content analysis is moving. The four forms are tonality analysis, prominence analysis, quality of coverage, and competitive analysis.

Tonality Analysis

Tonality is an analysis that uses a subjective assessment to determine if the content of article is either favorable or unfavorable to the person, company, organization, or product discussed in the text.

There are a variety of different ways to assess tone. One of the most common is a simple classification of positive, neutral, or negative. However, the preferred scale uses five points of analysis ranging from one meaning very negative to five meaning very positive. A rating of three on this five point scale is typically given to articles that are neutral. Neutral is commonly interpreted as an unbiased presentation of facts without an appraisal.

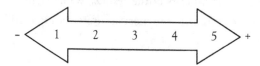

Other options include scales with positive and negative ratings. An example is would be a scale with a rating of –50 to +50. In this instance, –50 is completely negative and +50 is completely positive. A neutral analysis would be recorded as zero on this scale. However, the amount of potential variation associated with this type of scale limits the ability to achieve consistent evaluations or intercoder reliability when multiple analysts are used to analyze articles.

This method can be applied using several different approaches. The first is an assessment of the tonality of an overall article. Other approaches assess the tone of a specific mention or code or assess the tone of a specific message that may appear in an article. Each article is typically assessed individually and the findings can be aggregated to present an overall assessment of the tone of the media.

Prominence Analysis

This analysis takes into account six factors: (1) the publication where the article appears, (2) date of appearance, (3) the overall size of the article, (4) where in the publication it appears, (5) the presence of photography or other artwork, and (6) the size of headlines. In a typical prominence analysis, each element is given a weight that is factored into an overall score for each article. That score determines the prominence of the article.

Certain publications (e.g., *The New York Times* or *The Wall Street Journal*) are generally rated as having higher prominence than others.

This assessment is generally based on the size and perceived quality of the readership. Date of appearance can also be a factor since readership can be much higher on specific days (e.g., Sunday or Monday).

In this analysis, articles that receive higher prominence scores are given more emphasis in the evaluation. It is assumed that either the higher readership, prominence of the publication, size and placement of the article, or a combination of these factors leads to higher communication effectiveness. The limitation of this approach is that prominence is typically a highly subjective measure. There are no reliable methods to assure that prominence is rated consistently from publication-to-publication or from evaluator-to-evaluator. This often results in inconsistency of results, thus making it difficult to compare results over time.

Recent efforts have attempted to develop an objective measure for article prominence. Some of these objective measures of prominence rely on an advertising value equivalency model that assumes that a high AVE reflects both the prominence of the publication (e.g., quality of audience) and the size of the placement as well as the location (e.g., cover page, center page, back page, etc.) of the article within the publication. However, there is no conclusive research as of yet that validates the use of advertising rates as a proxy for determining article placement.

Quality of Coverage

Quality of coverage is often based on a combination of factors. The factors typically included in this measure are tonality (positive, neutral, or negative), prominence, or placement location, the inclusion of specific messages in the article, as well as the overall volume of articles generated. Each of these factors is entered into a computation that generates a score for each individual article in the analysis. This generates a *quality of coverage score* that is similar to the scales discussed earlier in this chapter. Many of these elements are, however, highly subjective and subject to the interpretation of the reader. The most significant limitation of this approach is that the evaluation is typically not tied to the outcomes that are anticipated from the public relations efforts. Therefore, while quality is assessed, the impacts of the messages placed are not taken into consideration.

Competitive Analysis

In addition to the analysis of an individual topic, event, brand, or company, a content analysis can also be conducted comparing the performance of companies, brands, topics, or events on their media coverage. This can range from comparisons of the total number of clips to the share of discussion to comparisons of the overall prominence one brand or company receives over another. This is often used as a way to assess relative performance in the media as well as identify where gaps exist and where there may be opportunities for further or enhanced communication efforts.

Other variations of content analysis also exist many of which use proprietary systems and employ a combination of many of the techniques discussed (Broom and Dozier 1990).

The Challenge of Current Approaches to Content Analysis

As widely available and diverse as each of these methods of content analysis are, public relations practitioners rarely make use of even the most rudimentary of these research methods. The only exception to this is high prevalence of clip counting—a method of content analysis that is almost universally applied among public relations consultancies as well as among their clients.

Even when a content analysis is conducted, the evaluation rarely, if ever, offers any insights more profound than the tonality of placements (e.g., positive, neutral, or negative) and consequently, these analyses fail to offer diagnoses of the situation or prescribe a solution that is tied to communication objectives.

We can speculate on the reasons for this lack of acceptance of one of the most basic and rudimentary forms for measuring public relations activities. However, in this chapter we contend that the issue is not lack of interest, lack of knowledge, lack of budget, or even a generalized fear of measurement and evaluation. Rather, it is a *perceived lack of usefulness* of these basic content analysis measures that lets them to fall in disuse and results in a general lack of measurement and evaluation by the public relations profession.

The Fatal Flaws of Common Forms of Content Analysis

As comprehensive as these common methods of content analysis appear, they still contains significant flaws that severely limit their utility:

- The first flaw is the absence of a basic analytic structure that determines the accuracy of coverage overall and more specifically determines the accuracy of specific messages included in the content of articles under analysis.
- The second flaw is an inability to link analysis to communication goals, objectives, and public relations messages.
- The third flaw flows from the first and second, a lack of understanding the communication lifecycle.

Flaw #1: Not Determining Message Accuracy

The basic accuracy of messages is not generally included among any of the methods of content analysis discussed or considered. Accuracy is a critically important consideration when attempting to link public relations outputs to outcomes of communication efforts. If a message is erroneous, false, incomplete, or misleading, then the communication efforts are significantly less likely to achieve their intent objectives (see Chapters 1 and 2 for a more detailed discussion on setting objectives).

To understand the value of message accuracy in a public relations measurement program, it is important to understand the elements that need to be taken into consideration when conducting this type of analysis. Message accuracy is based on an analysis of four basic elements which become the main units of analysis coded into at least four categories:

- The inclusion of *basic facts*.
- The inclusion of *misstatements* about these basic facts.

- The inclusion of *incomplete, deceptive, or misleading information* that biases the interpretation about basic facts.
- The *omission* of basic facts.

Basic Facts.   Basic facts are the fundamental information that is central to any communication program. Facts can be such fundamental information as a product definition, or a description of the product or service under study. They can also include statements, opinions, or points-of-view that can be supported and documented. Examples of opinions or points-of-view that can be considered basic facts are statements about *relative value* or *comparative information* that is used to place information in context.

Misstatements.   Misstatements are generally understood as errors or incorrect information included in an article or publication. Misstatements typically result from incorrect data but can also include unsubstantiated opinions or points-of-view from a reporter or interviewee that states a falsehood.

Incomplete Information.   Incomplete information is a statement, opinion, or point-of-view that selectively includes some information, but excludes other relevant facts. These apparently accurate statements often create misleading impressions or a deception about a product or service and, while factually accurate, are in actuality erroneous.

Omissions.   Omissions are the absence of key information that *should be included* in a specific article or publication. Not all basic facts can be considered omissions if they are not included in an article or publication. The key to understanding omissions is in the context of the article. The focus or subject matter of the story has to be relevant to the specific omission and the story or article will be considered incomplete unless that basic fact is included.

Flaw #2: Not Linking Messages to Communication Objectives

The second challenge involved in conducting effective content analysis is linking communication objectives with the actual message analysis. Typically communication objectives are directly related to the information needs dictated by a communication's life cycle. In public relations, there are two key recipients of these messages. The initial recipient is the media, who, in turn, serves as the conduit for transmitting messages to intended recipient (i.e., their readers).

Flaw #3: Not Understanding the Communication Lifecycle

All messages have specific goals or objectives. In most cases, these goals or objectives involve having the message recipient take a specific action or indicate intent to take a specific action. These actions can range from making an inquiry about a product or service to voting for a particular candidate to developing a favorable image of a brand, a company, an issue, or an organization.

Effective messaging is a process that requires the recipient to go through five stages before a desired action takes place. These five stages of communication effects include the following:

1. Establishing *awareness* of the brand, the category, or the issue
2. Building *sufficient knowledge and understanding* about the brand, category, or issue in order to make an informed decision
3. Developing a *level of interest in and preference* for the brand, category, or issue or at least a recognition of its relevance to the message recipient
4. Creating a *change in behavior or intent or commitment to take a specific action* based on the received messages
5. Establishing *advocacy* for the brand, the category, or the issue among current users or supporters.

Advocacy is a particularly important evaluation when conducting analysis of social media. As noted earlier, the unique nature of social media is the two-way interaction between an author and a reader that results in sharing this interaction with broader audiences that often takes the form of advocacy for a brand, a product, or an issue.

Simply communicating the desire to have a message recipient take an action is unlikely to have the impact a communicator is hoping to achieve. In most cases the analysis fails to account for the stage of the communication life cycle that needs to be addressed. For example, at the initial stage of the communication life cycle, communicators should be measuring the proportion of messages that are strictly designed to develop awareness. At later stages in the lifecycle, the analysis needs to shift to determine the proportion of messages that communicate knowledge, interest, or intent to act. (See Chapters 2 and 3 for a detailed discussion of these factors.)

When this type of analysis is applied, content analysis not only goes beyond a simple diagnostic of the accuracy of messages, but also expands to provide data and evaluation that become an integral part of the strategic communication planning process. Not only can accuracy be measured, but this accuracy can also be directly linked to communication goals that, in turn, can be measured and evaluated among the target audiences for these messages. This analysis is particularly important when each message must be delivered through the media.

The communication lifecycle must be understood for both the media as well as from the target audience. In many cases, each can be at a different level of understanding and may have different communication needs. An example is when the media may be completely knowledgeable about a product or service, but the target audience has only marginal awareness and little or no understanding about it. In these instances, the media may make assumptions about the level of knowledge held by the target audience and not report as completely and thoroughly as they should. This can inadvertently create a gap or omission in an article that needs to be corrected. As was pointed out by New York Yankee Hall-of-Fame catcher Yogi Berra, "You've got to be very careful if you don't know where you're going, because you might not get there."

Lessons Learned

The lessons learned from the application of this approach are remarkably simple. In order for content analysis to function as a useful tool, it has to be applied in direct relation to the communication goals and objectives that the content analysis is tracking. While this seems to be a simple and obvious conclusion, the challenge is that these linkages are rarely made and when they are made, they typically only go part way in meeting the goal or adequately evaluating specific outcomes.

Typically, even when content analysis delves deeply into published materials, these analyses fail to assume that erroneous reporting or commentary can be the primary barrier to achieving a program's communication goals. As a result, most content analysis tends to concentrate on tonality of an article rather than the fundamental correctness of the reporting. This concentration on tonality, consequently, fails to provide the information that is necessary to implement a corrective strategy with media, which can in turn result in an increase in accurate and appropriately positioned messages.

Content Analysis Case

MetLife and Accuracy of Coverage[2]

Recent award-winning cases involving research on behalf of MetLife are some of the few examples where a concentration on the accuracy of coverage has been applied in content analysis and, as the results demonstrated, implementing the findings from the initial analysis created measurable improvements in both the quality and accuracy of the coverage as well as the overall volume, resulting in significantly improved media relations.

As these cases showed, between 60 and 85 percent of published articles on the key issues of concern to MetLife included an error in reporting, a misrepresentation of key information or an omission of basic information that should have appeared in the contexts of the articles in question. By concentrating media relations efforts on those reporters and publications where the errors and omissions in reporting occurred, the eventual result was a significant decline in the proportion of articles with either errors or omissions as well as an overall increase in the number of articles by 45 percent on the issue at hand. While tonality was not a part of this analysis, the overall effect was that reporting on the issues was much more favorable and more in line with MetLife's media relations goals. The key conclusion drawn from these studies is that shifting the analysis to determining the accuracy of reporting can offer significant benefits that are

---

[2] Michaelson and Griffin (2005).

not available when only tonality is considered. However, this approach has some significant limitations, particularly in comparison with more traditional forms of content analysis.

The primary factors that limit the application of this form of content analysis are the need for in-depth knowledge of the issues in order to determine both erroneous and omitted messages as well as the skill level required to code each article not only for the presence of correct and incorrect messages, but also to determine when basic messages should have been included. The latter is particularly critical since it requires that the reader understand the full context of the article in order to code accurately. To date, artificial intelligence systems do not have the capacity to make these determinations. Consequently, highly skilled human coders are required to perform these assessments.

However, human coders need to be rigorously trained and supervised in order to analyze the content both correctly and consistently. In addition, it is highly desirable for these coders to have an intimate knowledge of the issues at hand in order to correctly identify errors in reporting as well as omissions of basic information that should have been included in the article. Without this training and skill sets, the findings from this research will be highly unreliable and inconsistent.

As a result, the costs for this type of analysis are much higher than other forms of content analysis. However, the return in a significantly improved quality of media relations as a result of this approach strongly justifies the investment, particularly on the types of products and issues discussed in the case histories on which the article is based. The end result: The overall results demonstrate substantially higher return than using other methods of content analysis specifically because the analysis concentrates on tying the objectives of the media relations to the content analysis.

A Research Case

Description of the Challenge

Americans often get information on financial planning through the media. This places a very heavy burden and responsibility on editors and reporters to ensure that the information they are sharing with their readers is both accurate and complete. For many middle market Americans, life insurance should be a significant component of their personal safety nets. Whether or not these consumers were getting the information they need to make informed life insurance purchase decisions—or encouraged by the news media to even consider the value of life insurance—prompted MetLife to commission a series of comprehensive research studies of the consumer media's coverage of various types of insurance as a product category.

The key challenge for MetLife was identifying how the media reports about types of insurance in order to develop a media relations strategy that provides critical information to the public and increases the overall level of accuracy of reporting on this issue.

Strategic Approach

The primary goal of the research projects was determining the degree to which correct, incorrect, and only partially correct information is included in news and other stories about various types of insurance. Going beyond traditional content analysis, an additional goal was the unique effort to determine the extent to which key information about specific type insurance was omitted or misreported from these articles. The analysis allowed MetLife to make a connection between the extent and depth of media coverage on different types of insurance and the consumers' comprehension of the significance of owning one of the many types of insurance policies available to them.

The information from this research was used to support broader public relations objectives on consumer insurance products:

- Educating consumers on when to buy specific types insurance, how much coverage they need and what type of insurance best fits their needs.
- Educating the media on the benefits of insurance as an essential life-planning and retirement tool.
- Continuing to position MetLife, the largest U.S. insurer, as a thought leader on insurance among the national media.

Audience Analysis

There was a broad range of audiences for this research. They included personal finance reporters who regularly write about financial issues and protection products as well as consumers who rely on the media for their investment and financial planning advice. While this is the general audience for this research, MetLife has a specific interest in those consumers who have the greatest need for reliable and accurate information about insurance and its benefits. Depending on the type of insurance under study, these audiences included young families, baby boomers, or older adults planning for retirement.

Strategy

Findings from this research served as the basis for media relations strategy and consumer education program that communicated the value and benefits of different types insurance to key financial planning reporters as well as provide supplemental information to these reporters to assure their reporting was accurate and complete. This in turn provided reliable information to the insurance buying public on these products.

Research Execution

The research for one of these types of insurance—life insurance—analyzed all articles on this type of insurance that appeared in the major market daily newspapers with the highest circulation in the United States, leading personal finance publications and websites (e.g., Money, Smart Money, etc.), newswire services and high circulation consumer magazines (Redbook, Self, O, Men's Health, etc.) from October 1, 2007, through September 30, 2008.

The articles included in the analysis were identified through a keyword search of the Factiva and Nexis databases. The Boolean search string: "life insurance" and ("purchase" or "purchasing" or "buy" or "buying" or "recommend" or "recommending") formed the basis of the search. The search yielded approximately 2,000 articles that met initial search criteria. Based on the initial search, each article was reviewed for content to ensure relevance to be included in final analysis.

Each article was assessed for overall content and messages. Articles were reviewed and analyzed to determine which messages were correctly reported, misreported, and completely overlooked. The analysis was based on codes organized around three areas: (1) basic facts about life insurance, (2) misstatements about insurance, and (3) omissions of basic facts about life insurance. Codes were developed by experts at MetLife in consultation with its research providers, as well as through a review of the articles included in the analysis. Coding was done in the context of each article. For example, if the article dealt with product features, codes dealing with cost issues were typically not included in the analysis. This was done to ensure a balanced and fair evaluation of content.

Key Research Findings

The key learning for this study is that life insurance is an essential component of a personal safety net for many Americans yet too little of its benefits are being conveyed in the media—the central resource that most consumers rely on for reliable information on personal financial planning.

This conclusion is based on the central finding of this research that identified 19 in 20 articles on life insurance from October 1, 2007, through September 30, 2008, had information gaps that need to be filled. Overall, 94 percent of all articles published in this period of analysis had at least one error or omission in its reporting on life insurance.

A typical article contained up to three omissions and one misstatement of basic facts about life insurance. Product features and costs were the most common categories where errors and omissions about life insurance occurred. Omissions of basic facts about life insurance were even more prevalent than the inclusion of misstatements. Thirty-two percent of articles contained a misstatement about life insurance. By comparison, 88 percent of articles omitted a basic fact on this subject. Omitted information is a missed opportunity to provide consumers with essential facts that enable them to make informed decisions on when to buy life insurance, how much coverage they need, and what type of policy best fits.

Surprisingly, the most frequent writers on life insurance were not always the most accurate, indicating the need for strong media education programs even among experienced personal finance writers. Journalists are omitting key information possibly because they either overestimate what the consumer knows about life insurance or they themselves require additional education on the topic. There were very few articles that featured life insurance as a product category. In fact, in 56 percent of coverage life insurance only received a passing mention. Only one in five articles mentioning life insurance (20 percent) went into any significant level of detail in a feature story.

The other key finding was that the overall volume of life insurance coverage of 170 articles in a one-year period was significantly lower than expected. While general mentions of life insurance is higher than other insurance products previously analyzed, overall coverage was much lower than anticipated based on the nature of the product and its universal use. While regional newspapers dominated life insurance coverage, most of the articles originated from wires or syndicated columns, indicating that life insurance is actually a national story rather than a local story.

Evaluations of Success

As a result of this analysis, MetLife is in the process of developing a proactive media relations strategy that will target personal finance reporters and other consumer media in order to close the key gaps highlighted in the research. These efforts include developing stronger relationships with personal finance reporters at the top tier media outlets to facilitate more accurate reporting on life insurance. This process has worked successfully in other areas including income annuities and long-term care insurance—two product areas where MetLife has established itself as the industry thought leader.

Social Media Content Analysis

How Do Web and Social Media Analytics Differ from Traditional Content Analysis?

In many respects, the analytic framework for web and social media analysis does not differ significantly from traditional media analysis. The operative basis for this analysis is not the online nature of the media. Rather, web and social media is first and foremost media that shares many of the same features as traditional print and broadcast. What differs, however, is *the source and the control of the media.*

Traditional media is a form of one-way communication. A reporter or editor from an established media outlook prepares a story that is in turn distributed to readers. Web and social media, however, operates with completely different rules. In this new media, anyone can be a journalist and readers—through comments and other types of postings—can be significant or even primary contributors to a story or article. These postings can range from long-format blogs, to posts on Facebook to 140 character Tweets.

While the source of the story may differ, the key measures remain those that demonstrate the degree of impact on the receiver of the messages included in the story. However, social media analysis, in order to be complete, should not be limited to simply message and sentiment analysis. Social media also provides an additional benefit that is unique to this form of communication—an understanding of a target audiences *unfiltered reaction* to messages and stories that appear in mainstream publications, online as well as print. This, however, leads to significant challenges in the coding process—identifying relevant social media posts.

Sampling Social Media

Although we will cover sampling in Chapter 8 in some detail it is important to briefly introduce it here. Because of the extensive volume of social media in comparison to traditional media sources, identifying relevant social media is one of the greatest challenges in social media analytics. In traditional media analysis, it is typical that a timeframe for analysis could yield several hundred to several thousand articles. This allows the researcher to use human coders to read each and every article for the time period in question. However, social media by its very nature often generates significantly greater volumes that can possibly reach millions of posts, many of which are irrelevant to the issue under study.

The solution to this challenge is fourfold. The first part of the solution is *the development of search strings that focus those posts* under consideration as close as possible to topic at hand. Sources for social media posts typically allow searches using Boolean search strings (see Chapter 5) as well as searches by specific timeframes and social media platforms.

The next consideration is *the proportion of the posts to be included* in the analysis. This consideration is particularly important since analytic platforms that rely on automated analysis and natural language processing (NLP) are generally inaccurate in their ability to interpret sentiment, identify relevant topics and understand irony and humor—common attributes of many online postings (see Lacy, Watson, Riffe, and Lovejoy 2015). The solution to this is to analyze a sample of relevant postings rather than the entire body of commentary. This sampling is best accomplished *through a random selection of posts.*

The third sampling consideration is a random selection of posts that starts with determining how many social media posts should be included in the final sample. Two factors weigh into this determination. The first is *how many posts can be accurately coded in the time allotted* to conduct the analysis. The second is *the proportion of the total number of social media posts that are included in the analysis.* As a rule of thumb, the higher the proportion of posts included in the sample will decrease any potential error in the sample. Under ideal circumstances, a sample of posts should include a proportion of 5 to 10 percent or greater of the total number of posts. At his level, the sample error diminishes significantly, thus increasing the overall accuracy of the analysis.[3]

However, even the inclusion of 5 percent of a universe of social media posts in a sample could yield a sample size that remains too large to efficiently code and analyze. Consequently, it is also critical for the researcher to consider the total number of posts that can be accurately coded and analyzed in the time allotted for the research.

The final consideration is the actual relevance of each post to the conversation and the topic under research. While search strings can narrow searches considerably, it is difficult to develop a search that is so precise that only relevant posts appear. As a result it is essential as an initial part of the coding process to determine this relevance.

---

[3] For a detailed description of sampling among finite populations refer to: www.reference.com/world-view/finite-population-correction-factor-92f64243cb1da073

Coding Social Media

Once the final sample is developed, the next step in social media content analysis is coding the posts so that they can be analyzed. There are a number of aspects of the social media coding process that are similar to coding traditional media sources. However, there are additional considerations that must also be taken in order to assure that the analysis provides the level of insight that will contribute to an understanding of program impact and effectiveness.

One of the factors that distinguishes social media from traditional media is the *publication process*. Traditional media is commonly written by accredited journalists or writers and is often put through a rigorous editorial review. By contrast, social media is basically unfiltered and anyone can publish or post their thoughts. While traditional media needs to be understood in light of the distribution of intended messages by reporters, social media is a reflection of the organic discussion among the target audience for these messages based upon messages disseminated through traditional media. Consequently, this raises the need to include social media analysis more than the inclusion of messages, topics, and sentiment, but also an understanding for *who is participating in the social media conversation*.

The actual coding of social media includes three distinct stages. Stage one is the determining if the post is actually relevant to the conversation being analyzed. Stage two is identifying the primary topic, messages included in the post and sentiment of the post from the perspective of the author. Stage three is where social media analysis is distinguished from traditional media analysis.

As noted earlier, social media is the organic reaction to news and information by members of the public who choose to share their opinions in an open forum. Borrowing from survey research (see Chapter 9), it is important to not only understand opinions and attitudes, but it is equally essential to also understand *who* shares these attitudes and opinions by key demographic variables—age, gender, occupation, and other relevant factors. To accomplish this, the third stage of coding is determining these characteristics about the person who posted. This provides insights into who is engaged in the conversation, the difference opinions included in the conversations, as well as the impact of these demographic variables on attitudes and opinions.

The Coding Process

As noted earlier, machine-based coding does not have the capability of accurately identifying these coding variables. The only viable approach currently available is to use trained human coders who are capable of accurate interpretation of an author's intent, as well as inferring the demographic characteristics of the author through their use of language, topic discussed, and secondary data sources.

However, the volume of social media, even if a sample is used rather than a census of all postings, precludes using traditional human coding methods. Recent developments through crowdsourcing applications such as Amazon Mechanical Turk and Crowdflower provide access to large volumes of coders and coders who can operate in a multitude of languages. While the process of using crowdsourcing requires skills in both survey research and data science, it is likely to become a viable and cost effective alternative to both automated analysis and traditional coding.

Limitations of Social Media Analytics

Social media analysis has provided unparalleled insights to communication researchers who need to measure the impact of communication programs. We can now understand in almost real time, target audience reactions to news and messages. Nonetheless, it remains essential for the public relations professional to understand the limitations of social media analysis in order draw accurate insights and conclusions.

The most significant limitation of social media analysis is the uneven levels of participation, particularly by different age groups. While overall participation in some form of social media is extremely high across all demographic groups, the type of participation—*active or passive*—can vary considerably. As expected, social media participation is significantly higher among Millennials than it is among Baby Boomers even though both cohorts have high levels of overall participation in Internet use. As a result of this difference in active participation levels (Pew Research

Center 2013, December 27), Millennials are typically overrepresented in social media conversations while Baby Boomers are dramatically underrepresented.

This does not mean that Baby Boomers have fewer or less strident opinions. Instead, careful interpretation of their conversations and level of participation by topic needs to be considered to determine how important they are to the overall conversation under analysis.

Evaluation and Interpretation

Content analysis is an important method for public relations researchers. It provides the researcher with an understanding of the actual messages being generated in response to planned campaign outputs. It serves as a way to measure outtakes in terms of third-party endorser understanding key campaign messages, amount of error that those messages contain, and the sentiment being conveyed to targeted audiences. One important aspect of content analysis—traditional or social—is the ability to benchmark campaign progress on motivational objectives. This is extremely true when looking at social messaging effectiveness, where actual responses and dialogues can be analyzed and interpreted for decisions regarding strategy and refinement of campaign messages if necessary. Using content analysis can be expensive in today's global, connected world. Multiple language mastery is becoming a necessary rather than sufficient ability. The speed at which messages are received, evaluated by audiences, interpreted, and shared is tremendous and becoming incrementally faster almost daily. As the researcher, you should be prepared to carefully break down message content by audience substrata or segmentation, adding to the normative analyses obtained in surveys for a deeper understanding of reactions to the campaign and using some as "pithy" commentary to the research report. Finally, content analysis is used in more than media analysis and should be considered when analyzing focus group or in-depth interview research.

PART III

Quantitative Methods for Effective Public Relations Research, Measurement, and Evaluation

Part III introduces the reader to the gathering of information from a *quantitative approach*. Quantitative methods differ from qualitative in three major ways. First, quantitative approaches are far less concerned with unique and individual responses; instead, they focus on the gathering of data from larger groups of individuals. Second, many use quantitative methods to generalize to a larger group of individuals through *sampling*. And, third, to understand quantitative methods, the researcher must have an understanding of basic *statistical procedures* and *analyses*. In reality, as will be pointed out later, both qualitative and quantitative methods are required in public relations research—the professional, unlike his or her marketing counterparts, must understand the unique perceptions of the opinion leaders who are targeted to serve as third-party endorsers of the messages being sent out by a campaign. In this way qualitative and quantitative methods are complementary to each other.

This section builds on the foundation for quantitative research for *sampling* (Chapter 8), which provides the researcher with ways conducting research which is representative of larger populations or public under study. It continues with a detailed discussion of the major quantitative method employed in public relations—the *survey* (Chapter 9). At the end of this chapter we introduce the concept of experimental methodology, through which precampaign testing and academic research focusing on questions of definition and fact are found. Chapter 10 examines *statistical analysis*, which is the cornerstone of quantitative analysis and evaluation.

CHAPTER 8

Sampling

One of the most significant challenges in any form of research is ensuring that respondents participating in a study are the right individuals. This process starts in the stating of study objectives where we define the research and information needs and, in turn, determine which stakeholder group is the most appropriate audience. As noted in Chapter 7, these individuals can be defined in a multitude of ways that range from simple demographic descriptions such as women who are 18 to 34 years old to complex definitions that incorporate geographic, demographic, and attitudinal characteristics.

Regardless of whether the description is simple or complex, the challenge remains the same for the researcher. That challenge ensures that those selected for inclusion in a study are representative of the larger universe of individuals who constitute the group that is the focus of the study. A representative group of study participants is crucial since the findings from the study are used to make decisions about the direction of a communication program, evaluate the success or failure of that program, or determine adjustments or modifications that need to take place to ensure communication and business objectives are being met. Without a sample that represents the broad opinions of the stakeholder group under study, it is highly likely that the essential decisions that are based on the research will be in error.

Why Do We Need to Sample?

In an ideal situation, we would ask each and every member of the population their opinions. We would ask them what they like and dislike, what they are aware of, and what their expectations are. That approach would, in theory, be error free, since everyone's opinion would be included and all subgroups, by definition, would be represented in their correct proportions in the overall population—this called a *census*. The practical reality is however that speaking to *every possible respondent* is a practical impossibility. Using that approach, a study employing a census of the adult population of the United States would require over 251 million individual interviews (United States Census Bureau, projections, 2015) (www. census.gov). A study of that magnitude would take years of planning, months to complete, and would require millions of dollars. Decisions on communication programs often need information that can be collected and analyzed in as short a period of time as a few days but rarely longer than a few weeks. These limitations render a census approach to survey research impractical except in very limited instances where an entire population is available for study and has a strong willingness to cooperate with the survey. An example of this type of research is an employee survey.

The solution is to talk to a group of individuals who are selected in a manner that ensures that their opinions are representative of the broader populations. That approach is called *sampling*, which in theory is based on the assumption that individuals who have shared or common characteristics such as demographic variables like age, gender, income, or marital status also are likely to share opinions or preferences since they are also likely to have similar backgrounds, interests, and lifestyles. The same is assumed true for psychographics or their attitudinal preferences and netgraphics or their use of the Internet or Internet-based communication (see Chapter 9). This method reduces the cost as well as the time required to complete a reliable survey, but unlike a census or the inclusion of all eligible respondents is subject to a certain margin of error.

Before we look at the two major types of sampling it is important to determine what the study's sampling frame will be. In Chapter 7 we introduced the idea of ensuring that the sample selected reflected the purpose and substrata necessary to analyze social message content analysis. This chapter extends that notion in more traditional ways when selecting respondents in a survey. In general, a sampling frame defines who are to be sampled from the universe of all possible respondents who reflect the purpose of the study and the target audience for the communication program in question, reduced to the population (or public or audience) being examined, and further reduced to the sample itself. The *sampling frame* does exactly what it implies. It frames the sample's respondents to particular demographic, psychographic, or other variables such as Internet use or product ownership. Furthermore, from secondary research the researcher should know the percentage or proportion of the population or public or audience and upon collecting data be able to compare the sample's breakdown against the population to check sampling reliability and validity (Stacks 2017). This secondary research on percentage or proportions of the population are also used to statistically correct the final sample by using weights to ensure all groups (e.g., men and women) are represented in their correct proportions in the final sample. *Statistical weighting* is particularly useful when it is necessary to examine the attitudes and opinions of a small segment of the population that would only have minimal representation in a probability survey. In those cases, the group in question is often over sampled to ensure statistically reliable analysis of the group. When this occurs, the group has to be weighted back into its correct proportion to gain an accurate understanding of the entire population under study.

The next section covers the two basic types of sampling used in research, explaining each type and providing methods within each. The section following that is more hands-on and walks through how an actual sample might be drawn. We turn next to the types of sampling.

Types of Sampling

Sampling can generally be divided into three basic types: probability, representative, and nonprobability. *Probability sampling*—"[a] sample drawn at random from a population such that all possible respondents or objects have an equal chance of being selected for observation or measurement" (Stacks and Bowen 2013, 23–24)—is used to make reliable and projectable predictions about the attitudes and opinions of an entire population being studied. Probability sampling has a unique benefit in that sampling error or the degree to which the attitudes, opinions, or preferences of a sample may differ from a population as a whole can be calculated. This error is commonly reported as a plus or minus *sampling error*. This allows the researcher to know how much sampling error and measurement error can be *expected* in one way and how much the researcher is willing to *allow* in another way. Probability sampling is most reliable when the entire population under consideration has an equal chance to be included in a study. For example, if one wanted to conduct a probability sample of the population of the United States, the sampling method would require that each household in the country be included in the available pool of respondents. Typically probability samples are conducted by telephone or door-to-door since all households have an equal chance of inclusion.

While probability sampling remains the most reliable approach, the difficulty and expense of reaching respondents by telephone or in-person has resulted in the shift to online surveys using prerecruited panels and are only represented (hence, *representative sampling*) of the true population under study. Because participation in online research panels is voluntary, respondents are not selected at random from the entire population. To address this change, research panels are selected to reflect the overall demographics of the broader population to be representative of the population rather than projectable to the entire cohort being studied. While representative sample typically reflect the population in question, sampling error that is commonly reported in projectable samples is not applicable. Finally, *nonprobability sampling* is selecting respondents for particular reasons—primarily dealing with access them—whereby the researcher has no way to adequately determine sampling error (see as follows).

Sampling and Measurement Error

Sampling error comes from a variety of areas, but most often involving sampling frame, list, and measurement error. First, if the sample frame is not specified exact enough, there will be *sampling frame error* due to the inability to correctly frame or correctly identify the population under study. Second, there are list errors. *List errors* occur when the contact lists—telephone books, voting records, purchaser data, and so forth—are not correct or have lapsed, thus while the sample frame may be fine, the list of respondents contains error. And, third, *measurement error* comes from respondents misunderstanding a question or not understanding a statement.[1]

---

[1] See discussion of question validity in Chapter 4.

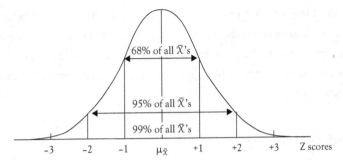

Figure 8.1 **The normal curve**

The amount of error is decreased as the sample size increases because as sample size increases, the data gathered become more equally distributed and approach what would be normally found in the population. This is reflected in what statistics reflect to as a "normal curve" (see Figure 8.1). Discussed in more detail in Chapter 10, under a normal curve we can estimate sampling and measurement error.

This is not to imply that a perfect sample would have no error; *there is always some error*, but we seek to minimize it. Without going into a lot of statistical formulae, if a sample needs to be at least 95 percent correct and the researcher is willing to accept up to 5 percent measurement error, then about 400 (384 actually) *randomly* sampled respondents from the population would be required. Reducing measurement error to 1 percent would require 9,604 respondents! And, to get a 1 percent sampling error (99 percent sample confidence) and 5 percent measurement error, you would need 663 randomly selected respondents (Backstrom and Hirsch-Cesar 1981). If it costs $100 per completed response, you can see where trade-offs in terms of expected error can come into play.

Nonprobability sampling—"[a] sample drawn from a population whereby respondents or objects *do not have an equal chance of being selected* for observation or measurement" (emphasis added) (Stacks and Bowen 2013, 20)—by definition cannot be projected to reflect the attitudes or opinions of a specific population group. In essence, the degree to which the sample differs from the population remains unknown. Nonetheless, this method is a valuable form of sampling that can provide insights and understanding of what a target population thinks, believes, and behaves. What needs to be remembered and stressed in the final report of the study is that results cannot be generalized away from the actual sample itself. In other words, the nonprobability sample yields a descriptive rather than a projective study.

Probability Sampling

Probability sampling takes several different forms. These forms include *random, systemic,* and *stratified samplings*. While each of these forms of sampling is distinct, they each have a common element that links them. The common linkage is that in each form of probability sampling, *every prospective respondent to a survey has an equal chance or a nonzero probability of being selected for a survey.*

Random sampling is the most elemental and basic form of probability sampling. In this method, each member of the surveyed population has an equal and known chance of being selected. For instance, the population of respondents would be placed in a box, mixed up, and the first name drawn would be selected as the first of x-respondents. The name would then be put back in the box, the box mixed up, and another name would be selected, placed back, and the process continue until the required sample size is reached. This can be a very long process!

Systematic sampling is another variation that is often used in place of random sampling. It is also called *nth name selection*. In this approach, a sample size is calculated and every *n*th record is selected from a list of population members that attempts to distribute the selected respondents throughout the list. This method is less robust and reliable than a purely random sample and has the potential to create a biased sample if the list used to select respondents is ordered in any hidden or unknown way. This approach is useful when there is a limited population to be interviewed, but where the population is too large to be effectively and efficiently studied using a census approach where every member of the population is contacted and agrees to respond.

Stratified sampling is a common sampling method used when there is a known subset of a population under study that is important to include in the final analysis, but whose population of that subgroup is too small to appear in sufficient numbers in a purely random sample and still allow for a meaningful analysis. An example of a subset that would be used in stratified sample would be large businesses. In a study of 500 randomly selected businesses, normally only 10 to 20 of these businesses might be present in the final sample. In this instance, the researcher would specify a subsample of 100 of these large businesses in order to have an analyzable segment. Random sampling is used to select a sufficient number of subjects from each subgroup. The final sample would be adjusted statistically to make sure large businesses are present in their correct proportion while a separate and statistically reliable analysis of this subgroup could also be conducted.

A special form of stratified sampling is the *systematic stratified sample*. In this case respondents would be randomly selected by either the *n*th record method or simple random sampling, but would be stratified within a particular variable, say respondents' sex, where so many males and so many females would be randomly selected.

Nonprobability Sampling

Like probability sampling, there are also several approaches to nonprobability studies. There are four basic variations of nonprobability sampling. These approaches include *convenience* sampling, *judgment* sampling, *quota* sampling, and *snowball* sampling. By definition, nonprobability sampling does not support projections or generalization of survey findings to a broader population or census. Nonetheless, it remains a useful tool when there are specialty populations that are of limited size, respondents that are hard to reach, or circumstances where traditional probability approaches would be prohibitive in terms of the cost and the time required to complete the studies.

Convenience sampling is typically used in exploratory research. In this instance, respondents are selected for inclusion in the sample because they are convenient and easy to reach. Researchers often use this approach when they are looking for a rough approximation of findings while they are also looking to minimize cost and the time required to conduct a probability study. This approach is also commonly used in qualitative research, particularly in the selection of respondents for participation in focus groups. In this instance, respondents are recruited from databases and have already indicated a willingness to participate in a research study. Another instance where convenience sampling is used is with mall intercept studies. These studies recruit respondents from shopping malls where respondents are solicited by interviewers soliciting their cooperation.

Judgment sampling is a variation of convenience sampling that often combines nonprobability and probability sampling. In a judgment sample, a single city or a neighborhood could be chosen to represent a wider population. In this case, the respondents within the area are chosen randomly using probability techniques. This type of sampling is often used for exit polling during political elections that rely on sample precincts to predict election outcomes. These sample precincts are selected based on prior voter behavior since they are likely to be indicative of actual voter preferences. Another use of judgment sampling is in test markets where specific cities or neighborhoods are selected to determine if a product has broad appeal prior to a national introduction. In both instances, substantial secondary, background research is required to make an informed decision of which markets are to be included in the study.

A variation of the judgment sample approach is *cluster sampling*. In cluster sampling an entire population is divided into groups, or clusters, and a random sample of these clusters are selected for inclusion in a study. For example, this method is used when a broad, geographically diverse population is under study. Under these circumstances, it is often expensive and time consuming to conduct a random study. Therefore, a geographic cluster of respondents is used in the study to represent the larger population. This approach can be used in probability and nonprobability sampling. Caution should be taken with this method since overall error rates are significantly higher than with traditional sampling methods.

Quota sampling is similar to stratified sampling in that the objective of the sampling approach is to ensure specific groups are represented in sufficient numbers in order to be analyzed. These groups are predetermined by the researcher who determines the desired sample. The final quota sample is then selected using convenience or judgment sampling methods. Like other forms of nonprobability sampling, the findings from the quota group samples cannot be projected to a larger population.

When a respondent group is particularly difficult to reach, then one solution is a procedure called *snowball sampling*. One of the challenges when a respondent group is rare or has a low incidence in the overall population is that it can be cost prohibitive to locate respondents. Snowball sampling asks referrals from initial respondents to generate additional respondents. An example of snowball sampling may be identifying individuals with a rare or unusual disease. Two factors influence the difficulty in finding these respondents. In one instance, there are few of these individuals in the overall population. Adding to this difficulty are privacy laws that limit access through third parties. It is not unusual, however, for those who have a specific condition to know others who experience the same challenges. They often meet in support groups and forge relationships that can lead to referrals. While this approach can quickly build samples, it is also fraught with the danger that the sample will be biased as it does not represent a true cross section of the overall population under study.

Sampling Applications

Chapter 7 introduced sampling as a way to work with the tremendous number of social media messages that might require analysis. Chapter 9 will review in detail the various types of survey methods and for each of these methods, there are specific considerations when developing a sample that needs to be taken to ensure the results of the survey are reliable. As an overview of Chapter 9, let's review each of these applications in greater detail.

Telephone Surveys

The most common sampling system used in telephone survey is a probability method called *random digit dialing* (RDD). An RDD sample randomly selects telephone numbers from known working residential or business telephone exchanges. The RDD approach is used as it includes listed and unlisted telephone numbers in their correct proportions. Some researchers have speculated that possibly half of these landlines may be unlisted (nefuri.com n.d.). This method assures their inclusion in a study. Further randomization is added to the study by requesting to speak to a resident at random. One method for selecting that individual is asking for an adult in the household who had the most recent birthday.

The RDD approach, however, is becoming increasingly difficult to use because of the continued rapid growth of cell or mobile telephones as a primary means of telephonic communication. Cell phones are the only telephone system in a high percentage of households. The proportion of cell-phone-only households is currently estimated at 47 percent (McGrath 2015, December 2), while about an additional 16 percent of all households "had both landline and wireless telephones but received all or almost all calls on the wireless phones" (Stephen et al. 2013). This is a particularly common phenomenon among younger adults and in less urban areas. These numbers are not commonly included in samples and therefore a significant bias is created because younger adults and those likely to live in outlying area are more likely to be excluded from the sample. Several research companies have recently introduced samples that include cell phones. However, challenges remain since many households have multiple cell phones, often one for each member of the household. This high incidence of multiple cell phone households potentially limits the ability of cell phone interviews to represent the broader opinions of a household rather than the opinions of an individual.

In some instances, nonprobability samples are used in telephone studies. These are referred to as *list samples*. These samples are typically drawn from directories or similar sources. This type of sampling approach is most commonly used when respondents have special characteristics (e.g., ownership or used of a particular type of product) or are a low-incidence group in the population and therefore difficult to reach through conventional random dialing. An example of a low-incidence group would be owners of small retail businesses. This nonprobability approach is significantly more cost effective than random respondent selection.

Door-to-Door Surveys

This is the original probability sampling approach and continues to be the "gold standard" of sampling. In door-to-door surveys, households are randomly selected from known clusters. This selection is based on known addresses. The database of known residences is available from the United

States Postal Service (USPS). USPS is responsible for delivering to all known households and, therefore, is required to maintain these lists and keep them updated regularly.

While this approach is highly reliable, it is time consuming and extremely expensive. It is also potentially dangerous for the interviewer to conduct the survey in areas that are not safe. Consequently, it is rarely used except under circumstances where the nature of the questions requires an in-person interview as well projectability to a larger population.

Online Studies

Online studies are by definition nonprobability studies since respondents are usually parts of panels who have agreed in advance to respond to a series of surveys in exchange for compensation or gifts. In many instances, the final sample is weighted to ensure that respondents in various demographic groups are present or *representative* in their correct proportions in the overall population. Weighting is a process that uses correction factors or weights to place each segment of the population in their correct proportions in the final sample. This process is used to approximate probability sampling methods, however, significant debate continued on the ability of this approach to provide *reliable* projections. However, the method is increasingly popular as the research can be completed quite quickly and at considerably lower costs than traditional telephone or door-to-door studies.

These interviewing systems are becoming increasingly sophisticated and respondents can review advertisements to be evaluated and be questioned without leaving their computers.

Intercept Studies

Intercept studies are nonprobability samples that are used when it is necessary to conduct an in-person interview and the time or cost required for a door-to-door study is prohibitive. Most shopping malls have exclusive research services that identify potential survey respondents that they invite to participate in a study. They are not selected randomly, but by their willingness to cooperate with the administration of an interview and they are not necessarily representative of a larger population since they

Table 8.1 Applications for each form of sampling

Type of data collection	Probability sample	Nonprobability sample
Telephone	✓	✓
Door-to-door	✓	
Online		✓
Intercept		✓
Content analysis	✓	✓

are engaged in an activity (shopping) they may distinguish them from the overall population. Consequently, their opinions could differ considerably from others. This approach is commonly used when communication materials are being tested for efficacy since it is easy to show test materials at a very low cost.

Content Analysis

As noted earlier in this chapter, probability sampling can also be used in content analysis (see Chapter 7). Sampling is used to randomly select articles for inclusion in an analysis when the overall volume of articles is too large to analyze efficiently. In some instances, thousands of articles can be generated, making it difficult to provide prompt and timely reporting of the findings. In this instance articles are randomly selected using a random number generator. This method determines which articles in a group of articles are chosen for deeper study and analysis.

Stratified sampling can also be used in content analysis. In this case, specific media, traditional as well as social, that are particularly important are selected separately to ensure that adequate proportions are available for analysis. Table 8.1 provides a simple breakdown of sampling by type of data collection.

Drawing a Sample

To this point the discussion has been theoretical; we've looked at what sampling *is* (census, probability, and nonprobability). To better understand the various sampling options, this section walks through the process of sampling for specific types of studies that typically may be conducted as part of a communication program.

Census

A census includes each and every individual who is eligible for a study according to the specified sampling frame. The challenge of a census is systematically assuring each and every individual who is eligible actively participates in a study. The only practical applications of a census are for very small populations such as employees of a small or mid-size company or similar types of populations. The other use of a census approach is for content analysis where it may be practical to include every available story in an analysis. Although the U.S. government conducts a required "census" of the U.S. population every 10 years, it is not actually a census since not all members are able to—or are actually available—to participate. A random sampling approach would probably be more appropriate, but law dictates that the population be sampled by census.

National Telephone Study

There are two general approaches for conducting a telephone study. One approach is called a *listed sample* or *directory* approach. An example of that method would start with a list or directory of all areas where the study is to take place. Names and their associated telephone numbers are randomly selected for the study. This approach has significant limits. While it is time and labor intensive, it also has several significant flaws that limit the ability of the study to be representative of the population under study. These flaws are that significant proportions of eligible respondents will not be included in this type of study. Those with unlisted telephone numbers as well as those with new or recent listings will not be included. In some localities, this could represent 3 in 10 potential respondents.

One of the solutions to that approach is something called the *Modified Waksberg Method* of *RDD* sampling (Waksberg 1978). In this approach clusters of known and working residential telephone exchanges are identified. A sample of these working exchanges is selected and telephone numbers that include the digits that comprise the exchange are generated.

The last two digits of the number are randomly generated. This procedure ensures that all working telephone numbers (listed, unlisted, and new listings) have an equal opportunity of appearing in the final study. Statistical adjustments are often applied to the final sample to ensure all demographic groups appear in their correct proportions.

With the advent of cell-phone-only households, this approach has lost a significant amount of efficacy since we can no longer sample using fixed locations or dedicated exchanges within an area code to randomly sample a population in its correct proportions. In addition, the use of cell phones by adolescents makes it extremely difficult to filter out ineligible respondents. An additional challenge is that a single household may have multiple lines thus making household sampling and screening challenging.

There are a number of leading survey research companies that have developed experimental protocols to compensate for these issues. However, these methods are evolving based on the increasing transition from landlines to cell phones and mobile computing systems. We anticipate further developments in this over the next several years.

Acceptance Rates

A particular challenge facing telephone sampling is declining willingness of potential respondents to cooperate with the interviewing process. According to the most recent study by Pew on this issue, current acceptance for telephone surveys have declined to as low as 9 percent, increasing the difficulties and costs associated with this type of research (Assessing the Representativeness of Public Opinion Surveys 2012).

Intercept Study

Since intercept studies are nonprobability studies, sampling issues focus on the sampling *frame* rather than the sampling *method*. In this type of data collection, the key to ensure the sample meets the specifications for the study is determining those characteristics that are desired for the respondents and creating a questionnaire that determines if prospective respondents are eligible to participate. This process, called *screening*, is similar to the screening process for focus groups described in the chapter on qualitative research (Chapter 6).

In an intercept study, prospective respondents are often identified visually by an interviewer who approaches these individuals according to specified instructions such as men 18 to 34 years old or young women who are shopping for new clothes. They are then asked a series of study qualification questions and, if they are eligible, then they are asked to participate in the full study. In some mall intercept studies, quotas are set for specific types of respondents. For example, as study design may require subsamples of different age groups. Once these quotas are filled, respondents are no longer eligible to participate in the study even though they meet all other qualifications for inclusion.

Online Study

Online studies present unique challenges in drawing or developing samples. Respondents to online studies are now often parts of panels of individuals who have been prequalified for participation in studies based on known characteristics. These characteristics include demographic variables such as gender, age, occupation, or education, as well as other variables such as product ownership or use and even the use of medication or presence of specific medical condition. They have also typically agreed in advance to participate in studies in exchange for compensation and are regular Internet users. They are often recruited from websites and e-mail solicitations as well as referrals from other panelists. All of these factors are variables that make it challenging to project the findings from this type of research to broader populations.

The most common sampling approach used for online studies is a random selection of panelists who receive invitations to participate in a particular study. They are selected based on their answers to earlier studies, but are usually "requalified" for new studies. The invitations are often sent over a several-day period to avoid potential biases associated with those who respond early. As in telephone studies, statistical adjustments are often applied to the final sample to ensure all demographic groups appear in their correct proportions.

A problem similar to telephone sampling is found with online surveys which can no longer use mass sampling techniques to gain responses. Survey companies are ethically required not to spam potential respondents and must have a prior relationship with the respondent in order to invite their participation (http://www.casro.org/?page=TheCASROCode). This has led to the use of prerecruited panels of potential respondents who participate based on the potential for some compensation. This approach has been strongly criticized since many respondents to online surveys over participate and thus limit the value and validity of their contribution. However, the costs associated with telephone and door-to-door surveys, as well as sociological and technological changes, have been so significant that online surveys are becoming the norm for the majority of studies.

These technological changes that are affecting this shift include caller identification that allows respondents to screen and reject calls and the proliferation of cellular telephones. Fewer than half of households have traditional landlines and often, these lines go unanswered. As a result of the shift to cellular telephone, everyone in a household often has their own line so that the sampling frame has also shifted from households to individuals.

Content Analysis

Most content analysis uses a census approach. However, in some instances it is impractical to include every article in an analysis. In that case there are two procedures that are used to determine which articles are analyzed as part of a study.

One approach is a random selection of articles. In this approach, the total number of articles to be included in the analysis is determined. This determination is made based on overall budgets to conduct the analysis, the time required or a combination of these factors. Two different random selections can be applied. One is the nth selection process where an every nth article is selected. The other approach is a random selection of articles.

The n is determined by the total number of articles in the census divided by the number of articles to be included in the analysis. This process yields an equal distribution throughout the list of articles. Ideally, the articles would be listed in an organized structure, most often chrono-logically that will minimize the bias of the selection process.

The random selection is determined by a *random number generator.* A random number generator is a device that generates a sequence of num-bers that lack any pattern. Articles are organized in a sequence similar to that used in the *n*th selection process and are numbered sequentially. Articles are selected according to the random number by matching that number to the article with the same number. Random number generators are available on numerous websites.

Another approach to content analysis sampling is to limit the number of articles to specific criteria. These criteria include types of publications or media outlets included and specific content of the articles. For exam-ple, earning reports on companies may be excluded from a study or at least two mentions of a company may be required for the article to be included. Articles can be limited to specific publications or categories of publications such as daily newspapers or weekly news magazines.

Best Practices

Best practices sampling takes into account the type of sampling required for the research. It begins with an understanding of the universe of pos-sible respondents, defines that universe down to a particular population and then sets a sampling frame. The particular kind of sample generated will depend on the research's goals and objectives. Best practices sampling *reporting* will include the number of respondents sampled, how they were sampled, and the measurement error associated with the sampling.

Evaluation and Interpretation

Sampling has taken on an increasingly important feature in public rela-tions research. Regardless of who or what you are studying, sampling allows you to more efficiently conduct your research and yet still be able to estimate sampling or measurement error. When evaluating your sample it is extremely important to review your sampling frame. Most mistakes or misinterpretation stems from a lack of understand who or what the population is. It is also important that the client know and understand any weighting or statistical balancing used when analyzing data and why it was necessary. Understanding the differences between probability, reprehensive, and nonprobability sampling and explaining to the client the advantages and disadvantages of each is crucial when you make your final interpretation of findings. Often clients will ask how the results generalize to the larger population, but for whatever reasons only allow for or underwrite nonprobability sampling. This sort of problem must be handled in the developmental phase of the research campaign.

Summary

Sampling is an important element of public relations research. Whether a sample is drawn randomly or not, sampling allows the researcher to conduct a study with a smaller number of respondents or participants within certain expectations of error in sampling and measurement. Even in a nonprobability sample, a comparison against expected demographic variables provides some estimate of sampling error and with a large enough sample (at least 400), some idea of measurement error within the sample can be estimated. Finally, sampling is something that goes beyond the survey or poll and can be used in experiments and even in content analysis. Understanding sampling and the advantages and limitations to each type of sampling provides the researcher a way to ascertain in secondary research whether the study being reviewed is a reliable and valid document that can be used to help define developmental and refinement phases of a public relations campaign or program.

CHAPTER 9

Survey Methodology

As noted earlier, research can take on many forms, some of it focusing on unique and individual responses that provide rich information about a problem or a project, but sometimes an understanding of how large groups of individuals perceive a problem or a project is required. This type of research is called *quantitative research*. When the researcher is asking questions about larger groups of individuals from a quantitative approach, that researcher is seeking *normative data*. Normative data provide information on larger groups that then can be further subdivided by nominal or ordinal, or both data (see Chapter 4) and compared or can be compared against data gathered by others from similar groups.

The primary method employed in public relations to gather such data is *survey methodology*. This chapter introduces the concept of a survey and its component parts. At the end of the chapter a special form of survey methodology is examined, one that is often used in academia and sometimes in marketing or advertising, but seldom in public relations—the *experiment*. The major difference between a survey and an experiment is *control* of the study. In a survey the researcher is seeking information without setting restrictive conditions. The respondent could be at home, on the telephone, with the television on and the survey would still be conducted. In an experiment, however, that same respondent would be in a controlled environment. Each respondent is in the same environment as all other respondents, which controls any intervening variables—things that may change responses that the researcher seeks to eliminate or contaminate the respondents perceptions of what was being studied.

The Survey as Quantitative Methodology

The Dictionary of Public Relations Measurement and Research defines a quantitative methodology as one "that produces generalizable findings by collecting and analyzing data in objective ways, such as experiments and closed-ended, forced-choice questionnaires of sufficiently large samples" (Stacks and Bowen 2013). Furthermore, it states that quantitative research "relies heavily on statistics and numerical measures" (Stacks and Bowen 2013, 25). Survey methodology is defined as "a formal research methodology that seeks to gather data and analyze a population's or sample's attitudes, beliefs, and opinions" (Stacks and Bowen 2013, 31). As such, a survey is appropriate when the researcher needs to better understand how a large group of individuals perceives some attitude object— whether it is an organization, an individual, or a product.

Qualifying Evaluation of Survey Data

Before turning to the conducting of a survey it is important to note three things that qualify how survey data are evaluated. First, how the data have been gathered qualifies what can be done with it. This is the qualifier of *sampling*, covered later in this chapter and in more detail in Chapter 8. Second, how responses are assessed qualifies how the data can be evaluated. This is the qualifier of *causality*, which states that what individuals perceive is a function of some particular public relations strategy conducted prior to respondent contact. And, third, the type of questions being asked qualifies how the data can be assessed and evaluated. This is the qualifier of *questionnaire construction*. All three of these qualifiers must be taken into account when evaluating the data gathered by survey.

Polls Versus Surveys

Polls and surveys are both quantitative approaches to gathering data on large groups of individuals. The primary differences between the two are simple. *Polls*, "a form of survey research that focuses more on immediate behavior than attitudes" (Stacks and Bowen 2013, 23) yield short, *behaviorally driven* quantitatively gathered data (Stacks 2017). They seek to quickly assess a sample or population's intended actions or immediate short-term perceptions. Surveys, on the other hand, seek to understand why groups hold particular opinions through an analysis of their attitudes, beliefs, and values on a particular topic. The survey is, therefore, much longer and requires more secondary research in writing the survey questionnaire. Both have places as quantitative tools in the public relations professional's research toolkit.

Designing a Survey or a Poll

Although it may be tempting to just sit down and write a survey or a poll questionnaire, there are at least five considerations the researcher must address. Those considerations, which come from secondary research, are in the following order: (1) What is known about the population under study and the concepts or behaviors or attitudes being assessed? (2) What is being studied: potential or actual behavior or attitudes, beliefs, and values? (3) What is the best way to contact potential respondents? (4) Given the research question and communication plan objectives, how many times are respondents contacted? And, (5) what sort of sampling, if any, is to be conducted?

The "Frame"

Unless the researcher has the resources to contact each and every respondent available, some sort of parameters needed to be placed on who will be studied. Basically, there is a *universe* of people that could be sampled, but some of those are not of interest and can be excluded for both that reason and economics. That leaves the researcher with a public of interest within what now might be considered a *population*. Populations, however, are quite large and may or may not need to be further broken down into an audience composed of several or more *demographics*. It is when the researcher has determined just exactly who will be contacted that he or she has defined the *frame* of his or her survey or poll. A survey frame, already defined in Chapter 8 as a *sampling frame*, might be interested in active voters of either sex of middle-class families who have at least three credit cards. Hence, the survey would not be interested in people who have not voted in a specified time or who are not registered voters or who are part of the upper or lower economic classes, but would include both males and females. The survey frame sets the conditions of who will be contacted and, with sufficient secondary research, can be compared against known data—typically census data—for estimates of sample reliability and validity.

Survey Type

The researcher must then consider what type of survey to conduct. Is this something more behaviorally oriented and does not require a more in-depth understanding of motivations or information? If so, then the researcher will conduct a poll—a short set of questions that can be answered quickly, usually on a yes or no basis. For instance, for people known to reside in an upper-income neighborhood based on census data, the poll may ask a couple of questions—"Are you planning on voting in the next bond election?," followed by "Will you support the bond proposal?" Since the researcher already knows a lot about the neighborhood from the census data, and if a telephone contact, be fairly certain about the respondent's sex, not much more is needed.

If the researcher needs to know if the respondent has seen a product, where they saw the product, and what the respondent thinks and feels about the product, then a survey is required. The survey will be much longer and require more thought. Hence, it will be more costly to run and take longer to analyze the data, but will yield considerably more information on respondents.

Contacting Respondents

There are numerous ways to contact respondents, each with advantages and disadvantages. Traditional approaches were introduced in Chapter 8 and include person-to-person, mail, and telephone. Contemporary approaches use the social media and computer networks and automated calling. Approaches to contacting respondents—and respondent reactions to being contacted—have changed dramatically over the past 30 to 40 years that your authors have conducted surveys. At one time, it was an honor to be contacted for your opinion on a product or political party or a company or individual. Contact was rare back in those days. Today, potential respondents are being bombarded with requests, often not from research firms but marketing agencies trying to sell a product under the guise of a survey or poll, and the respondent response has been to filter requests and most often simply either refuse to open an e-mail or letter or to ignore the request.

Regardless of the contact approach, all surveys and polls should report three things: (1) how the respondents were selected; (2) how the respondents were contacted; and (3) how many respondents participated, to include the percentage of completed surveys compared against attempts of contact. A good response rate will vary by approach, but in general, response rates have dropped significantly over the past 20 years (Stacks 2017). Sometimes an incentive will be offered to increase response rates. For instance, a coupon for a discount on a product or an advanced copy of the results or report may be offered for completion. When this is done, the researcher must follow through and keep the promised action.

Traditional Contact Approaches

Perhaps the oldest form of contact is the *person-to-person* approach. Here individual interviewers are sent out to conduct survey interviews face-to-face with the respondent. These are expensive when you take into consideration the costs of transportation and duplication of materials, but the advantage is that the *selected* respondent, if available, is identified as the *correct* respondent. A downside of this approach is that interviewers have to often go to areas or a location that may not be safe, thus incurring another consideration when selecting respondents. The typical person-to-person approach aims to survey a little over 400 individuals. Why 400? This is the magic number that survey researchers and pollsters use to ensure that their sample is 95 percent who they intended it to be and that respondents will error in their responses no more than 5 percent of the time. Because the researcher is targeting specific individuals through a process where she basically knows who and where the respondents live, a 60-percent response rate for completed surveys is considered good (Backstrom and Hirsch-Cesar 1981).

A variation of the person-to-person contact approach is the *intercept*. As the label implies, contact is made by intercepting people in a particular location. This is a variation of the "man on the street" intercept.

In the intercept, respondents are selected because of their location and this is reported in the write up of the results. Typically, these interviews are conducted in enclosed shopping malls. The mall intercept allows the researcher to target specific respondents, as well as can be used when getting responses or reactions to particular products. As will be seen later, it is a way to bring an experiment to the field.[1]

Almost all of us have been approached to participate in a *telephone survey* at one time or another. The telephone approach has several advantages over other contact methods. First, if the calls are to individuals from an identified list, we have a pretty good idea of who the respondent is and basic census data can be obtained for the telephone exchange and number. Second, the number of call attempts and completed calls for each numbers provide us with easily computed response rates. And, third, if a respondent is not available we can establish a systematic method to choose another respondent for the call. Telephone calls can be made into areas that might be dangerous for an interviewer to go or may be so far from the researcher as to be impossible for contact to be made. And, finally, telephone surveys can be conducted fairly fast. The downsides? First, telephone surveying is relatively expensive as the researcher will have to either invest in a bank of telephones, or rent a phone bank from a provider. Second, calling times are generally restricted. No one likes having their dinner interrupted, so the researcher needs to understand local eating norms and try to call between dinner and bedtime, usually 7:00 p.m. to no later than 10:00 p.m. Third, the type of questions asked is restricted. Although open-ended questions may be necessary, they are hard to get respondents to complete and the interviewer must write exactly what the respondent said (this is often done by having the interviewer record all answers on a computer). Finally, language can be a problem. If a respondent does not speak English, for instance, the interview cannot translate the survey or questions or provide guidance as to what a particular word or phrase may mean. Good telephone response rates used to be in the 50 to 60 percent range; however, given all the filtering equipment now available on the

---

[1] The intercept is particularly useful in marketing public relations.

normal telephone set (to include caller ID, answering machines being used to filter out calls, and cell phones) a typical response rate is often in the range of 9 percent.[2]

Finally, there is the *mail* approach. In this approach respondents are contacted through the mail, typically a national postal service such as the U.S.P.S. or Royal Mail, and asked to complete a paper-and-pencil questionnaire and return it to the researcher. The advantages to the mail survey include respondents being able to see the questionnaire, complete open-ended questions, and provide the researcher with different opinion or attitude or belief measures (see Chapter 4). For instance, while a telephone survey is limited to category-centered measures, such as the Likert scale, the mail survey can use *Semantic Differential* scales or visual scales. The disadvantages to the mail survey include costs (duplicating, stuffing, postage), now knowing exactly who completed the questionnaire, and problems with mailing lists and datedness of addresses. A good response rate used to be in the 60-percent range, but today it is considered to be good in the 20-percent range. According to one survey researcher, however, employing a five-step process can still yield response rates in the 60-percent range, but the costs associated with the method are rather high (Dillman 2007). However, because of the development of other data collection methods, specifically online or Internet surveys, the use of mail surveys has declined significantly.

Contemporary Contact Approaches

Contemporary contact approaches employ most of the bells and whistles that modern communications provide. Some of the approaches, however, have yielded a harsh backlash for people engaged in honest survey research or polling. The worst offenders are companies that utilize *computer-generated calls or robocalls* with computerized responses—no actual human is interviewing respondents. Most of us have received a computer-generated survey; typically it begins with a short-time delay

---

[2] Pew Research Center; "The Challenges of Polling When Fewer People Are Available to Be Polled" http://www.pewresearch.org/fact-tank/2015/07/21/the-challenges-of-polling-when-fewer-people-are-available-to-be-polled/

and then a voice. They typically ask for the respondent to provide responses via selecting a particular number on the phone keypad or reply with a yes or no response.

Perhaps the biggest push lately has come in the area of *Internet or web-based surveys*. The Internet survey combines the advantages of the mail survey with the speed of the telephone survey. The researcher employs a web-based survey program (e.g., Survey Monkey, Qualtrics, or mrInterview) or contracts with a vendor who manages and deploys online surveys and to create a questionnaire, link it to a file of Internet addresses, and send it out. Internet surveys are fast but response rates are generally low; indeed, many marketing survey companies have sprung up that actively seek panels of people who are paid or offered some form of payment to evaluate products. Specialized samples may yield higher survey responses, but general population responses are lower than might expected with traditional contact methods. A downside of Internet surveys is a problem with anonymity and confidentiality. This can be addressed by hiring an Internet survey firm to conduct the survey and strip all Internet addresses prior to sending the responses back. An advantage of the Internet survey using web survey programs is that basic statistical analysis is provided as part of the package (see Chapter 10 for more on statistical analysis). Internet-based surveys, however, have an inherent bias due to the fact that only those who are Internet users and who have registered for surveys are invited to participate.

Problems with Internet surveys have led to a *social network approach*. Instead of asking potential respondents to complete a survey sent to them (called the *opt-out* approach), a plea is made for interested respondents to go to a website and participate in the survey (called the *opt-in* approach). As will be briefly discussed a little later in this chapter and in more detail in Chapter 10, this approach does not allow the researcher to generalize his or her findings to the larger population.

Data Gathering Approaches

Once the survey contact approach has been decided, the next question is what type of survey or poll will be employed. There are two basic survey designs that are employed—cross-sectional and longitudinal. The difference between them deals first with how many times contact is made and second, who are contacted if the particular study requires study over time.

Cross-Sectional Design

Surveys or polls employing a *cross-sectional design* only run their survey once and for a specified period of time. The cross-sectional survey or poll is probably the most used design in all of survey research. As the name suggests, it seeks to report on a specific cross-section of a population at a specific time. The *longitudinal design*, as the label implies, is a study that is done over time and usually employing the same questionnaire over time. (Using different questionnaires over time is equivalent to comparing apples to oranges.) The longitudinal survey can be further broken into three types: trend, panel, and cohort. The *trend* survey employs *different* respondent samples from the *same* population over time. That is, the survey is administered over a time period multiple times, but with different samples from the same population. The *panel* survey employs the *same* respondents from the population over time. It takes a relatively large sample of respondents (because respondents will drop out—fail to continue to participate for any of a number of reasons) and asks them to complete the survey questionnaire over a specified period of time. The *cohort-trend* survey employs *different* respondents from the population over time, but respondents are selected from a *subpopulation* of interest that is referred to as its constant (Stacks 2017). The subpopulation may be a sample of first-time purchasers of a product taken yearly or it could be from an organization's retirees yearly.

Sampling

Sampling refers to the actual selection of respondents for a survey or a poll. It was covered in detail in Chapter 8 but a quick overview should put survey planning into perspective. There are three basic ways to select respondents. First, you can contact each and every respondent in your population, which is a *census* of that population. The key is that you cannot miss any respondent. Second, you can conduct a *random* or *probability sample* of the population. A random sample means that you are selecting respondents through a process whereby *each and every respondent has an equal chance of being chosen to participate* in the survey. A random sample allows the researcher to draw inferences from the sample and generalize them to the larger population within specified degrees of sampling and measurement error. Finally, you can conduct a *nonprobability or convenience* sample. A nonprobability sample draws from respondents who are available to the researcher and inferences can only be made to those who completed the survey.

Summary

Conducting a survey or a poll should be approached with a thorough understanding of how and why the research is being conducted. Often surveys will generate results that dictate more research of a qualitative nature be conducted. Sometimes qualitative studies are used to prepare for survey research. Clearly, the qualitative and quantitative methodologies should be approached as complimentary to each other. When both qualitative and quantitative methods are used, the research is said to be *triangulated* (Stacks 2017; Hickson 2003). We turn next to the actual writing of a survey instrument—the questionnaire.

Questionnaire Construction

Creating a poll questionnaire is fairly straightforward, while creating a survey questionnaire is much more difficult. The poll questionnaire is short, to the point, and is focused on intended or actual behavior; thus yes and no questions are about all that are required. The survey questionnaire, however, seeks to assess and evaluate respondents' attitudes, beliefs, and values toward some expected behavior in the future. As such, it is much longer on average and requires considerable thought. However, the questionnaire can be approached from its four main sections—introduction, body of questions, demographics, and closing. Before actually starting on writing a questionnaire, however, the way it will be transmitted to respondents must be considered as it will change how the questions are stated and respondents will answer.

Introduction

It would seem intuitive that a questionnaire should begin with an introduction, but this isn't always the case. There is a difference between an introduction and directions on how to complete the questionnaire. A survey or a poll questionnaire should begin with a short introduction that does three things. First, it introduces the respondent to the sponsor and whatever research organization is conducting the survey. This serves to establish the credibility of the project. Second, it should assure respondents that their responses will be kept anonymous and confidential. Anonymity and confidentiality are especially important in surveys where respondents are asked questions about their attitudes and beliefs. And, finally, it affords a bit in interpersonal communication. If telephone or person-to-person contact is employed, it should also allow the respondent to refuse to participate (Stacks 2017). The telephone or person-to-person introduction is a script that is spoken, while the other contact approaches are read. Regardless, the introduction should be short and to the point. A written example might be:

> The survey you are being asked to complete is being conducted for X company by ABC Survey Research. We are engaged in a study assessing the public's perception of product Z. The survey will take approximately XX minutes and requires that you simply respond by indicating the most appropriate responses. There are no right or wrong responses, only your perspective on them. You will remain anonymous at all times and all responses will be held in strictest confidence. Please take XX minutes to complete the survey and return it to us by ...

An adaptation of this introduction for verbal transmission might begin with, "Hi, my name is___, and I'm conducting a survey for X Company...."

Body

The questionnaire body contains the meat of the survey. Usually the questionnaire begins with general questions and statements and then moves to more specific questions and responses. All questionnaires should use transitions such as "Next," or "Please answer the following questions by…" between sections. In a telephone or person-to-person survey the transitions, called signposts, keep the respondent's interest up and simultaneously maintain a steady rate of completion. A special type of body question is the *filter question*. A filter question moves respondents from one part of the body to another, to include the moving the respondent to the closing section. For instance, if the study was only concerned with respondents who regularly read newspapers (defined by the study's purpose), a filter question might be "Are you a regular newspaper reader? Yes or No?" If no, the respondent would be sent or skipped to the closing section in a written survey or the interviewer would move immediately to the closing section. A filter question can serve as a filter to a previous filter question: "Do you read a newspaper at least five times a week? Yes or No?" with the same decisions made depending on response.

How the questionnaire's questions and statements are laid out depends again on the contact method employed. For instance, Likert-type statements (see Chapter 4) in a questionnaire might be written thusly:

Please respond to the following statements as to whether you Strongly Agree (SA), Agree (A), Neither Agree Nor Disagree (N), Disagree (D), or Strongly Disagree (SD) with each.

I think that abortion is a woman's choice   SA   A   N   D   SD

Third trimester abortions should be legal   SA   A   N   D   SD

In a written format the respondent sees the instructions, the statements, and can see that the responses are equal appearing. The verbal format, however, requires that the instructions and statements be read exactly *as is* and the response categories *stated for each and every statement.* In the verbal format respondents quickly pick up the responses and will respond before the interviewer finishes the categories.

Demographics

All surveys or polls have a section that seeks to better understand who is responding to the study. This is the *demographic section* and will include not only *demographic data*, such as gender, age, income, education, and so forth, but can also include *psychographic data* (interests, hobbies, likes, and dislikes) and *netgraphic data* (social media used, social networks belonged to). Respondents are often unwilling to provide demographic data, so most surveys put the demographic section at the end of the questionnaire. The exception to this is when a demographic is used as a filter question and it must be asked early, such as found in voting studies or studies where use or knowledge of a product is required. Many surveys will use a demographic filter question seeking to avoid respondents who have backgrounds in public relations, marketing, and advertising or work for the company or client for whom the survey is being conducted. Please note that several of these questions can be quite sensitive and caution needs to be taken in their wording. These questions typically concern age ("How old are you?," "In what year were you born?"), education ("What is the highest educational level completed?" usually asked in the form of an ordinal list beginning with elementary school through graduate school), and household or personal income (usually an ordinal list tied to known income demographics). A typical signpost used is "Finally, for statistical purposes, please answer the following questions."

Closing

Finally, the closing section ends the survey. It serves a couple of purposes. First, it takes the time or space to thank the respondent for his or her time. Second, it provides information that the respondent can use to follow-up on participation or provides contact information on how to get in touch with the survey team. And, finally, it often is used when some promise is made regarding getting a coupon for participation or a copy of the results and tells respondents how to provide that information and assuring of anonymity and confidentiality. A sample closing statement might be:

> Thank you very much for completing this survey. Your responses will help us better understand X. If you would like more information or have any questions regarding the survey, please contact XX at XXX. (Should you wish to claim your coupon for X, please include your contact information here:_____. We will not include this information in the study and your responses remain anonymous and confidential.)

(The material in brackets would be if an incentive were used to increase response rates.)

The Experiment as a Special Case

Earlier in this chapter we noted that a survey can also be used as part of an experiment. An *experiment* is a research project that attempts to carefully control any outside influence on the results. When we think of an experiment, we think of the traditional *laboratory experiment*.[3] Although laboratory experiments are conducted in public relations, they are conducted mostly by academics testing relationships between variables. Because they are highly controlled, they cannot be generalized beyond the carefully controlled conditions, but they do provide evidence of *causal relationships*.

Causal relationships state that because one thing happened, another happens as a result. To establish causation three things must occur.

- First, *it must be established beyond doubt that changes in one thing (variable) causes changes in another thing (variable)*.
- Second, it must be established whether the variable associated with causing change actually precedes the change in the second variable; or that *the effect actually follows the cause*.
- Finally, it must be shown beyond doubt that no other variables influenced the causal relationship.

Only a carefully controlled experimental study can do this. An experimental study interviews a randomly selected group of people (subjects or participants) who are randomly assigned to *conditions* in which certain variables are manipulated and also includes a *control group* which receives no manipulation or exposure to the variables that are expected to create a causal effect (Campbell and Stanley 1963).

What makes the survey qualify as a special experimental case? There are four specific conditions that have to be met:

---

[3] For a complete analysis of public relations experimentation, see Stacks (2017), Chapter 14.

1. Randomly selecting participants.
2. Screening them for specific qualities that meet the conditions set forth by the research.
3. Randomly assign some to experimental conditions where they are manipulated (they are exposed to the experimental stimulus) and respond to the questionnaire.
4. Randomly assign some to control conditions where they receive no manipulation (they only complete the questionnaire).

This is exactly what the public relations *multiplier effect* studies did, but they went further (Michaelson and Stacks 2007; Stacks and Michaelson 2009). To ensure that the results were not biased due to where people lived, the study was conducted at six malls across the United States. In one study 350 shoppers who were daily newspaper readers participated, in the second study over 600 shoppers who read daily newspapers and shopped those same malls participated. The results failed to find the multiplier effect for public relations over advertising, but did provide data that the public relations efforts increased product knowledge and could be correlated to participant feelings toward the product.

Most public relations professionals will not engage in experimentation, but a true understanding of experimental studies published by academics and others is invaluable when conducting secondary research that will lead to qualitative or quantitative research. Understanding what variables should cause an effect provides a strategic advantage in coming up with public relations programs or campaigns.

Case Study: Broward County Public Schools Community Involvement Department Survey

In 2003 the Community Involvement Department of the Broward County Public Schools determined that they needed to establish a baseline of knowledge, awareness, and perceptions of its community involvement program by county school administrators and teachers. The department's programs involved a number of initiatives that brought community leaders and parents into the classroom. In particular, they wished to ascertain the baseline on what were the schools that had received Five Star ratings of excellence and which had participated in the department's community involvement programs.

Background

The Broward County Public School's Community Involvement Department ran a number of programs they thought enhanced student and teacher educational experiences. While the department had in place extensive mentor, parent, community partner, and volunteer programs, no systematic assessment of teaching and administrative awareness, knowledge, and attitude regarding the program had been undertaken. It was hoped that research would accomplish two objectives. First, it would provide a baseline of awareness, knowledge, and attitudes toward the department's programs from top-ranked, Five Star schools. Second, the research would serve to validate the department's vision and mission as related to the Broward County Public School's vision and mission.

Secondary Research

The department brought in a survey researcher to work with them on the research project. Prior to a first meeting, he was sent materials relevant to the project, including larger Broward County Public Schools mission and vision background information and data, summaries of the department's own discussions of their mission and vision, and other relevant information. During a face-to-face discussion, study parameters were established and a decision was made to target successful schools as best practices examples, with the target audiences split between Five Star elementary, middle school, and high school teachers and administrators.

Sample

The sample consisted of administrators and teachers from 34 Five Star schools (14 elementary, 9 middle, and 11 high schools) active in the department's community involvement programs. The decision to sample only Five Star schools sought to gather data from best practices schools. The sample was split into administrators (a census of all 110 administrators) and teachers (400 were randomly selected across the three school levels from a listing of all teachers' home addresses at the 34 schools). The survey employed a mail format and a modified Dillman five-step process (Dillman 2007) was followed with warning cards sent to all respondents in late May, 1 week prior to sending out the questionnaire packet, two weeks after that a reminder card was sent, two weeks after the reminder a new packet was sent, and a final reminder card was sent to all respondents two weeks after that. The study was conducted during the summer of 2003. Because the survey was conducted over the summer months and knowing that there would be address errors due to movement and reassignments, it was decided that any selected respondent whose initial card was returned by the post office would be replaced by a simple random selection of a new respondent; 80 respondents were thus dropped from the sample due to address errors and 80 replacements were added using a random number generator. Ten administrator cards were returned as undeliverable, so the sample consisted of 100 of 110 possible administrators.

Questionnaire Development

The survey sought to assess teacher and administrator awareness, knowledge, and attitudes toward the department's mentor, parent, partner, and volunteer programs and the extent to which respondents believed that five special audiences (school board, teachers, parents, students, and community partners) identified with 15 specific values the department felt served to enhance their mission in regard to the larger school board mission. The questionnaire began with an introductory paragraph describing the project, how respondents were selected, and a guarantee of anonymity and confidentiality and ended with a short thank-you-for-participation paragraph. The working elements were broken into five sections, beginning with individual demographic data dealing with school-related questions (e.g., what grade was taught, how many years at the current school) and four personal questions (highest degree earned, year born for age calculations [i.e., "In what year were you born? 19."]), sex, and race (White, Black, Hispanic, Asian, or Other with space for input). Because all respondents were involved in some way with the community involvement programs which were being assessed, demographic data were collected first unlike many surveys where the data are obtained last. The second section addressed their participation in the community involvement program. The third section asked about respondent perceptions of the community involvement program. The fourth section addressed community involvement identified across the five special audiences. And the fifth section asked open-ended questions.

Because there were two subsamples, slightly different questionnaires were created for teachers and administrators. The teacher questionnaire was phrased in the first person (e.g., "I believe," "I have," "your"), while the administrator questionnaire was phrased toward the school, as well as the respondent (e.g., "My school," "My faculty," and "I have"). The demographic data questions for administrators only differed from teachers in terms of duties (administering versus teaching; title versus grade level taught). The second section's instructions differed in terms of orientation; administrators were asked to provide information regarding "your school's Community Involvement Division programs and your relationship with it," while teachers were instructed to provide information regarding "programs you indicated participating in above program [from the demographic section] and your relationship with them."

The third section contained a large number of 5-point Likert-type statements using a strongly agree to strongly disagree continuum written to assess the Department's community involvement strategies and priorities. Again, two different sets of questions were created, one for teachers that employed 45 statements from the teacher's perspective (e.g., "I visit") and included statements from parent input, staff input, resource availability, community input, their school improvement plan, and student input; in addition, several statements assessed perceptions of school administrators. The administrator section employed 40 statements (e.g., "My faculty visit") at the individual school level, but did not seek administrative data.

The fourth section provided respondents with a matrix with the department's 15 core values as identified in the developmental phase, across the five selected audiences. Respondents were asked to check which core values they felt each specific audience identified with (school board; administrators focused on teachers, while teachers focused their school; parents; students; and community partners). The resultant matrix provided data of departmental values that could be broken by audience or by value.

Finally, a number of open-ended questions were asked to help better understand respondents' perceptions of the department. Teachers and administrators were asked how other teachers and administrators or friends would describe community involvement program, what recommendations they had that might make the community involvement program better, and anything that was positive or negative that the department should know about.

Results

By the end of the summer 45 administrators and 132 teachers, representing all three school levels, had returned questionnaires yielding a total response rate of 35.4 percent (45 percent administrator; 33 percent teacher). The sample size was considered acceptable due to moves and vacations during the summer months when teachers were not teaching.

The results were instructive and the department was provided data that helped them to better understand how their programs were being received, where there might be problems, and how the department's values are identified with across key audiences.

Summary

The survey established a baseline against which future surveys dealing with information flow, perceptions and attitudes, and identification with the Community Involvement Department could compare against for progress in meeting departmental goals and objectives. It also pointed out areas of commonality between administrators and teachers, as well a need for better communication flow from the department to the administrator to the teacher.

Best Practices

What makes a best practice survey? First, the study objectives clearly reflect the overall communication program goals and objectives. Second, secondary research is conducted that links what is known regarding the survey object of study to what is needed to be known. If the survey is attempting to gain behavioral indicators, then a poll may be most appropriate; if it attempts to better understand attitudes, beliefs, or values, a survey is likely most appropriate. Third, sampling decisions are made based on what is known about the population and a sampling frame is established. Fourth, the questionnaire is designed, written, and checked to ensure that it flows well. This requires several decisions regarding transitions, mainly a function of how the survey is to be conducted—mail, telephone, Internet, person-to-person all require slight modifications in terms of instructions and transitional statements. Fifth, the sample design is determined and the survey type selected. Finally, if time allows, a pretest with a sample from the larger population is conducted. Best practice survey research is not something done at the spur of the moment; as with other methods, it should be planned and executed according to a plan that is closely tied to the larger communication and business plan.

Evaluation and Interpretation

The survey is an important method in your research toolbox. It is flexible and can be approached as either a poll or survey, depending on the intended outcomes. When analyzing the survey, the data collected are typically first described and then put to further statistical examination. Interpretation of survey results is dependent, however, on the sampling frame and then on the type and design of the questionnaire employed. It is extremely important that clients understand the rationale behind attitude measures, how reliability and validity was established, and, most importantly, the response rates per question asked. Interpretation of large samples is best when the responses are statistically tested with inferential statistics (see Chapter 10), which allow you to establish how much error there is in expected versus obtained responses. Usually, we expect such statistics to be employed with experiments, but surveys as quantitatively generated data can be tested for group differences (e.g., male versus female responses) within tolerable degree of error. In this way the survey has three important benefits: (1) we know the sampling error if conducted randomly; (2) we know or can approximate the measurement error; and (3) we can state whether certain variables or strata are "truly" or "significantly" different from each other. All of this provides the researcher with important information with which to answer client queries about the validity and reliability of the data and projections to the population.

Summary

Survey research provides a way to gather data from a large and diverse population. If conducted through random selection, it allows a researcher to generalize the results within degrees of sampling and measurement error to the larger population. If conducted as a nonprobability sample, the researcher must confine drawing conclusions and summarizing findings to the sample drawn. Regardless, the survey is a popular quantitative method employed in public relations as a way to gather data that will lead to a better understanding of how the targeted sample or population perceive the object under study.

CHAPTER 10

Statistical Reasoning

Quantitative research by its very nature is closely associated with numbers and coming to conclusions based on those numbers. When a researcher uses a quantitative method, he or she takes numerical data and interprets it through *statistical reasoning*. Statistical reasoning can be approached in two ways, depending on the nature of the research and its uses. The first way is to use the numerical data to simply *describe* variables in the study; this is called *descriptive statistical reasoning*. Often surveys will report what was found through the research in terms that simply describe how many respondents answered statements or as levels of a particular variable, such as sex (48 females or 48 percent of the sample as compared to 52 males or 52 percent of the sample felt the product was a good buy for its price). The statistics simply describe the results. The second way is to use the numerical data to *infer* differences between levels of a variable; this is called *inferential statistical reasoning*. Here the numerical data are used to establish the *probability* that groups of people are truly different on a variable. In the preceding example, for instance, is 48 actually smaller than 52? Or, is there no real difference between female and male perceptions on that product? Inferential statistical reasoning provides a way to test— to infer—for differences.

This chapter covers both descriptive and inferential statistical reasoning from a practical perspective. It will not require the understanding of complex statistical formulae, but instead will demonstrate how numerical data can be used to present findings and then interpret those findings in terms of what the probability of differences are. As such, there is very little mathematics involved; indeed, statistical analysis, especially today with computerized statistical packages such as IBM

Statistical Package for the Social Sciences (SPSS) Statistics,[1] is more about understanding how to read a map and what that map represents. The analogy to a map is appropriate in that statistics provide the directions from which inferences can be made about numerical data. As with maps, however, there are slightly different maps for different purposes. Examples of these are maps used to travel differ between geographical points and maps used to show political representations of the same territory. Simply put, different statistical programs provide different ways of looking at the data being analyzed. Before we turn to descriptive statistical reasoning, a quick review of data and how we define and label that data is necessary.

Describing Data

In Chapter 4 we noted that data can take many different forms. For statistical purposes, however, data are associated with numbers and numerical thinking. Because of this, people will often assume that data—numbers—have some direct meaning. From the outset, let's agree that *numbers have no meaning in and of themselves but meaning is interjected into them by people collecting, analyzing, and reporting those numbers.* That is, a number is simply an indicator, an often imprecise indicator that provides us with the ability to make comparisons. In Chapter 4 numbers were defined by the type of data being collected or observed. We noted that there were two major types of data—categorical and continuous—and within each major type there were two subclasses.

Categorical and Continuous Data

When employing statistical reasoning, especially when we are attempting to infer differences from data, how the data are initially defined becomes important. Although covered in detail in Chapter 4, categorical analyses

---

[1] SPSS has been around for at least 30 years. Initially known as the "Statistical Package for the Social Sciences," it is used by many academic and professionals to compute statistics. In 2009 SPSS was purchased by IBM and is now known as IBM SPSS Statistics.

resulting from either nominal or ordinal data that in the former simply differentiate levels of an object or a variable and in the later propose an ordering effect for levels of the object or variable. For instance, nominal-level data for sex would be defined as female or male, with each being equated equally and simply a way to distinguish the levels. However, for ordinal-level data, such as socioeconomic status, lower class, middle class, and upper class are not only different, but also ordered in terms of lowest to highest status. Note, too, that categorical data are *always* categorical data, even when analyses may *appear* to be continuous (e.g., percentages). Continuous analyses resulting from interval-level data (e.g., age) or ratio (e.g., monetary data such as dollars or pounds sterling) put the data on a range or continuum. As noted in Chapter 4, continuous data can be reduced to categorical data, but categorical data cannot be modified to become continuous data.

The first step in statistical reasoning is to understand how the data were defined before the data were collected. This provides the basic information required to decide on which statistic is most appropriate to report and interpret. The second step is to actually compute the statistic by running the data either by hand or via a computer.

Using Computer Programs to Calculate Statistics

The computer has made all of us statisticians. This is not necessarily a good thing. A computer will compute any statistic asked for, whether it is the appropriate statistic for the data or problem. Furthermore, new statistical packages will often help in deciding what statistic should be run. A rule of thumb is that the computer is actually only as smart as the user, so understanding what statistic to run should come from the research objectives, which of course reflect the larger public relations and business objectives. Some statistical packages have evolved into large programs that not only run the statistics requested, but also have fairly good graphing programs. Other computer programs simply run the statistics requested and provide output for analysis. There are a large number of computerized *statistical* packages available, to include IBM SPSS Statistics and SAS (large comprehensive programs) and MiniTab or small Stats (smaller less comprehensive programs) (Stacks 2017). In addition, there

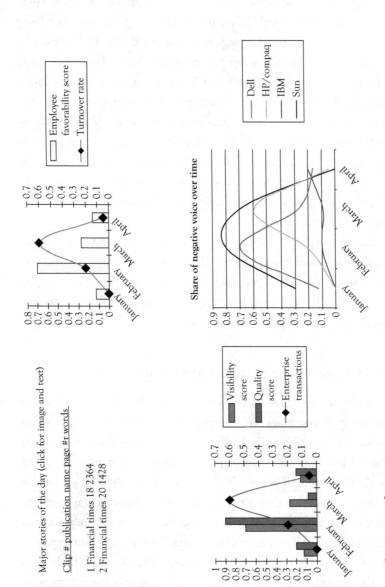

Figure 10.1 Sample scorecard

are analytical packages which combine both the analytics, such as content analysis and basic statistical analyses. These programs include survey packages such as Survey Monkey and Qualtrics, as well as dedicated statistical analysis programs such as Mentor and statistical add-on programs that can be used in conjunction with Microsoft Office applications like Excel. "Analyse It" and "SPC-XL" are two of the commonly used of these add-on programs. The computer also allows researchers to provide clients with sophisticated visual presentations of the data. These "dashboards" or "scorecards" are simply descriptive statistics that are updated at intervals ranging from daily to monthly to quarterly. Figure 10.1 presents visual representations of a number of variables representing verbal descriptions, categorical data, and continuous data. We will refer back to them when discussing visualizing descriptive data.

Descriptive Statistical Reasoning

Descriptive statistics, as noted earlier, simply describe or summarize the data. All quantitative research and some qualitative research describe its data. The simplest level of description is to summarize the data for one variable, or to conduct a *univariate descriptive analysis*. More complex analyses summarize the data for two or more variables, or conduct *bivariate* or *multivariate descriptive analyses*. Bivariate and multivariate analyses summarize the data by each variable's levels, such as sex (male or female) and socioeconomic status (lower, middle, and upper):

	Lower class	Middle class	Upper class
Female			
Male			

Categorical Descriptive Statistical Analyses

Categorical statistical analysis deals basically deals with *frequency counts*—the actual number of observations found in each level of a categorical variable. It is important to remember that the frequency count is the basis for all other descriptive statistics, the most frequent of which is the percentage. The *percentage* is simply the number of observation in a category divided by the total number of observations. Percentage data is often used when the data are to be reported as quartiles (25 percent segments) or deciles (10 percent segments). Finally, the ratio can be calculated from the frequency counts. The *ratio* is a comparison of two frequencies, say we had ten males and five females, the ratio of males to females would be 2 to 1, stated as 2:1.

Univariate

Univariate descriptive statistics deal with a single variable. For instance, if a content analysis was run with the following categories for story rating, "favorable," "neutral," and "unfavorable," there would be three categories (plus the "other" category, which we will ignore for now). If there were 100 placements the descriptive statistics might break down as follows: 50 were favorable, 30 neutral, 20 unfavorable. The data could also be described in terms of percentages, with the number of observations per category divided by the total observations: 50 percent were favorable, 30 percent neutral, 20 percent unfavorable. Percentages are often reported with small sample sizes, which may make interpretation difficult. For instance, it seldom happens in large samples that the results come out at 50 percent or 33.3 percent, unless they were rounded off. If so, the descriptive analysis should state so. A third descriptive statistic is the ratio. If a survey's results found that males represented 40 out of 400 respondents, while females represented 360 respondents, the proportion of females to males would be 10 to 1, or 10:1.

Visualizing. Categorical descriptive statistics are usually visualized as either a univariate table or as bar or column charts (bar charts are horizontal, columns are vertical), or pie charts, although there are other formats that can be used (e.g., surface, donut, bubble, and radar or spider web). The following table visually presents the story placement results as a univariate table.

Sex of respondent		Story rating	
Female	400	Favorable	50
Male	40	Neutral	30
		Unfavorable	20

Many public relations research firms now provide visualizations of statistics. Several different univariate statistics were visualized in Figure 10.1.

Bivariate and Multivariate

Bivariate and multivariate descriptive statistics describe the relationships between two or more categorical variables. Of the two, bivariate analyses are most common in public relations research reports. A bivariate analysis on the story placement by respondent sex would result in a two column (sex) by three row (story rating) table:

Sex/story rating	Female	Male
Favorable	230	20
Neutral	138	12
Unfavorable	92	8
Total	460	40

A multivariate descriptive analysis would produce extra tables. If a third variable were being analyzed, say socioeconomic status of the respondent (low, middle, high), there would be three tables, one for each level of one of the three variables. In our previous example, we would have a table for low socioeconomic respondents, a table for middle socioeconomic respondents, and a table for high socioeconomic respondents.

Visualizing. Visualizing bivariate or multivariate is typically done through bar or column charts, although the data also can be visualized through other chart types (e.g., pie, spider).

Continuous Descriptive Statistical Analyses

Continuous data are found on some continuum, hence the label, *continuous*. Continuous data are considered stronger than their categorical counterparts because of the statistical procedures and what they tell researchers. As noted in Chapter 4, continuous data are either *interval*, where the distance between data points is considered to be equal, or *ratio*, where the distance between data points are absolute. The demographic variable *age*, when calculated from year born, would be interval data (e.g., if I were to

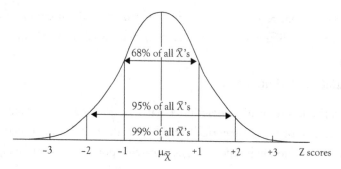

Figure 10.2 The normal curve

respond to a survey question, what year were you born, and filled in 1949, when subtracted from 2017 would yield my age as 67 years). My bank account, which would run from 0 or higher (or lower since it is ratio it can be ±), would be ratio data.

What makes continuous data so powerful is that along its continuum, the data will fall under some type of curve (which you first encountered in Chapter 8), which is a function of the distribution of all data points gathered for whatever continuous variable is being examined. All continuous data have their own normal distribution which has certain properties that provide continuous statistical analysis with more ways to describe them. The hypothetical *normal curve* is shown in Figure 10.2. Of importance is the area *under* the curve, which can be expressed in deviations from the mean or average of all data points. This underlies the concept of continuous data to have a *central tendency*—to distribute around that mean. Without going into statistical detail, all continuous data can be demonstrated to fall within X-number of *standard deviations* (based on the mean and its *variance*, or distribution from the mean). All curves find that 34 percent of all data will fall 1 standard deviation from the mean, or 68 percent of the data will fall ±1 standard deviation from the data's mean. This is powerful in terms of description in that it provides much more information than simple frequencies, percents, or ratios. While there are many continuous statistics available, we will concentrate on six.

Univariate

The five most commonly employed continuous statistics are the mean, median, mode, variance, and standard deviation. The *mean* typically refers to the average of data points for a variable. There are, however, a number of different means used by statisticians (Blalock 1972; Williams and Monge 2001), but the mean usually found in public relations research is the *average*. Means are highly influenced by data points that are extremely far from the average. *Outliers* are data points that influence the mean. Take 10 data points: 1, 2, 3, 4, 5, 6, 7, 8, 9, and 10. The mean for this dataset would be 5.5; if one of the data points were an outlier, say instead of 6 it was 22, the mean would be much larger (7.1). When there are outliers, it is essential that the *median*, or the data point that is 50 percent of the dataset scores, be examined. When calculating the median, the data are lined up in order and the middle data point is the median (for datasets with an even number of data points, the median is the average of the two scores around the 50th percentile). In the case of the 10 scores, the median would be 5.5, same as the mean; in the case of the outlier, the median would be 6.0. The *mode* is the data point(s) that reoccurs most in the dataset. In this case there are no recurring numbers, each number is unique. However, if the data points were 1, 2, 3, 3, 4, 5, 6, 7, 8, 9, the mode would be 3. A dataset where the mean, median, and mode are identical would indicate adherence to the hypothetical normal curve, as shown in Figure 10.2. When the mean, median, and mode differ the shape of the curve changes by becoming flatter, part of this is due to the variance or distribution of scores.

As noted earlier, all data for a continuous variable are distributed around the mean for that dataset. The *variance* provides an indicator of the distribution of data points around the mean. Interestingly, the variance is typically larger for small datasets than larger datasets. Why? Think of an auditorium with 100 seats. For the first 10 people to sit, the distribution will be large—there are many seats and few people, so their seating may be anywhere. As the number of people increases, the distribution of people in seats decreases as fewer and fewer seats are left. The variance describes how normal the dataset is, but is unique to the dataset. The *standard deviation*, which is the square of the variance, normalizes the data and can be used to compare datasets of different variables, even if those variables are measured differently (e.g., 5- or 7-point measure) through the *standardized score* for each variable, which is expressed in terms of the number of standard deviations each score is from the mean. Thus, from these continuous statistics, we know the distribution of data around a mean. For instance, age for a sample might be 21.2 years, with a standard deviation of 3.2 years. This would tell us that 68 percent of the sample was aged 18.0 to 24.4 years old.

Visualizing. Univariate continuous statistics typically are reported as numbers in a table. It is difficult to create a graph of only one variable. When we do, however, we typically find that a line graph is used to visually portray the data (see Figure 10.1). For that we need to turn to bivariate and multivariate variable analyses.

Bivariate and Multivariate

As with categorical variables, more than one variable can be described in relation to another. This is done typically by describing the relationship between means for two or more variables or for two variables, examining the correlation between the two variables; however, one of those variables must be categorical, which provides points of reference for the analysis. For instance, age and sex can be described by looking at the mean and standard deviation for males and the mean for females. When we look at two continuous variables, we typically describe their correlation. A *correlation* is the relationship between the variables data points. A correlation can only reflect the relationship between the two variables and ranges from a perfect correlation of +1.00 through no correlation at all at 0.00 to a perfect negative correlation of −1.00. According to Hocking, Stacks, and McDermott (2003), correlations below ±0.30 are *weak*, ±0.30 to ±0.70 *moderate* and ±0.70 to ±0.90 are *high*, and above ±0.90 are *very high*. In communication research, most correlations are typically found below ±0.50 and if higher they may be restricted by controlling the data range in some way often making the relationship unclear.

Visualizing. Visualizing bivariate and multivariate relationships are easier than univariate relationships because there is a comparison. The usual visualization is via the line or fever graph with separate lines indicating different variables in relationship to each other (see Figure 10.1). A correlation is visualized as a scatter graph, where one variable is found on the X-axis and the other on the Y-axis. Figure 10.3 shows that the relationship between sales and consumer ratings of an advertisement are positively

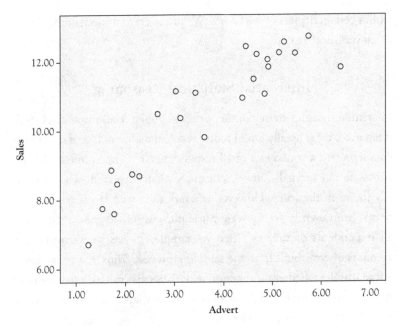

Figure 10.3 Scatter graph

related. If you were to draw a line through the data points, it would go from the lower-left corner just above the six on the sales axis and continue at an angle upward toward the six on the advertisement ratings axis.

Using Categorical and Continuous Data to Describe Simple Relationships

Categorical and continuous are now commonly intermingled in visualizing data from several variables that provide the public relations professional an indication or snapshot of the relationships between variables of interest. Note that in Figure 10.1's first visual on the second row, some variables are univariate and some are bivariate (and, like comparing means, one axis is categorical and the other continuous).

It is important at this point to emphasize that *descriptive statistics do not analyze the data or the relationships between variables.* To make judgments about variables being larger or smaller than others, or that the relationships are truly "significantly different," requires that inferences be made. This moves us to a more advanced set of statistics that allow researchers to state the strength of a relationship or lack of relationship within certain degrees of *confidence*. We turn next to understanding inferential statistical analysis.

Inferential Statistical Reasoning

Inferential statistics are seldom reported in public relations research and, if reported, are generally put in footnotes. As a matter of fact, if the study's data represent a true *census* of all respondents or sources, inferential statistics are not needed—any descriptive statistics represent what is actually found in the study. However, when dealing with larger populations drawn from even larger universes, it is not possible to collect data from all respondents or sources. Then we sample, and as we know, certain amounts of error built in to the sampling process. Thus, the researcher is left to wonder whether the descriptive statistics are true representations of the larger population and differences among variables are real or whether they due to chance—or *random error*.

One of the reasons survey researchers run inferential statistics on their demographics is to test sampling error. If there were 400 randomly selected respondents to a survey, the researcher is willing to accept up to 5 percent sampling error—but this does not mean that there was sampling error, just that there might be. Therefore, running inferential tests on the data against known data (and hoping for *no* differences), gives a researcher the ability to say that he or she is 90 percent, 95 percent, or 99 percent confident that the sample is representative of the larger population.

In much research where *differences* are expected, inferential statistics provide a researcher with the amount of confidence that variables are different from each other. In survey research the second form of error is measurement error. Inferential statistics allows us to test for measurement error among the outcome variables when analyzing the descriptive statistics. For instance, if purchase intent of a product was the outcome of interest and the study used measures of product awareness, product knowledge, and liking as indicators of purchase intent, the researcher needs to test whether the variables truly indicated purchase intent, and if so, how much confidence can the researcher have in the results of the tests. The *standard* accepted confidence that there are differences is put at

95 percent. This means that 95 times out of 100 the results were due to purchase intent and not to measurement or other error.

There are many inferential statistics that can be run on data. Some simply look to see if levels of a categorical variable (e.g., sex) describe differences in the outcome variable. For instance, do males intend to purchase the product more than females, or is the difference in purchase intent due to error? Others look to try and predict from a number of variables (almost always categorical) which are related to the outcome of interest. Which of three variables, operationalized as dichotomous variables (i.e., high awareness, high knowledge, high liking versus low awareness, knowledge and liking) best predict purchase intent? Those statistics that look at differences are fairly simple and we will look at the chi-square (χ^2) as representative of categorical variables and the t-test and analysis of variance (ANOVA) as representative of continuous tests. Regression is what most use to try and model predictive tests. As noted in the first part of this chapter, it is not our intent to make statisticians out of readers, but we hope that after the short descriptions that follow, you will have a basic understanding of what the test does.

Categorical

The *chi-square* (χ^2) test is one of the most utilized of categorical inferential statistical tests. The chi-square tests whether the frequency of observations in a given category or level of a variable are different from what would be expected. The chi-square is often used in surveys to test demographic variables against known results, typically against census or industry data. For instance, suppose a random survey of shoppers in a large metropolitan area finds that 56 percent of the respondents were female and 44 percent were male. Going to the census data (easily available through the U.S. government), we find that for this particular area females constitute 51 percent of the metropolitan area and males 49 percent. The chi-square would test the female data obtained (56 percent) against the census data (51 percent) and test the male data obtained (49 percent) against the census data (44 percent). A chi-square test, if run, would find that the sample **not** differ significantly (the probability of differences was confirmed at with 95 percent confidence) from the census data (there was a greater than

5 percent chance that the data were due to sampling error). Thus, we can claim that our sample did not differ from the reported census data.

Continuous

While categorical inferential statistics look for differences between categories, continuous look for differences between means for different categories. The most commonly used inferential test is the *t*-test. The *t*-test looks at differences in continuous outcome variables between variables with two and only two groups (e.g., male or female; high or low; expensive or inexpensive). This is a major limitation, but the *t*-test is easy to interpret and any means found different must be significantly different because there are only two of them. The *t*-test has another limitation—it is sensitive to differences in small samples (under 150) because of the way it is calculated (Blalock 1972, 192–93).[2] Suppose we have two means, male purchase intent on a 5-point scale was found to be 4.5, while female purchase intent was found to be 2.5. The question the *t*-test answers is whether 4.5 is truly different from 2.5 (notice that it is not stated as larger or smaller, but as different). A *t*-test run on the means would find that, the two groups were significantly different and that the researcher can be 95 percent confident in making a claim that males were more intent to purchase than were females. There are three *t*-tests: the one we just discussed is labeled an "independent *t*-test;" when you get data from the same people twice (and only twice), it labeled a "paired *t*-test;" and when you are comparing against a known test score, it is known as a "one group *t*-test." All three are of use in public relations research.

For larger samples or for studies where there are more than two levels of a variable or more than one variable, a different test is run. The Analysis of Variance (ANOVA or *F*-test) is a more general test that is not sensitized to large samples. Instead of using a special variance measure, it simply looks for the variance that can be explained by being in a category (high, moderate, low awareness) as compared against the variance for being in

---

[2] This is beyond the scope of this book, but the *t*-test is based on a sensitive measure of variance for each mean. As a sample gets larger, the variance becomes larger and the test's ability to take that into account reduces.

any group (called "between group" or systematic variance for the category and "within group" or error variance for all respondents across groups) for the outcome variable (purchase intent). The ANOVA then tests to see if there is less variance for groups as compared against all respondents. With a larger sample, the results for dichotomous variables are similar to the t-test. However, with three or more groups, a significant overall finding (that being in a group did make a difference in the outcome variable) does not indicate how the groups differed. In that case, more tests must be run, which are a specialized form of the ANOVA—the *one-way* ANOVA (Williams and Monge 2001).

Finally, there are times when researchers want to predict which variables best predict an outcome. The most commonly used statistical test here is to run a *simple* or *multiple regression*. What the regression does is first look for differences between variables and then look for how the variables correlate. By drawing a line through the correlation matrix outcomes can be predicted for individual variables or can test to see which variables of several can best predict outcomes (Allison 1999). The variables that are examined are the "dependent variable" and the "independent variables" that impact or affect the dependent variable. An example of a dependent variable is "willingness to purchase" a product or a service. What regression does is examine a series of other variables that impact or "drive" a "willingness to purchase" and determines the overall contribution each of these independent variables makes toward that decision. Examples of independent variables may include overall awareness of a product, levels of knowledge about the product or affinity toward or prior relationship between the company and the purchaser.

Best Practices

Best practice public relations employs descriptive and inferential statistics in analyzing the effect of public relations variables on outcomes of interest. Running appropriate statistical tests and being able to discuss the descriptive findings is the first step in best practices statistical analysis. The second step is to run the appropriate inferential statistics to test for confidence in those differences or which variables best predict specific outcomes.

Evaluation and Interpretation

All public relations campaigns use statistical analysis to demonstrate that what was done during the campaign had some impact. In most cases this impact is a number greater than that at baseline, when the campaign started. However, sometimes the goal is to have *no* change among respondents. This is often the case in corporate public relations where some outside controversy may impact on stakeholders and your campaign is to minimalize any change. Using statistics helps to drive home results. Normally, statistical reports are descriptive, but at times you may be asked "How sure are you of these findings?" You can respond if you ran the appropriate inferential statistics by stating you are extremely confident (1 percent error allowed or 99 percent confident), confident (5 percent error), somewhat confident (10 percent error), and so forth. Regardless, you will need to visualize your results so that the client can see the relationships you are talking about. Therefore, running statistics has become a necessity when reporting and interpreting results. You don't have to be a statistician, but you do need to know what to ask your data management people and how to make your own analysis and interpretation of that data.

Summary

Continuous inferential statistics are powerful tests of differences between potential predictors of variables relating to some outcomes. With the increased emphasis on proving value, public relations research is moving quickly to employing more inferential tests. Public relations researchers employ inferential tests all the time. However, insimple presentation and final reports they are often not included in the report body but as notes (see, for example, Li and Stacks 2015). The inferential test provides the public relations professional with the information necessary to state with confidence whether or not variables in a program or campaign are effective in demonstrating return on expectations and ultimately return on investment.

PART IV

Wrapping Up

Part IV wraps up and reviews the key factors that need to be considered when conducting public relations research, measurement, and evaluation. This part places in context the key information from Parts I, II, and III and presents a series of nine best research and measurement practices and standards based upon these parts that form the foundation for creating communication programs that are effective in achieving their goals. The part includes a review on setting objectives, the use of specific research methods, and the applications of a research, measurement, and evaluation program.

CHAPTER 11

The Application of Standards and Best Practices in Research and Evaluation for Public Relations[1]

The Current State of Public Relations Measurement

Companies specializing in public relations measurement and evaluation have traditionally focused on evaluating only the outcomes of public relations. These outcomes are most commonly the media or press coverage that is a direct result of media relations activities (outputs). The primary limitation of these companies is their limited focus on an intermediary in the public relations process—the media—rather than on the target audience for these communication activities.

Relying strictly on evaluations of intermediaries in the communication process fails to create effective measurement and evaluation systems that provide a diagnostic appraisal of communication activities which, in turn, can lead to enhanced communication performance. The failure to include diagnostic measures ignores one of the fundamental best practices in communication research and is the key reason why public relations measurement and evaluation has failed to progress significantly over the past 30 years.

---

[1] Sections of this chapter were originally published in Michaelson and Macleod (2007) and Stacks (2016, 2017).

Standards in Public Relations Research

Setting standards for public relations research—ethical, measurement, evaluation standards—should be the first thing a client looks for when hiring a research firm. As noted in Chapter 2, these standards are only now being seen as important (Stacks 2016). Why? First, because standards are necessary conditions for professionalism. Second, because standards tell us what to research and lead to how to conduct that research. Third, because standards provide the only way to effectively and efficiently provide comparative evaluation of communication programs for their efficacy and for their ability to meet communication objectives.

Ethical standards address how researchers should approach research, the research participants, and the nature of business. Unethical research calls into question the validity of the research and the researcher's professionalism and, perhaps more importantly, it calls into question the researcher's neutrality and impartiality in assessing the data, evaluating it, and making recommendations. An ethical researcher should be above the fray, providing pure and unbiased data and evaluation.

Measurement standards address how data should be created, assessed, and evaluated. Furthermore, all measures should report reliability and validity information and include the actual reliability statistics.

Evaluation standards provide the researcher with a tool that allows him or her to compare results against others. Evaluation standards include how much statistical error the researcher was willing to accept (usually no more than 5 percent) and results against other recognized research findings.

Best Practices in Public Relations Research

In public relations research, academic as well as professional,[2] there are nine best practices that can serve as the foundation for establishing a standardized set of measures for public relations activities that are essential elements in advancing public relations measurement and evaluation.

---

[2] For a detail discussion of academic evaluation methods, refer to: Stacks (2016, 2017).

These practices are divided between two broad areas: (1) the use of specific research methods and procedures and (2) the application of measures that examine both the quality and the substance of public relations activities.

Research Methods and Procedures

There are three research methods and procedures that are an essential part of best practices in public relations research. These methods and procedures include every key step in the research process from the inception of the project through the delivery of the research report itself. These three steps are as follows:

1. Setting clear and well-defined research objectives.
2. Applying rigorous research design that meets highest standards of research methods and ensures reliable research results.
3. Providing detailed supporting documentation with full transparency.

Clear and Well-Defined Research Objectives

Setting clear and well-defined research objectives is the critical first step in the public relations research process. Unfortunately, it is the aspect of best research practices that is typically either overlooked or not given the level of attention that it requires in order to create an effective and reliable measurement and evaluation system. The establishment of clear and well-defined definitions is particularly critical since research objectives function as the foundation upon which the rest of the research program rests (Stacks 2017). The key to setting these objectives so that they can effectively contribute to a measurement and evaluation program that meets best standards involves answering the following five questions.

- *Is the information need clearly articulated?*
  - o In order for any form of measurement and evaluation to be effective, it is essential that the information be specific and unambiguous. A generalized information need such as, "How well did the program perform?" is unlikely to serve as an effective basis for any research-based decisions.

The more appropriate questions are: "What is the level of awareness of the product, issue, or situation?" "How knowledgeable is the target audience about the material being communicated?" "Is the information relevant to the target audience?"

"How has the attitude of the audience been impacted by exposure to communications?" "Is the target audience willing to take any form of action as a result of exposure to the communication program?" These questions result in setting specific information objectives that can be reliably measured and provide data that can be used to improve communication performance.

- *Are the target audiences for the communication program well defined?*
    - o It is essential to understand who the target *audience* is as precisely as possible.[3] This is important for several reasons. The primary and foremost reason is practical. To conduct research that reliably measures and evaluates a communication program, it is essential that those to whom the program is directed also serve as the source of the information about the audience. A poorly defined audience is typically one that is so broad in its scope that it includes those unlikely to express an interest or need. An example of an audience that may be too broad in its scope is "women aged 18 to 49 years old." By contrast, a more narrowly defined audience is "mothers of children that are 12 years or younger." While the former group includes the latter group it is less precise and depending on the product or service, less likely to yield the same information.
- *Are business objectives being met through the information gathered from the research?*
    - o The central reason for conducting any type of measurement and evaluation research is to address a business issue or

---

[3] We can no longer get away with measuring publics; they are too heterogeneous in a global business environment that is so clearly interconnected via the Internet.

concern. Consequently, as the objectives for the research are being established, it is critical that a detailed assessment of the business takes place as a first step in the process. For example, if the issue is assessing the introduction of a new product category, then measuring awareness is a highly relevant and essential measure. However, if the business issue concerns a prominent national brand, then purchase intent may be a more relevant and important measure to include in the research program. The more closely research is tied into delivering business objectives, the more valuable and strategic it will be.

- *Is there a plan for how the findings from the research will be used?*
  - o Just as it is important to have a clear understanding of the research objectives, it is equally essential to understand the types of actions that can be taken as a direct result of the information that is gathered in the research process. The intent is to create research that functions as an aid in the decision-making process, rather than having it serve as an end in and of itself. For this reason, it is best to consider likely internal users or customers for the research findings at the outset (e.g., marketing, investor relations, new product development, human resources, market, or business units). Human nature being what it is, it is also advisable to secure their involvement and buy-in first, so that the findings are welcomed and applied constructively, not just as an afterthought. Objective listening research and the insights derived from it are tremendously powerful in terms of internal education for management and appreciation for the strategic focus of communication.
- *Is the organization prepared to take action based on research findings?*
  - o Just as important as having a plan for applying the research is having an understanding of the actions the organization is willing to take based on the findings. If the senior decision makers are unwilling to undertake specific

actions, then creating a research program that measures
and evaluates that action will have little value to the
organization and may actually be counter-productive to the
organization's long-term goals and objectives.

Rigorous Research Design

Once objectives have been established, it is important to design research
that both supports the objectives and is rigorous enough to provide usable
and actionable information. This rigor not only assures reliable research
results, but also provides a foundation for measuring and evaluating
communication performance over time. Again, a series of nine questions
needs to be addressed in order to ensure that rigorous research designs are
applied.

- *Is the sample well defined?*
    - The research sample, just like the target audience, needs
      to be precise in order to make sure it is the actual target
      audience for communication that is included in the
      research. The recommended approach is to screen potential
      research respondents for these defining characteristics
      before the start of the study. These defining characteristics
      can be demographic (e.g., age, gender, education,
      occupation, region, etc.), job title or function, attitudes,
      product use, or any combination of these items. However,
      while it is important to define the sample precisely, caution
      must also be taken to make sure that key members of
      the target group are included in the sample. In some
      instances, samples require minimal quotas of specific types
      of respondents to ensure that analyzable segments of each
      quota group are included in the study.
- *Are respondents randomly selected?*
    - One of the most significant and immeasurable biases
      that can occur in a study is the exclusion of potential
      respondents who are difficult to reach and therefore are
      less likely to participate in the study. Special attention

needs to be paid to ensure that these individuals have an equal opportunity to participate. This is equally true for telephonic as well as online surveys. This is typically accomplished through multiple contacts over an extended period with a random sample or replica of the group being studied. It is also essential to be sensitive to the audience being studied and appropriately adapt the ways that responses to questions are secured. Examples of these very specific groups of individuals that require increased sensitivity are young children or other groups where there are special laws and regulations guiding data collection, night-shift workers, ethnic minorities, and disabled or disadvantaged groups. (See Chapter 8 for a detailed discussion of sampling.)

- *Are appropriate sample sizes used?*
  - o Samples need to provide reliability in two distinct manners. The primary need is to make certain the overall sample is statistically reliable. The size of the sample can vary considerably from a few hundred respondents to over 1,000 individuals. The decision to use one sample size over another is contingent on the size of the overall population represented by the sample, as well as the number of subgroups that will be included in the analysis. For example, a national study of Americans typically requires a sample of 1,000 respondents. This assures geographic and demographic diversity as well as adequately sized subgroups between which reliable comparisons can be made. By contrast, a survey of senior executives may require only 200 to 400 completed interviews to meet its objectives.
- *Are the appropriate statistical tests used?*
  - o Survey research is subject to sampling error. This error is typically expressed as range of accuracy. A number of different standards can be applied to determine this level of accuracy as well as serve as the basis to compare findings between surveys. The most common standard used is the 95 percent measure. This standard assures that the

findings, in 19 out of 20 cases, will be reliable within a specific error range for both sampling and measurement. This error range varies depending on the size of the sample under consideration with a larger sample providing a corresponding smaller range of error. With that standard in place, a number of different statistical tests can be applied. The key is to select the proper test for the situation being tested. (See Chapter 10 for a detailed discussion on statistical testing.)

- *Is the data collection instrument unbiased?*
  - o A questionnaire can impact the results of a survey in much the same way as the sample selection procedures. The wording and sequence of questions can significantly influence results. Therefore, it is essential to make sure that wording is unbiased and the structuring of the questionnaire does not influence how a respondent answers a question. Paying attention to this concern increases the reliability of the findings and provides a better basis for decision making.
- *Are the data tabulated correctly?*
  - o Special concern needs to be taken to make sure that the responses from each questionnaire are properly entered into an analytic system so that data from the entire study can be reliably tabulated. Data preferably should be entered into a database with each questionnaire functioning as an independent record. This will also allow for subsequent verification if errors are detected and will also allow for the greatest analytic flexibility. Accuracy will also be significantly enhanced with this approach. Spreadsheets do not provide the same analytic flexibility as specialized statistical packages (i.e., SAS or SPSS) and it is significantly harder to detect errors when using that type of data entry system.
- *Are the data presented accurately?*
  - o Assuming the data are tabulated properly, it is equally important that it be presented in a manner that accurately

represents the findings. While data is often selectively presented, the omission of data should not be allowed if it presents misleading or inaccurate results. Consequently, the full dataset needs to be available, even if the data is only selectively presented.

- *Is qualitative research used appropriately?*
  - o Well-executed qualitative research (focus groups, individual in-depth interviews, and participant observation) can provide unique insights that are not available from other sources. While these insights are invaluable, this form of research is not a substitute for survey data. Qualitative research is particularly useful with three applications: development of communication messages, testing and refinement of survey research tools, and providing insights as well as deeper explanations of survey findings. (See Chapter 6 for a detailed discussion on qualitative research methods.)
- *Can the study findings be replicated through independent testing?*
  - o If research is properly executed, reproducing the study should yield similar results. The only exception is when significant communication activity has occurred that will impact attitudes and opinions. Unless the study is reliably constructed so that it can be replicated, it will be difficult to produce studies that can be reliably compared and which will demonstrate the actual impact of communication activities. (See Chapter 9 for a detailed discussion of experimental design.)

Detailed Supporting Documentation

While it is essential to employ a rigorous research design when measuring and evaluating public relations activities, it is just as critical to document how the research was conducted. This documentation provides a clear understanding of the issues being measured and a detailed description of the audience being studied. Just as important, it provides the information required to replicate the study so that consistent measurement and evaluation can be applied. The three questions that need to be answered to ensure that the documentation meets the standards of best practices are as follows:

- *Is the research method described fully?*
  - o The description of the method includes not only *how* the study was conducted (telephone, in person, online, etc.), but also the *timeframe* when the interviews took place, *who* conducted the interviews and a description of the *sample*.
- *Is the questionnaire—as well as any other data collection instruments—available for review?*
  - o This ensures that the reader understands the context of the questions by being able to refer back to the questionnaire when reviewing the dataset. It also allows for easier replication of the study.
- *Is the full dataset available if requested?*
  - o Availability of the data provides full transparency of the findings, as well as the foundation for doing comparative analyses with subsequent waves of the research. It also allows for additional tabulation of the data and other analyses that may be useful in a subsequent analysis.

Quality and Substance of Research Findings

The second broad area contributing to best practices in public relations research involves six practices which ensure that the research findings contribute to improving communication programs. These six practices are as follows:

1. Designing the research to demonstrate the effectiveness of public relations activities.
2. Linking public relations outputs to outcomes.
3. Using the findings to aid in the development of better communication programs.
4. Demonstrating an impact on business outcomes.
5. Being cost effective.
6. Having applicability to a broad range of public relations activities.

Demonstrating Effectiveness

The central reason to conduct measurement and evaluation research is to determine if a communication program works. Consequently, every set of research objectives and each research design needs to ask the following two questions:

- *Is the research designed to show the potential impact of a message, program, or campaign?*
  - o This is the primary acid test when designing a measurement and evaluation effort. Unless the research has this capability built into the design, it should be reconsidered. These designs can vary considerably from situation-to-situation. However, a common element of many measurement and evaluation programs is setting a baseline or benchmark at the initial stages of the research and using that benchmark as the basis for evaluating performance, preferably throughout the campaign at specified intervals.
- *Is the research designed to function as a benchmark to gauge future performance?*
  - o A benchmark study has to examine basic communication measures. The importance of each of the measures may vary over time. However, basic measures of awareness, knowledge, interest or relevance, and intent to take action need to be considered for inclusion in most studies.

Linking Outputs to Outcomes

Significant proportions of public relations measurement and evaluation focuses attention on the evaluation of media placements. While media placements are often critical in the evaluation and measurement process, they only represent one limited aspect of the public relations process. More importantly, concentrating analysis only on that one area fails to take into account the fundamental issue that public relations activities take place in order to impact a target audience. While the media are a key target for this activity, they actually function as an intermediary or conduit. The fundamental question that needs to be asked is:

- *Does the research examine the entire public relations process?*
  - o This process needs to include an examination of the program's communication objectives and media placement, as well as the impact of these placements on the target audience.

Developing Better Communication Programs

The goal of a measurement and evaluation program is not to determine the success or failure of a public relations program. The goal is to improve the overall performance of these efforts. There are two best practices in this instance that need to be applied:

- *Is a diagnostic element built into the research that provides insight and direction to improve program performance?*
  - o Research needs to do more than measure communication performance. It also needs to provide insight into the communication objectives and the target audiences in what we have labeled an "end-to-end" process. Consequently, the research needs to offer direction for public relations programs and their content and to also identify corrective strategies so the programs achieve their goals. Measurement in this instance is not an end in itself. Rather, it is a diagnostic, feedback-oriented tool.
- *Is research conducted early in the program to take advantage of the information?*
  - o Ideally measurement and evaluation should take place at the onset of a communication program so that the findings can be incorporated into the program planning and strategy. The benefit of this research is lost if the only research conducted takes place at the end of the effort.

Demonstrating Impact on Business Outcomes

While a more effective communication program is a central reason to conduct research, the real goal is to have a demonstrable impact on business objectives. The key questions that need to be asked about the research design, therefore, need to concentrate on evaluating communication performance—outcomes—as well as mediating variables such as reputation and relationships (and trust and transparency [Rawlins 2007]) to business outcomes. Establishing appropriate benchmarks and building in key performance indicators are increasingly a valued part of research activity which further cements communication into organizational improvements.

- *Did the product sell (outcome); were attitudes changed (outtake); did reputations improve as a direct result of the public relations program (outcome)?* (Stacks and Bowen 2013)
  - o Each of these is a specific business outcome that has an impact on the operations or an organization. It is essential to determine if it is the program that affected these changes or was it other actions.
- *How did the public relations effort contribute to overall success?*
  - o If the public relations program contributed to these changes and shifts, then it is equally important to determine which elements of the program had the greatest impacts (correspondence between outputs and outcomes).

In Chapter 1 we introduced the concept of best practices (Michaelson and Macleod 2007) as Figure 11.1 demonstrates—and by now it should be readily apparent—there is a strong interrelationship between the organization setting communication objectives, messages sent by the organization, how those messages are received, and how the outtakes from those messages impact on the objectives goals set by the organization.

Cost Effectiveness

There are a number of formulas that provide guidelines for the proportion of a public relations budget that should be devoted to measurement and

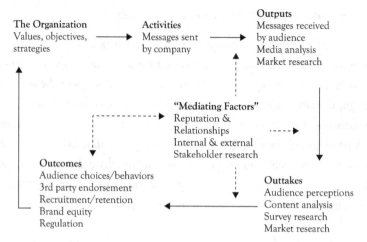

Figure 11.1 Best practices

evaluation systems (see Pritchard and Smith 2015). The issue, however, is not about how much should be spent, but if the inclusion of research in the program increased effectiveness, that it has a value that is greater than the cost of the actual research.

- *Did the research enhance the effectiveness of the public relations efforts?*
  - This is the first question that needs to be answered. If the program did not improve as a result of the research or if the direction to improve future programs was not gathered, then the research needs to reevaluated and redesigned to ensure these goals are met.
- *Was the return on investment for conducting the research program greater than the actual cost of the research itself?*
  - However, even if the research is effective in improving program performance, the cost of the research still needs to be considered. Research that costs $10,000 but only offers incremental performance of $1,000 is a poor investment. This does not mean that research should not be conducted in this situation. Instead, the research design and the research objectives need to be reevaluated.

Applicable to a Broad Range of Activities

While the direct intent of public relations measurement and evaluation is to improve communication performance, it is also essential to note that public relations does not operate in a vacuum. It is typically integrated with other aspects of an organization and these needs to be taken into consideration so that the benefits of the research can be used as widely as possible.

- *Is the information gathered applicable to other areas?*
  - These areas can include new product development, corporate reputation, other marketing communication methods as well as promotional use.

Benefits of Best Practices in Public Relations Research

The benefits of best practices go beyond merely "doing it right." Following these practices offers specific business advantages. These advantages stem from generating highly reliable results that go beyond merely providing information. They are results that are actionable, improve decision making based on the availability of highly reliable data, and yield a potential database that allows a comparison of findings from case to case that can also be applied to parallel communication programs. Just as important is the increase in overall quality that will lead to consistency in the application of research and the findings from that research.

Implementing Best Practices

The primary best practice that needs to be followed is the inclusion of research, measurement, and evaluation as a *core part* of a public relations program. Ideally, an individual in each organization should be charged with managing this process—to know the best practices and to assure that these best practices are followed. While there is no standard approach for how public relations research should be conducted, following best practices yield reliable and usable results. By following these basic guidelines, research will provide the requisite insights for improved planning, effectiveness, and demonstration of the importance and value of strategically linked communications to organizational success.

Evaluating and Interpreting

Once the research has been completed it is important that the final presentation of results and interpretations be made. Typically, this is done in two forms. First, a written report that begins with an executive summary of the findings and followed with an in-depth discussion of what was found, how reliable and valid those findings were, and tables and graphics that visualize those findings for the client. Second, an oral presentation to senior client leadership is presented that takes the written report down to its essence and is used as a baseline itself to foster questions and answers. If you have followed the standards and best practices reported in this volume, you should have no problem with evaluating the research, its methodology, and its results. With the appropriate other business function data (i.e., marketing, human resources, information technology, and so forth), you can establish relationships between campaign outtakes and outcomes as they relate to business-driven results during that same timeframe. Looking at the final outcome(s) and correlating them to other function outcomes provides a measure of the return on investment (ROI) that the public relations campaign has for that investment.

APPENDIX A

Standardized Measures for Public Relations Impact

Table A1 Recall measures

Data collection method	Prototype question	Response categories
Interviewer administered* (unaided)	Thinking back to what you have just *(read/observed/reviewed/saw)*, tell me the *(brands/products/services/issues/topics)* that you remember *(reading/observing/reviewing/seeing)*.	Open-ended responses with prelist of likely responses and an open response field.
Self-administered** (unaided)	Thinking back to what you have just *(read/observed/reviewed/saw)*, place an X in the boxes for the *(brands/products/services/issues/topics)* that you remember *(reading/observing/reviewing/seeing)*.	Open response field.
Interviewer administered (aided)	Thinking back to what you have just *(read/observed/reviewed/saw)*, tell me if you remember *(reading/observing/reviewing/seeing)* about any of the following *(brands/products/services/issues/topics)*.	List of brands, products, services, issues, or topics that are or could have been included in the communication. These are typically presented in a random order.
Self-administered (aided)	Thinking back to what you have just *(read/observed/reviewed/saw)*, place an X in the boxes if you remember *(reading/observing/reviewing/seeing)* about any of the following *(brands/products/services/issues/topics)*.	List of brands, products, services, issues, or topics that are or could have been included in the communication. These are typically presented in a random order.

Source: Michaelson and Stacks (2011). Used with permission.

*Interviewer administered studies include telephone surveys, in person surveys and intercept studies where a trained research asks questions of a respondent and records their responses.

**Self-administered studies include online studies and any other type of study where the respondent records their own answers to questions. The recording medium can include paper questionnaires as well as computer-based recording.

Table A2 Knowledge measures

Data collection method	Prototype question	Response categories
Interviewer administered	Next, I am going to read you a series of statements about a (brand/product/ issue/service/topic). That (brand/ product/service/issue/topic) is a (insert category) called (insert name). After I read you each statement, please indicate if you "strongly agree," "somewhat agree," "neither agree nor disagree," "somewhat disagree," or "strongly disagree," with each statement about (insert name).	List of attributes that describe the brand, product, services, issues, or topics that are or should have been included in the communication. These attributes are typically read to respondents in a random sequence.
Self-administered	Next, you are going to read a series of statements about a (brand/product/ service/issue/topic). That (brand/ product/service/issue/topic) is a (insert category) called (insert name). After you read each statement, please indicate if you "strongly agree," "somewhat agree," "neither agree nor disagree," "somewhat disagree," or "strongly disagree," with each statement about (insert name).	List of attributes that describe the brand, product, service, issues, or topics that are or should have been included in the communication. These attributes are typically presented to respondents in a random sequence if an online survey method is used. Answer categories are shown with each statement.
Interviewer or self-administered	Based on everything you have read, how believable is the information you just saw about the (brand/ product/service/issue/topic)? By believable we mean that you are confident that what you are (seeing/ reading/hearing/observing) is truthful and credible.	The response categories for this question are typically a scale that measures an overall level of credibility or believability. One of the most common and reliable scales consists of five points ranging from "very believable" to "very unbelievable" with a neutral midpoint.*

Source: Michaelson and Stacks (2011). Used with permission.

*This type of scale is often referred to as a Likert scale. The scale was developed by Rensis Likert at the University of Michigan Institute for Social Research. The scale is noted for its high degree of reliability in survey research.

Table A3 Measures of interest

Data collection method	Prototype question	Response categories
Interviewer or self-administered	After *(seeing/reading/hearing/observing)* this material would you say you are "very interested," "somewhat interested," "neither interested nor uninterested," "somewhat uninterested," or "very uninterested" in this *(brand/product/service/issue/topic)*?	The response categories for this question are typically a scale that measures an overall level of interest. One of the most common and reliable scales consists of five points ranging from "very interested" to "very uninterested" with a neutral mid-point. The scale is similar to that used in the credibility or believability measure described in Table A1.
	This product is a value for its price. The product has been presented honestly. Based on what I know of it, this product is very good. This product is something that is like me. Based on what I know of it; this product is an excellent choice for me. Based on what I know of it, I find this product quite pleasant to use. This product is used by people in my economic class. I think the product is very consumer unfriendly. People who buy this product are very much like me. I think this product is very reliable. This product reflects my social background. I would purchase this product because it reflects my lifestyle. This product is awful. People who use this product are culturally similar to me.	The response categories for these questions would range from "strongly agree" to "strongly disagree."

Source: Michaelson and Stacks (2011). Used with permission.

Table A4 Measures of relationship

Data collection method	Prototype question	Response categories
Interviewer administered	I am going to read you a series of statements about the (*brand/product/ service/issue/topic*). There are no right or wrong answers, we are interested in how much you agree or disagree with the statements. Do you strongly agree, somewhat agree, neither agree nor disagree, somewhat disagree, or strongly disagree? Place an X in the box that best represents your answer for each statement.	The response categories for this question are typically a scale that measures an overall level of agreement. One of the most common and reliable scales consists of five points ranging from "strongly agree" to "strongly disagree" with a neutral midpoint. The scale is similar to that used in the interest measure previously described.
Self-administered	Please respond to the following statements about the (*brand/product/ service/issue/topic*). There are no right or wrong answers, we are interested in how much you agree or disagree with the statements. Place an X in the box that best represents your answer for each statement.	The response categories for this question are typically a scale that measures an overall level of agreement. One of the most common and reliable scales consists of five points ranging from "strongly agree" to "strongly disagree" with a neutral midpoint. The scale is similar to that used in the interest measure previously described.

Source: Michaelson and Stacks (2011). Used with permission.

Table A5 Measures of preference and specified action

Data collection method	Prototype question	Response categories
Interviewer administered	I am going to read you a list of different (brands, products, services) that you can buy at your local store follows. Which *one* of these (brands, products, services) do you prefer most?	List of brands, products, services, issues, or topics that are or could have been included in the communication. These are typically presented in a random order.
Self-administered	A list of different (brands, products, services) that you can buy at your local store follows. Which *one* of these (brands, products, services) do you prefer most? Place an X in the box that best represents your answer.	List of brands, products, services, issues, or topics that are or could have been included in the communication. These are typically presented in a random order.
Interviewer or self-administered	Based on everything you have *(seen/read/heard/observed)* about this *(brand, product, service, issue, topic)*, how likely are to *(purchase/try/support)* this *(brand, product, service, issue, topic)*. Would you say you are "very likely," "somewhat likely," "neither likely nor unlikely," "somewhat unlikely," or "very unlikely" to *(purchase/try/support)* this *(brand/product/service/issue/topic)?*	The response categories for this question are typically a scale that measures an overall level of intent to take a specific action. One of the most common and reliable scales consists of five points ranging from "very likely" to "very unlikely" with a neutral midpoint. The scale is similar to that used in the credibility or believability measure described in Table A1.

Source: Michaelson and Stacks (2011). Used with permission.

Table A6 Measures of advocacy

Data collection method	Prototype question	Response categories
Interviewer administered	I am going to read you a series of statements about the *(brand/product/service/issue/topic)*. There are no right or wrong answers, we are interested in how much you agree or disagree with the statements. Do you strongly agree, somewhat agree, neither agree nor disagree, somewhat disagree, or strongly disagree? Place an X in the box that best represents your answer for each statement.	The response categories for this question are typically a scale that measures an overall level of agreement. One of the most common and reliable scales consists of five points ranging from "strongly agree" to "strongly disagree" with a neutral midpoint. The scale is similar to that used in the interest measure previously described.
Self-administered	Please respond to the following statements about the *(brand/product/service/issue/topic)*. There are no right or wrong answers, we are interested in how much you agree or disagree with the statements. Place an X in the box that best represents your answer for each statement.	The response categories for this question are typically a scale that measures an overall level of agreement. One of the most common and reliable scales consists of five points ranging from "strongly agree" to "strongly disagree" with a neutral midpoint. The scale is similar to that used in the interest measure previously described.
	I will recommend this (brand, product, service, issue, topic) to my friends and relatives. People like me can benefit from this (brand, product, service, issue, topic). I like to tell people about (brands, products, services, issues, topics) that work well for me. Word-of-mouth is the best way to learn about (brands, product, services, issues, topics). User reviews on websites are valuable sources of information about (brands, products, services, issues, topics).	The response categories for these questions would range from "strongly agree" to "strongly disagree."

Source: Michaelson and Stacks (2011). Used with permission.

APPENDIX B[*]

Dictionary of Public Relations Measurement and Research

This booklet was prepared and edited by
Dr. Don W. Stacks and
Dr. Shannon A. Bowen

_____

[*] Available in Arabic, Chinese (simple and traditional), English, Italian, Portuguese, Russian, and Spanish at: http://www.instituteforpr.org/dictionary-public-relations-measurement-research-third-edition/

Commission on Public Relations Measurement and Evaluation Dictionary Editorial Board

Dictionary of Public Relations Measurement and Research[1]

@ Replies—*sm/s/*engagement. A key performance indicator (KPI) metric that provides evidence of Twitter activity; see also: Twitter, Retweets

-A-

Active Advocates—*m/s/outtake/outcome.* People or groups who are actively advocating, supporting or promoting for the object of the research; see also: Advocacy, Objective

Advertising Value Equivalents (AVE)—*s.* A discredited output score that suggests an equivalent cost of buying space devoted to editorial content; also referred to as Equivalent Advertising Value (EAV); see also: Opportunity to See

Activity—*m.* Content creation such as blogs, videos, tweets, press releases, speeches, and so on

Advertorial—*m.* Space in a publication bought to advertise an organization's position on an issue

Advocacy—*m/engagement.* The advocating or supporting of an object that is a planned outcome of a campaign; change or engagement driven by an agenda

Affective Attitude—outtake/*outcome.* An attitude dimension that reflects changes in interest, desire, and commitment levels

Aided Awareness—*m/outtake.* Measurement of how much people are aware of an object by providing hints, examples, or descriptions; see also: Awareness, Unaided Awareness

---

[1] *Terms* are identified as either statistical (s) or methodological (m). In addition terms associated with the social media are identified as (sm) and identifiers include output, outtake, outcome, and ethics. Common usage is used when determining whether the term is listed as either statistical or methodological when terms have dual meanings (e.g., regression).

Algorithm—*s*. A step-by-step problem-solving procedure, especially an established, recursive computational procedure, for solving a problem in a finite number of steps

Alpha Level (α)—*s*. The amount of error or chance allowed in sampling or inferential testing

Analysis of Variance (ANOVA)—*s*. An inferential statistical test of significance for continuous measurement of dependent variables against a number of groups as independent variables

Analytics—*m*. The evaluation of data by some planned method, usually quantitative in nature

Articles—*m/output*. Typically printed stories or news items, but also found on the Internet; see also: Items

Attitude—*m/outtake/outcome*. A predisposition to act or behave toward some object; a motivating factor in public relations; composed of three dimensions: affective (emotional evaluation), cognitive (knowledge evaluation), and connotative (behavioral evaluation)

Attitude Change—*m/outtake/outcome*. The change or shift in direction of a target audience during and after a campaign; see also: Advocacy, Opinion

Attitude Research—*m/outtake/outcome*. The measuring and interpreting of a full range of views, values, feelings, opinions, and beliefs that segments of a public may hold toward a client, issue, or product

Attitude Scale—*m/outtake/outcome*. A measure that targets respondent attitudes or beliefs toward some object; typically interval-level data and requires that an arbitrary or absolute midpoint ("neutral" or "neither agree nor disagree") be provided to the respondent; also known as Likert-type or Semantic Differential measures; *s*. an output measured as an interval or ratio measure

Audience—*m*. A specified group from within a defined public with whom the organization wishes to communicate, build relationships, or influence

Authenticity—*m*/ethics. Being genuine; having the individual or organization act or behave internally as it appears to stakeholders and external publics

Automated Monitoring and Analysis System—*m*. Computer programmed systems that monitor the traditional and social media and analyze specific metrics for a client

Autonomy—*m*/ethics. The ability to act independently through the use of one's objective rationality

Average Basis—*sm/s/outtake*. A metric that averages unique visitors to a social media site or platform

Awareness—*m/outtake/outcome*. A metric that provides indication of the how much people have heard of a brand, client, issue, and so on; awareness may be with unaided (top-of-mind) or aided; see also Aided Awareness, Unaided Awareness

-B-

B.A.S.I.C.—*m/outtake*. A research planning model that focuses on where in the communication lifespan a particular object is: Build awareness, Advance knowledge, Sustain relevance, Initiate action, Create advocacy

Balance—*m/ethics*. An ethical value indicating objectivity or fairness

Banner—*sm/output*. A graphic used in social media platforms much like an ad to position a client, individual, issue, and so on

Bar Graph—*s*. A representation of a frequency distribution by means of rectangles (or other indicators) whose widths represent class intervals and whose heights represent corresponding frequencies; see also: Graph

Baseline—*s*. An initial measurement against which all subsequent measures are compared; *m*. a data point established for comparison at the developmental stage of a research campaign

Behavior Change—*m/outtake/outcome*. An alteration in an audience's or individual's behavior; this change is typically the objective of a communication or public relations campaign; see also: Outtake, Outcome

Behavioral Event Interview (BEI)—*m*. An interview technique used to solicit evidence or examples of a specific competency or skill you possess; BEI is based on the premise that a person's past behavior is the best predictor of their future performance

Behavioral Objective—*m*. An objective that specifies the expected public relations campaign or program outcome in terms of specific behaviors; *s*. a measure that is actionable in that it is the behavior requested (e.g., outcome) of a target audience; see also: Outcome

Belief—*m*. A long-held evaluation of some object, usually determined on a basis its occurrence; clusters of beliefs yield attitudes

Benefit-Cost Ratio (BCR)—*outcome*. Expected Benefits (or financial returns) over Expected Costs (a BCR of 2:1 means that for every one dollar invested, the financial benefit or return will be two dollar); similar metric to ROI but BCR used to predict benefits or returns while ROI measures actual benefits or returns; BCR used in evaluating decisions about a proposal or to choose between several alternative ones by comparing the total expected costs of each option against the total expected benefit

Benchmarking (Benchmark Study)—*m*. A measurement technique that involves having an organization learn something about its own practices, the practices of selected others, and then compares these practices; sometimes referred to as a baseline against which results are compared

Benchmark—*m/s/outtake*. A planned KPI testing whether a campaign is on target and phase against baseline expectations; see also: Refinement Stage

Best Practices—*m*. The technique, method, or process that is more effective than any other

Big Data—*m*. Large and complex datasets from a wide range of sources including structured and unstructured data; analyses require the use of advanced computing systems or resources

Bivariate Analysis—*s*. A statistical examination of the relationship between two variables

Blogger—*sm/output*. An individual or organization that owns and is responsible for providing content for a blog; see also: Blog

Blog—*sm/output*. Online journals maintained by an individual or business with regular entries; short for weblog; see also: Blogger

Bookmark—*sm/s/outtake/engagement*. The tagging of web pages, social media links or posts; a metric of influencers or third-party endorsers

Bots—*sm/outtake*. Internet web robots that run automated tasks; see also: Chatterbot

BRAD—*s*. British Rate And Data measure; provides circulation and advertising costs data

-C-

Campaign (Program)—*m*. The planning, execution, and evaluation of a public relations plan of action aimed at solving a problem or taking advantage of an opportunity

Case Study Methodology—*m*. An informal research methodology that gathers data on a specific individual or company or product with the analysis focused on understanding its unique qualities; is not generalizable to other cases or populations; see also: Informal Methodology, Qualitative Research

Categorical Data—*s*. Measurement data that are defined by their association with groups and are expressed in terms of frequencies, percentages, and proportions; see also: Nominal Data, Ordinal Data

Category—*m*. In content analysis the part of the system where the content (units of analysis) are placed; also referred to as "subjects" or "buckets"

Causal Relationship—*m*. A relationship between variables in which a change in one variable forces, produces, or brings about a change in another variable; s. the result of a significant interaction term in an analysis of variance or regression, often displayed in path analyses or sequential equation models

Census—*m*. Collection of data from every person or object in a population

Central Tendency—*s*. A statistic that describes the typical or average case in the distribution of a variable; see also: Mean, Median, Mode, Range, Standard Deviation, Standardized Score, Variance, Z-Score

Characters—*m*. A manifest unit of analysis used in content analysis consisting of individuals or roles (e.g., occupations, roles, race); see also Keystrokes

Chat Sessions—*sm/outtake*. Synchronous Internet discussions where individuals communicate with others; see also: Bot

Chatterbot—*m/sm/output*. A program designed to create conversation designed to increase interaction and relationships on the Internet

Chi-Square (χ^2)—*s*. An inferential statistical test of significance for categorical data (nominal or ordinal)

Churn Rate—*m/sm/s/outtake*. A metric that calculates the attrition rate of stakeholders who no longer subscribe or participate or have cut ties with an organization or social media platform

Circulation—*s*. Number of copies of a publication as distributed (as opposed to read)

Clicks—*sm/s*. The process whereby a visitor to a social media platform selects and enters that platform; a metric measuring visits to a platform; see also: Clickthroughs

Clickthroughs—*sm/s/outtake*. Social media KPI metric of how many visitors to a web page go beyond the initial web page and into site content

Closed-Ended Question—*m*. A question that requires participants to answer selected and predetermined responses (e.g., strongly agree, agree, neither agree nor disagree, disagree, strongly disagree)

Cloud Computing—*m/sm*. The use of files and resources available through remote locations. Data and processes are accessed online and does not reside on local computers

Cloud—*m/sm*. An Internet location for files that allow researchers to share data, analyses, and evaluations; see also: Cloud Computing

Cluster Analysis—*s*. An exploratory data analysis tool which aims at sorting different objects into groups in a way that the degree of association between two objects is maximal if they belong to the same group and minimal if otherwise

Clustered Sample—*m*. A type of probability sample that involves first breaking the population into heterogeneous subsets (or clusters), and then selecting the potential sample at random from the individual clusters

Cognitive Attitude—*outcome*. An attitude dimension that reflects changes in awareness, knowledge, and understanding toward some object

Coefficient Alpha (α)—*s*. A statistical test for a measurement's reliability for interval and ratio data; also known as Cronbach's coefficient alpha

Cohen's Kappa—*s*. An intercoder reliability measure used in content analysis when there are more than two coders; see also: Reliability, Content Analysis

Cohort Survey—*m*. A type of longitudinal survey in which some specific group is studied over time according to some criteria that stay the same (e.g., age = 21) while the samples may differ

Column Inches—*s/outtake*. Measurement of a print article's column physical space, often used in content analyses

Comment—*sm/outtake/output*. Social media generated responses to Tweets, blogs, or Facebook or YouTube messages or news sites or various other forums

Communication—*m*. The process that deals with the transmission and reception of intentional messages that are a part of a natural language system (e.g., words, phrases, sentences, paragraphs)

Communication Life Cycle—*m*. A planning model that focuses on where in the cycle of awareness through advocacy an object may be; see also: B.A.S.I.C.

Communication Product (Product)—*m/output*. The end result of the communication product process resulting in the production and dissemination of a brochure, media release, video news release, website, speech, and so forth; see also: Output, Outtake

Communication(s) Audit—*m*. A systematic review and analysis of how effectively an organization communicates with all of its major internal and external audiences by identifying these audiences, by identifying the communication programs and their communication products utilized for each audience, by determining the effectiveness of these programs and their products, and by identifying gaps in the overall existing communication program; uses accepted research techniques and methodologies; see also: Formal Methodology, Informal Methodology, Case Study, Content Analysis, Survey, In-Depth Interview, Focus Group, Experiment, Secondary, Historical, Participant-Observation

Communication(s) Research—*m*. Any systematic study of the relationships and patterns that are developed when people seek to share information with each other

Community Case Study—*m*. A methodology whereby the researcher takes an in-depth look at one or several communities—subsections of communities—in which an organization has an interest by impartial, trained researchers using a mix of informal research methodologies (i.e., participant-observation, role-playing, secondary analysis, content analysis, interviewing, focus groups)

Computer Generated Sentiment—*m/outtake/output*. An analysis done by computer that measures sentiment toward an object; see also: Sentiment

Concurrent Validity—*m*. A measurement device's ability to vary directly with a measure of the same construct or indirectly with a measure of an opposite construct; it allows you to show that your test is valid by comparing it with an already valid test

Confidence Interval—*s*. In survey methodology based on a random sampling technique; the range of values or measurement within which a population parameter is estimated to fall (e.g., for a large population we might expect answers to a question to be within ±3 percent of the true population answer; if 55 percent responded positively, the confidence interval would be from 52 to 58 percent); sometimes called measurement error

Confidence Level—*m*. In survey methodology based on a random sampling technique, the amount of confidence we can place on our confidence interval (typically set at 95 percent, or 95 out of 100 cases truly representing the population under study, with no more than 5 cases out of 100 misrepresenting that population); sometimes called sampling error; *s.* the amount of confidence a researcher has that a finding between groups or categories is statistically significant; see also: Statistical Significance

Connotative Attitude—*outcome.* An attitude dimension that reflects intended behavior

Consistency—*m/ethics.* Using a rigorous and codified ethical decision-making paradigm to lessen capricious actions; allows an organization to be known and trusted by publics

Construct Validity—*m.* A dimension of measurement; *s.* a statistically tested form of measurement validity that seeks to establish the dimensionality of a measure; see also: Validity, Face Validity, Criterion-Related Validity, Content Validity, Discriminant Validity, Divergent Validity

Content Analysis—*m.* An informal research methodology (and measurement tool) that systematically tracks messages (written, spoken, broadcast) and translates them into quantifiable form via a systematic approach to defining message categories through specified units of analysis; the action of breaking down message content into predetermined components (categories) to form a judgment capable of being measured

Content Validity—*m.* A form of measurement validity that is based on other researchers or experts evaluations of the measurement items contained in a measure; see also: Validity, Fact Validity, Construct Validity, Criterion-Related Validity, Discriminant Validity, Divergent Validity

Contingency Question—*m.* A survey question that is to be asked only to some respondents, determined by their responses to some other questions; sometimes called a *funnel question*

Contingency Table—*s.* A statistical table for displaying the relationship between variables in terms of frequencies and percentages; sometimes called a *cross tabulation table* or *cross tab*

Continuous Data—*s.* Data that are measured on a continuum, usually as interval or ratio data; see also Interval Data, Ratio Data

Contour Plot—*s*. A graphical technique for representing a three-dimensional surface by plotting constant z slices, called contours, on a two-dimensional format; for example, given a value for z, lines are drawn for connecting the (x, y) coordinates where that z value occurs; the contour plot is used to answer the question "how does Z change as a function of X and Y?"

Convenience Sample—*m*. A nonprobability sample where the respondents or objects are chosen because of availability (e.g., "man on the street"); a type of nonprobability sample in which who ever happens to be available at a given point in time is included in the sample; sometimes called a *haphazard* or *accidental* sample

Convergent Validity—*s*. A type of construct validity that refers to the principle that the indicators for a given construct should be at least moderately correlated among themselves; see also: Coefficient Alpha, Validity, Face Validity, Content Validity, Construct-Related Validity, Criterion-Related Validity, Discriminant Validity, Divergent Validity

Conversation—*sm/s/engagement*. A relationship whereby people interactively respond to others through blogs, tweets, or comments; see also: Owned Media, Earned Media

Conversation Index—*sm/s/engagement*. A social media metric that measures number of visitor comments and posts

Conversation Rate—*sm/s/engagement*. A social media metric that measures the feedback received as compared to postings

Conversion—*sm/s/outtake*. Desired social media activity you want stakeholders to engage in, such as clickthroughs, visit, comments, or "likes" of your page

Correlation (*r*)—*s*. A statistical test that examines the relationships between variables (may be either categorical or continuous); measures the degrees to which variables are interrelated; see also: Correlation Coefficient, Pearson Product Moment Coefficient, Spearman-rho, *r*

Correlation Coefficient—*s*. A measure of association that describes the direction and strength of a linear relationship between two variables;

usually measured at the interval or ratio data level (e.g., Pearson Product Moment Coefficient, *r*), but can be measured at the nominal or ordinal level (e.g., Spearman-rho)

Cost Per Mille (CPM)—*s/outtake*. The cost of advertising for each 1,000 homes reached by the media; a measure of efficiency

Cost-Benefit Analysis (CBA)—*outcome*. A variation of Benefit Cost Ratio; initially developed for the evaluation of public policy issues specifically; see also: Benefit Cost Ratio

Cost-Effectiveness—*s/outcome*. An evaluation outcome that may be measured in public relations research which evaluates the relation between overall expenditure (costs) and results produced, usually the ratio of changes in costs to change in effects; used to compare the costs of different media distribution channels against their degree of effectiveness in terms of reach, message accuracy, timeliness, and so on; used to compare different campaign effectiveness outcomes against their costs; a measure of efficiency

Covariance—*s*. A statistic that measures the degree that variables influence each other

Covariation—*s*. A criterion for causation whereby the dependent variable takes on different values depending on the independent variable

Criterion Variable—*m*. The variable the research wants to predict to; see also: Dependent Variable

Criterion-Related Validity—*m*. a form of validity that compares one measure against others known to have specified relationships with what is being measured; the highest form of measurement validity; see also: Validity, Face Validity, Content Validity, Content Validity, Discriminant Validity, Divergent Validity

Crossbreak Analysis—*s*. A categorical analysis that compares the frequency of responses in individual cells from one variable against another; see also: Contingency Table, Crosstabulation, Frequency, Frequency Table

Cross-Sectional Survey—*m*. A survey based on observations representing a single point in time; see also: Snapshot Survey

Crosstabs—*s*. Statistical tables used to array the data; allows the analyst to go beyond total data into frequencies and averages as well as to make possible overall as well as subgroup analyses (e.g., comparisons of the opinions expressed by sell-side analysts with those stated by buy-side investment professionals); see also: Contingency Table

Crosstabulation—*s*. The result of a comparison between two categorical variables in a table; see also: Crossbreak Analysis, Frequency, Frequency Table

Cumulative Scale (Guttman Scale or Scalogram)—*m*. A measurement scale that assumes that when you agree with a scale item you will also agree with items that are less extreme; see also: Outcome, Guttman Scalogram, Likert Scale, Semantic Differential Scale

Cyber Image Analysis—*m*. The measurement of Internet content via chat rooms or discussion groups in cyberspace regarding a client or product or topic; the measurement of a client's image everywhere on the Internet

-D-

Dashboard—*m/s/outtake*. A concise visual presentation of data intended for management decision making, using graphs and tables that are kept up-to-date on a regular basis; the elements of the data display can show measures of activities, outputs, engagement, outtakes, outcomes, and business result

Data—*m*. The observations or measurements taken when evaluating a public relations campaign or program; *s*. the frequencies, means, percentages used to assess a campaign or program; see also: Nominal Data, Ordinal Data, Interval Data, Ratio Data

Database—*s*. A collection of data arranged for ease and speed of search and retrieval

Database Mining—*m*. A research technique utilizing existing data; see also: Secondary Methodology, Big Data

Data-Mining—*s/outtake/outcome*. Analysis of extant data to find commonality or relationships in the data; can be done in any stage (developmental, refinement, evaluation) of a campaign; see also: Big Data

Deduction—*m*. A philosophical logic in which specific expectations or hypotheses are developed or derived on the basis of general principles

Delphi Technique—*m*. A research methodology (usually survey or interview) where the researcher tries to forecast the future based on successive waves of interviews or surveys with a panel of experts in a given field as a means of building a "consensus" of expert opinion and thought relating to particular topics or issues

Demographic Analysis—*m*. Analysis of a population in terms of special social, political, economic, and geographic subgroups (e.g., age, sex, income-level, race, educational-level, place of residence, occupation)

Demographic Data—*m*. Data that differentiate between groups of people or things (e.g., sex, race, income)

Deontology—*m*/*ethics*. A principle or duty-based, nonconsequentialist approach to ethics based on the three categorical imperatives of moral duty, dignity and respect, and good intention

Dependent Variable—*m*/*outtake*/*outcome*. The variable that is measured or collected and evaluated

Depth Interview—*m*. An extensive, probing, open-ended, largely unstructured interview, usually conducted in person or by telephone, in which respondents are encouraged to talk freely and in great detail about given subjects; also known as an *in-depth interview*; see also: In-Depth Methodology

Descriptive Research—*m*. A form of research that gathers information in such a way as to paint a picture of what people think or do

Descriptive Statistics—*s*. The reduction and simplification of the numbers representing research, to ease interpreting the results

Descriptive Survey—*m*. A type of survey that collects in quantitative form basic opinions or facts about a specified population or sample; also known as a *public opinion poll*

Design Bias—*m*. research design bias is introduced when the study fails to identify the validity problems or when publicity about the research fails to incorporate the researcher's cautions

Developmental Phase—*m*. The precampaign phase where strategies are explored and secondary or historical data are examined; the phase where benchmarks are set and baseline data are set

Diggs—*sm/s/*engagement. A bookmarking site often used to indicate how influencers are linking to blogs or posts; see also: Bookmark

Digital Advertisements—*sm/s/output*. Advertisements employed in social media platforms often in the form of banners; see also: Banner

Dignity—*m/ethics*. A public relations ethics principle that guides interaction with publics *or* stakeholders; also a tenet of ethical research with human subjects

Disclosure—*m/ethics*. An obligation to inform publics and stakeholders truthfully, quickly, and accurately of information affecting them; also, a public relations ethical research principle

Discretion—*m/ethics*. An obligation to engage in an objective and thoughtful ethical analysis before acting

Discriminant Validity—*s*. A type of validity that is determined by hypothesizing and examining differential relations between a test and measures of similar or different constructs; it is the opposite of convergent validity and is also known as divergent validity; see also: Convergent Validity, Divergent Validity; *m*. a way of establishing if a measure is measuring what it is supposed to measure; see also: Validity, Criterion-Related Validity

Distributed File Systems—*m*. A client-server model that allows the storage and retrieval of files stored on a server with an appropriate indexing mechanism that are served to multiple clients requesting them

Divergent Validity—*s*. A type of validity that demonstrates variables does not correlate with each other; see also: Discriminant Validity

Double-Barreled Question—*m*. A question that attempts to measure two things in one question; a source of measurement error

Duty—*m/ethics*. By obligation of rationality, one's responsibility to uphold moral law and engage in ethical analyses

-E-

Earned Media—*m/output*. Publicity or coverage gained through the newsworthiness or topicality of information or editorial influence; social earned media refers to publicity or coverage gained the Internet

Editorial—*m*. The content of a publication written by a journalist, columnist, or guest writer, as distinct from advertising content which is determined by an advertiser; an article expressing the editorial policy of a publication of a matter of interest (also known as a "leader" or "leading article"); space in a publication bought by an advertiser that includes journalistic copy intended to make the reader think it originates from an independent source (also known as an "advertorial"); *s.* an outcome or measured variable

E-Mail Campaigns—*m*. A social media campaign that employs e-mails as a direct marketing tool; a grassroots campaign targeting specific audiences

E-Mails Sent—*sm/output*. A metric that counts the number of e-mails actually sent out

E-mail Survey—*m*. A survey technique whereby a link (URL) to a programmed questionnaire is sent to a respondent via e-mail, the respondent self-administers the questionnaire, and the survey program system accumulates the responses

Endorsement—*m/s/outtake/engagement*. The advocating of a plan of action or campaign of influence by influencers; the advocating for another entity, be it individual, product or body, with a view to influence others

Engagement—*m/s/outtake/engagement/outcome*. Any action or response from a target audience resulting from proactive communications that creates a psychological motivation or bond, an emotional involvement, and empowerment to engage through participation

Environmental Scanning—*m*. A research technique for tracking new developments in any area or field by carrying out a systematic review of what appears in professional, trade, or government publications

Equal Appearing Interval Scale—*m*. A measurement scale with predefined values associated with each statement

Equivalent Advertising Value (EAV)—*s*. A discredited output score that suggests an equivalent cost of buying space devoted to editorial content; also referred to as Advertising Equivalency Value or Advertising Value Equivalents (AVEs); see also: Opportunity to See

Error Bar—*s*. A graphical data analysis technique for showing the error in the dependent variable and optionally, the independent variable in a standard *x-y* plot

Ethics—*m*. The approach to acting with rectitude, reflection, and responsibility in the public relations context; also, treating research participants, data gathered, and sponsor/client results with rectitude and deliberation; see also: Deontology, Utilitarianism

ETL—*m*. Abbreviation for extract, transform, load; three functions that need to be performed to move data from one database to another one; see also: Extraction, Transformation, and Loading (writing to the destination database)

Ethnographic Research—*m*. A qualitative research method that relies on the tools and techniques of cultural anthropologists and sociologists to obtain a better understanding of how individuals and groups function in their natural settings; see also: Participant-Observation

Evaluation Research—*m/outtake/output*. A form of research that determines the relative effectiveness of a public relations campaign or program by measuring program outcomes including cognitive changes (to levels of awareness, knowledge and/or understanding), affective changes (to attitudes and opinions), or connotative changes (behaviors) of a targeted audience or public) against a predetermined set of objectives that initially established the level or degree of change desired

Evaluation Stage—*m*. The campaign stage whereby the outputs, outtakes, and outcomes are evaluated for impact; see also: ROI, ROE, SROI

Events—*s/output*. A community affairs or sponsorship output

Experimental Methodology—*m*. A formal quantitative research methodology that imposes strict artificial limits or boundaries on the research in order to establish some causal relationship between variables of interest; is not generalizable to a larger population

Explanatory Research—*m*. A form of research that seeks to explain why people say, think, feel, and act the way they do; concerned primarily with the development of public relations theory about relationships and processes; are typically deductive

Exploratory Research—*m*. A form of research that seeks to establish basic attitudes, opinions, and behavior patterns or facts about a specific population or sample; are typically inductive and involve extensive probing of the population or sample or data

External Research—*m*. Primary and secondary research on target stakeholder groups conducted to identify which social media or traditional tools will be used in a campaign

Extraction—*m*. The moving of data from a source database; see also: Transformation, Loading

-F-

Face Validity—*m*. A form of measurement validity that is based on the researcher's knowledge of the concept being measured; the lowest form of measurement validity; see also: Validity, Content Validity, Construct Validity, Criterion-Related Validity, Discriminant Validity, Divergent Validity

Facebook—*sm/s/engagement*. A social media outlet that provides a conversation among "friends," as well as a channel for advertisers; see also: Likes, Conversations

Facilitator—*m*. An individual who leads a focus group; also known as a moderator

Factor Analysis—*s*. A statistical tool that allows researchers to test the dimensionality of their measures, to express a number of correlated variables in terms of a smaller number of uncorrelated factors; used to assess a measure's construct validity

Fairness—*m/ethics*. Seeking to create balance or justice through discretion, objectivity, reflexiveness, and autonomy

Fever Graph—*s*. A form of line graph that expresses peaks and valleys of data along a continuum that is either continuous or whose classes represent categories; see also: Graph

Field Study Methodology—*m*. A formal research methodology that imposes fewer restrictions or limits or boundaries on the research in order to test some causal relationships found in experimental research and generalize them to a larger population

Filter Question—*m*. A question which is used to move a respondent from one question to another; a question that is used to remove a respondent from a survey or interview; also called a screener question; see also: Funnel Question, Structured Interview

Financial Metrics—*s/outcome*. Outcome measures that place some financial value on the outcome of a campaign; see also: Return on Investment, Return of Expectations

Focus Group Methodology—*m*. A qualitative research method that uses a group discussion approach to gain an in-depth understanding of issues, an organization, or product; is not generalizable to other focus groups or populations

Followers—*sm/s/engagement/outtake*. The number of people who are engaged in or observing a particular individual, event, or brand, and so on; see also: Facebook, Twitter, Tweet

Formal Methodology—*m*. A set of research methodologies that allows the researcher to generalize to a larger audience but often fails to gain in-depth understanding of the client, object, or product; a set of methodologies that follow scientific or social scientific method; a set of methodologies that are deductive in nature

Formative Evaluation—*m/outtake*. A method of evaluating the process by which programs occur while activities are in their early stages with the intent of improving or correcting activities

Frequency—*s*. A descriptive statistic that measures how often something occurs

Frequency Table—*s*. A listing of counts and percentages in tabular form; may report a single variable or multiple variables; see also: Crossbreak Analysis, Crosstabulation

F-Test—*s*. An inferential test of significance associated with Analysis of Variance (ANOVA); see also: Analysis of Variance

Full Disclosure—*m/s/ethics*. An ethical research value that provides research participants or report readers about a survey, experiment, focus group, in-depth interview with relevant background information about the study and truth about any deception that was used

Funnel Question—*m*. A question used in a questionnaire or schedule that moves an interviewer or respondent from one part of a survey to another (e.g., "Are you a registered voter?" If the respondent says yes, certain questions are asked and if not, then other questions are asked); see also: Filter Question, Structured Interview

F-Value Score—*s*. The calculated score obtained from analysis of variance that is tested against tabled values; see also: Analysis of Variance

-G-

Goal (Objective)—*m/outtake/outcome*. The explicit statement of intentions that supports a communication strategy and includes an intended audience or receiver, a proposed measurable cognitive, affective or connotative outcome (or desired level of change in that audience), and a specific timeframe for that change to occur

Good intention—*m/ethics*. Acting upon the basis of goodwill alone; having a pure moral intent to do the right thing

Grand Mean—*s*. A descriptive statistics which represents the mean of all sample means in a study, weighted by the number of items in each sample; the grand mean treats the individuals in the different subsets (groups) as if there were no subgroups, but only individual measures in the set; it is thus simply the mean of all of the scores; see also: Mean

Graph—*s*. A graphical representation of a variable; see also: Bar, Pie, Line, Fever

Gross Rating Points (GRP)—*m*. Measures of weight or readership or audience equivalent to audience exposure among 1 percent of the population; see also: Targeted Gross Rating Points (TGRP)

Guttman Scale (Cumulative Scale or Scalogram)—*m*. A measurement scale that assumes unidimensionality and that people when faced with a choice will also choose items less intense than the one chosen

-H-

Hadoop—*m*. An open-source software that is used to analyze cloud databases; see also: Cloud, Big Data, Open Source

Hashtag—*sm/s/outtake*. A Twitter tag that annotates a message for ease of retrieval by others; a number symbol; typically a hashtag is preceded by #, such as #PR; see also: Twitter, Tweet

Histogram—*s*. A representation of a frequency distribution by means of rectangles whose widths represent class intervals and whose heights represent corresponding frequencies; a bar chart representing a frequency distribution; heights of the bars represent observed frequencies; see also: Graph

Historical Methodology—*m*. An informal research methodology that examines the causes and effects of past events

Holsti's Reliability Coefficient—*s*. A fairly simple reliability measure used in content analysis; see also: Reliability, Content Analysis, Intercoder Reliability, Intracoder Reliability, Scott's Pi, Krippendorf's Alpha

Hypothesis—*m*. An expectation about the nature of things derived from theory; a prediction of how an independent variable changes a dependent variable; formally stated as a predication (e.g., males will purchase more of X than females), but tested via the null hypothesis (males and females will not differ in their purchases of X)

Hypothesis Testing—*m.* Determining whether the expectations that a hypothesis represents are, indeed, found in the real world

-I-

Image Research—*m.* A research program or campaign that systematically studies people's perceptions toward an organization, individual, product, or service; sometimes referred to as a *reputation study*

Impact—*sm/s/outtake/outcome.* A metric that analyzes how much influence an individual, group, or organization might have on stakeholders; the outcome of outputs, engagement, and influence; see also: Influencer, Output, Engagement

Impressions—*m/s/output.* A metric that indicates the number of possible exposures of a media item to a defined set of stakeholders; the number of people who might have had the opportunity to be exposed to a story that has appeared in the media; also known as *opportunity to see* (OTS); *s.* usually refers to the total audited circulation of a publication or the audience reach of a broadcast vehicle; see also: Circulation

Inbound Links—*sm/s/outtake.* A metric that indicates whether the earned media has contextual links from well-ranked sites and blogs; see also: Earned Media

Incidence—*s.* The frequency with which a condition or event occurs in a given time within a population or sample

Independent *t*-Test—*s.* An inferential statistical test of significance that compares two levels of an independent variable against a continuous measured dependent variable

Independent Variable—*m.* The variable or variables against which the dependent variable is tested

In-Depth Interview Methodology—*m.* An informal research methodology in which an individual interviews another in a one-on-one situation; see also: In-Depth Interview (IDI)

Induction—*m*. A philosophical logic in which general principles are developed from specific observations

Inferential Research—*m*. Statistical analyses that test if the results observed for a sample are indicative of the population; the presentation of information that allows us to make judgments whether the research results observed in a sample generalize to the larger population

Inferential Statistics—*s*. Statistical tests that allow a researcher to say within a certain degree of confidence whether variables or groups truly differ in their response to a public relations message; see also: Analysis of Variance, Chi-Square, Bivariate Analysis, Correlation, Pearson Product Moment Coefficient, Spearman-rho, Regression, Path Analysis, Sequential Equation Model, *t*-Test

Influence—*s/outtake*. An outcome of engagement based on proactive messaging that seeks to sway attitudes or behaviors

Influencer—*m/s/outtake*. An individual with specialized knowledge on a subject or highly recognized by an audience; an individual who has the ability to sway others' thoughts; see also: Active Advocate, Opinion, Attitude Change, Behavior Change

Informal Methodology—*m*. A research methodology that does not allow the researcher to generalize to a larger audience but gains in-depth understanding of the client, object, or product; see also: Qualitative Research

Informational Objective—*m*. An objective that establishes what information a target audience should know or the degree of change in knowledge levels after the conclusion of a public relations campaign or program

Inputs—*m/s*. The research information and data from both internal and external sources applied in the conception, approval, and design phases of the input stage of the communication production process

Inquiry Research—*m*. A formal or informal research methodology that employs systematic content analysis, survey methodology, or interviewing techniques to study the range and types of unsolicited inquiries that an organization may receive from customers, prospective customers, or other target audience groups

Instrumental Error—*m*. In measurement, error that occurs because the measuring instrument was poorly written; *s*. tested for via reliability analyses; see also: Coefficient Alpha, KR-20

Intangible Metrics—*s/outtake*s. Data that reflect social science variables that impact on a campaign; see also: Nonfinancial Metrics

Intellectual Honesty—*m/ethics*. Veracity and truth telling in public relations communication, management, and research

Intellectual Integrity—*m/ethics*. Ethical conduct in determining what is an issue, relevant facts, and the way to proceed with integrity and honesty

Intercoder Reliability—*m*. The reliability or agreement of content coding done by two or more coders; see also: Reliability, Intracoder Reliability, Holsti's Reliability Coefficient, Scott's Pi, Krippendorf's Alpha, Cohen's Kappa

Internal research—*m*. Research conducted on key internal stakeholders; see also: Developmental Phase

Interval Data—*m*. Measurement data that are defined on a continuum and assumed to have equal spacing between data points (see also: Ratio Data); *s*. includes temperature scale, standardized intelligence test scores, Likert-type scale, semantic differential scale, Guttman Scalogram; see also: Attitude Research, Attitude Scale, Data, Variable, Likert Scale, Guttman Scalogram

Interview Schedule—*m*. A guideline interviewers use to ask questions to research participants; it can consist of structured questions, semistructured, or a suggestive list of questions

Intracoder Reliability—*m*. The reliability of content analysis coding when the coding is done by only one coder, usually the researcher; *s*. obtained from statistical tests which analyze coder decisions versus chance; see also: Reliability, Intercoder Reliability, Cohen's Kappa, Holsti's Reliability Coefficient, Krippendorf's Alpha, Scott's Pi

Issues Research—*m*. A formal or informal research methodology that systematically studies public policy questions of the day, with the chief focus on those public policy matters whose definition and contending positions are still evolving

Items—*s/output*. A manifest unit of analysis used in content analysis consisting of an entire communication product or tactic (e.g., an advertisement, story, press release)

-J-

Judgmental Sample—*m*. A type of nonprobability sample in which individuals are deliberately selected for inclusion in the sample by the researcher because they have special knowledge, position, characteristics, or represent other relevant dimensions of the population that are deemed important to study; see also: Purposive Sample

Judgment—*m/ethics*. Using moral autonomy and discretion in planning, conducting, and assessing public relations activities

-K-

Key Messages—*m/output*. The essential communication ideas or concepts that underlie a campaign which should be endorsed by third-person advocates; see also: Active Advocates

Key Performance (Performance Result)—*m*. The desired end effect or impact of a program of campaign performance

Key Performance Indicator (KPI)—*m/s/outtake*. Data that provide evidence of campaign performance against key preagreed criteria, such as sales, number of inquiries, clickthroughs, comments, visitors, and so on

Keystroke—*s*. The pressing of a computer or typewriter key; a measure of efficiency

Keyword Searches—*m/sm*. Determining stakeholder interest by the key words they search with

Klout—*sm/output*. A social media platform for social media influence

Known Group *t*-Test—*s*. An inferential statistical test of significance that compares the results for a sampled group on some continuous measurement dependent variable against a known value; see also: Inferential Statistics, Independent *t*-Test

KR-20—*s*. A reliability statistic for nominal or ordinal-level measurement; also known as Kuder-Richardson Formula 20; see also: Reliability, Coefficient Alpha

Krippendorf's Alpha—*s*. A fairly simple measure of intercoder agreement for content analysis; see also: Reliability, Intercoder Reliability, Intracoder Reliability, Holsti's Reliability Coefficient, Scott's Pi, Cohen's Kappa

-L-

Lack of Bias—*m/s/ethics*. Moral autonomy using rationality to seek independence from external constraints and to objectively assess and report data

Latent Content—*m*. From content analysis, an analysis of the underlying idea, thesis, or theme of content; the deeper meanings that are intended or perceived in a message

Length of Depth of Visit—*sm/s/engagement*. The amount of time an individual spends on a particular web page

Likert Scale—*m*. An interval-level measurement scale that requires people to respond to statements on a set of predetermined reactions, usually strongly agree, agree, neither agree nor disagree, disagree, strongly disagree; must possess an odd number of reaction words or phrases; also called *summated ratings method* because the scale requires at least two, if not three, statements per measurement dimension

Like—*sm/s/engagement*. A metric of people who indicate that they like a posting on the social media; see also: Facebook

Line Graph—*s*. A representation of frequency distribution by means of lines representing data points at various intervals along a continuum; see also: Graph

Linkbacks—*sm/s/engagement*. A metric of the number of clickthroughs on links to blogs or tweets; see also: Blog, Tweet, YouTube

LinkedIn—*sm/output*. A social networking site that allows people to be linked by professional interests or duties

Loading—*m*. The writing of data extracted and transformed to a destination database; see also: ELT, Extraction, Transformation

Longitudinal Survey—*m*. A type of survey that consists of different individuals or objects that is observed or measured over time (e.g., multiple snapshot samples)

-M-

Mail Survey—*m*. A survey technique whereby a printed questionnaire is completed by a respondent and the respondent returns it via postal mail

Mall Intercept Research—*m*. A special type of person-to-person surveying in which in-person interviewing is conducted by approaching prospective participants as they stroll through shopping centers or malls; a nonprobability form of sampling

Manifest Content—*m*. From content analysis, an analysis of the actual content of a message exactly as it appears as opposed to latent content that must be inferred from messages

MapReduce—*m/s*. A database programming model and an associated implementation for processing and generating large datasets where users specify a map function to process a key or value pair to generate a set of intermediate key or value pairs, and a reduce function that merges data associated with the same intermediate key; see also: Big Data, Computing

Market Mix Model—*m*. A sophisticated model that looks at all parts of a marketing program to determine cause and effect of specific communication vehicles on an overall program

Market Research—*m*. Any systematic study of market trends, market effects of entry and innovation, or studies of pricing models and competitive effects on purchasing behavior

Mean—*s*. A descriptive statistic of central tendency that describes the "average" of a set of numbers on a continuum; also called "average"; the process of applying a precise number or metric, which is both valid and reliable, to the evaluation of some performance

Measurement—*m*. A way of giving an activity a precise dimension, generally by comparison to some standard; usually done in a quantifiable or numerical manner; see also: Data, Scale

Measurement Bias—*m*. Failure to control for the effects of data collection and measurement, for example, tendency of people to give socially desirable answers

Measurement Error—*m*. The amount of error found in a research campaign; in surveys it is the amount of error in individual responses; *s*. a term that expresses the amount of doubt that a researcher may accept in terms of findings; see also: Confidence Interval

Measurement Reliability—*m*. The extent to which a measurement scale measures the same thing over time; *s*. a statistical reporting of how reliable a measure is; see also: Coefficient Alpha, Test-Retest Reliability, Split-Half Reliability

Measurement Validity—*m*. The extent to which a measurement scale actually measures what it believed to measure; see also: Face Validity, Content Validity, Construct Validity, Criterion-Related Validity

Media—*m*. Includes newspapers, business and consumer magazines and other publications, radio and television, the Internet; company reports, news wires, government reports and brochures; Internet websites and discussion groups

Media Evaluations—*m*. The systematic appraisal of a company's reputation, products or services, or those of its competitors, as expressed by their presence in the media

Median—*s*. A descriptive statistic of central tendency indicating the midpoint in a series of data; the point above and below which 50 percent of the data values fall

Mention Prominence—*s*. An indication of the prominence of a mention in the media of an issue, company, or product; typically measured in percent of article and position within the output (e.g., headline, above the fold, first three minutes)

Mentions—*s/sm/outtake/outcome*. An output or outcome consisting of counts of incidents of a company or product or person appears in the media, one mention constitutes a media placement; the number of times a tweet, blog, or other social media output is talked about by other social media users

Message Content—*m*. The verbal, visual, and audio elements of a message; the material from which content analyses are conducted; *s*. analysis of media coverage of messages regarding a client, product, or topic on key issues; a trend analysis factor that measures what, if any, of planned messages are actually contained in the media

Message Strength—*s*. A trend analysis factor that measures how strongly message about a client or product or topic was communicated

Metric—*m/s/outtake/outcome*. A numeric value associated with campaign research demonstrating statistically whether outtake or outcome objectives are being reached; see also: Output, Outtake, Refinement Stage

Mode—*s*. A descriptive statistic of central tendency indicating the most frequently occurring (the most typical) value in a data series

Modeling—*m/s*. An approach to show how variables influence outcomes through relationships

Moderator—*m*. An individual who leads a focus group; also known as a facilitator

Monitoring—*m*. A process by which data are systematically and regularly collected about a research program over time; see also: Environmental Scanning

Moral Courage—*m/ethics*. Ability for a public relations professional to act as an ethics counsel; courage in advising when assessments are unpopular or go against management's desires and directives

Moral Objectivity—*m/ethics.* The ability to autonomously weigh perspectives of many varied publics on a moral issue using one's objective rationality; see also: Autonomy

Motivational Objective—*m.* An objective that establishes the desired level of change in a target audience's specific attitudes or beliefs after a public relations campaign

Multiple Regression—*s.* A statistical technique that employs multiple independent variables to predict an outcome variable (dependent variable); see also: Regression, Independent Variable, Dependent Variable

Multivariate Analysis—*s.* An inferential or descriptive statistic that examines the relationships among three or more variables

-N-

Network Analysis—*m.* A formal or informal research method that examines how individuals or units or actors relate to each other in some systematic way

Neutral Point—*s.* A point midway between extremes in attitude measurement scales; in Likert-type scales usually defined as "neutral" or "neither agree nor disagree"; see also: Attitude, Attitude Scale, Likert Scale, Semantic Differential Scale

Nominal Data—*s.* Measurement data that are simple categories in which items are different in name only and do not possess any ordering; data that are mutually exhaustive and exclusive; the simplest or lowest of all data; categorical data; example: male or female, where neither is seen as better as or larger than the other

Nonfinancial Metrics—*m/s/s/outtake/outcome.* Data gathered that do not include "hard" data such as sales, profits, attendance; data that are social in nature and reflect attitudinal variables such as credibility, relationships, reputation, trust, and confidence

Nonparametric Statistics—*s.* Inferential and descriptive statistics based on categorical data; see also: Chi-Square, Spearman-rho

Nonprobability Sample—*m*. A sample drawn from a population whereby respondents or objects do not have an equal chance of being selected for observation or measurement

Nonverbal Communication—*m*. That aspect of the communication that deals with the transmission and reception of messages that are not a part of a natural language system (e.g., visual, spoken [as opposed to verbal], environmental)

Norm—*s*. Short for "normative data"; see also: Normative Data

Normal Curve—*s*. Measurement data reflecting the hypothetical distribution of data points or cases based on interval-or ratio-level data that are "normally distributed" and error free; all continuous or parametric datasets have their own normally distributed data that fall under its specific normal curve

Normative Data—*s*. The set of scores that allow comparison of results to other studies and see "where you stand" and provide a context

Not Using Misleading Data—*m/s/ethics*. A moral responsibility and imperative to report data accurately and fully; not slanting data to support a preferred outcome or assessment

Null Hypothesis—*s*. The hypothesis of no difference that is formally tested in a research campaign or program; its rejection is the test of the theory; it is the formal hypothesis that all inferential statistics test; see also: Inferential Statistics

Number of Comments—*sm/s*. A metric that indicates the number of comments on a social media conversation

Number of Fans—*sm/s/outtake*. A metric that analyzes the number of fans on a social media site, especially on Facebook

Number of Followers—*sm/s/outtake*. A metric that analyzes the number of individuals who are actively following a blogger, a tweeter, or individual, company, and so on, on Facebook

Number of Likes—*sm/s/outtake*. A metric that analyzes Facebook likes; see also: Like

-O-

Objective—*m*. A measurable outcome in three forms: informational (cognitive), motivational (attitudinal or belief), behavioral (actionable); an explicit statement of intentions that supports a communication strategy, and to be measurable, includes an intended audience or public, a proposed change in a communication effect, a precise indication of the amount or level of change, and a specific timeframe for the change to occur

Omnibus Survey—*m*. An "all purpose" national consumer poll usually conducted on a regular schedule (once a week or every other week) by major market research firms; also called *piggyback* or *shared-cost* survey

Online Survey—*m*. An approach to show how variables influence outcomes through relationships

Open-Ended Question—*m*. Open-ended questions ask respondents to answer in their own words; some longer forms may probe the dimensions of attitudes and behavior held by a particular respondent through an interactive conversation between respondent and interviewer

Opinion—*m/s/outtake/outcome*. The statement of an attitude by an influencer or third-party endorser as part of proactive communication planning; a verbalized or written evaluation of some object; see also: Influencer

Opportunities to See (OTS)—*m/s/outtake*. The number of times a particular audience has the potential to view a message, subject, or issue; *s*. a statistic based on outputs serving as a dependent variable in some research; see also: Dependent Variable, Impressions, Outcome, Output

Ordinal Data—*s*. Measurement data that are categories in which items are different in name and possess an ordering of some sort; data that are mutually exhaustive and exclusive and ordered; categorical data; example: income as categories of under $25K, $26K–$50K, $51K–$75K, $76K–$100K, over $100K

Outcomes—*m/s*. Quantifiable changes in awareness, knowledge, attitude, opinion, and behavior levels that occur as a result of a public relations program or campaign; an effect, consequence, or impact of a set or program of communication activities or products, and may be either short-term (immediate) or long-term; *s.* the dependent variable in research; see also: Dependent Variable

Outgrowth—*m/s.* The culminate effect of all communication programs and products on the positioning of an organization in the minds of its stakeholders or publics; *s.* an outcome statistics used as a dependent variable in some research; see also: Dependent Variable, Outcome

Output—*m/s.* What is generated as a result of a PR program or campaign that may be received and processed by members of a target audience, and may have cognitive impact on outtakes: the way a target audience or public feels, thinks, knows, or believes; the final stage of a communication product, production, or process resulting in the production and dissemination of a communication product (brochure, media release, website, speech, etc.); *s.* the number of communication products or services resulting from a communication production process; the number distributed or the number reaching a targeted audience; sometimes used as an outcome serving as a dependent variable in research; see also: Independent Variable, Dependent Variable, Outtake, Outcome

Outtake—*m/s.* Measurement of what audiences have understood or heeded or responded to a communication product's call to seek further information from PR messages prior to measuring an outcome; audience reaction to the receipt of a communication product, including favorability of the product, recall and retention of the message embedded in the product, and whether the audience heeded or responded to a call for information or action within the message; *s.* sometimes used as an outcome serving as a dependent variable in research; see also: Dependent Variable, Outcome

Owned Sites—*sm.* Social media platforms that are controlled or "owned" by a company or organization; see also: Social Media Platform; Facebook; Twitter

-P-

Page Rank—*sm/s*. A metric for the likelihood of website being found by seeker of relevant information

Page Views—*sm/s/outtake*. A metric that analyzes the number of times a web page has been viewed

Paid Media—*m/sm/output*. Outputs placed in the media as a function of advertising

Paired *t*-Test—*s*. An inferential statistical test of significance that compares data that are collected twice on the same sample; see also: Inferential Statistics, Independent *t*-Test, Known Group *t*-Test

Panel Survey—*m*. A type of survey that consists of the same individuals or objects that is observed or measured over time; a type of survey in which a group of individuals are deliberately recruited by a research firm because of their special demographic characteristics for the express purpose of being interviewed more than once over a period of time for various clients on a broad array of different topics or subjects

Parameter—*s*. In sampling, a characteristic of a population that is of interest

Parametric Statistics—*s*. Inferential and descriptive statistics based on continuous data; see also: Data, Descriptive Statistics, Inferential Statistics

Participant-Observation—*m*. A research methodology where the researcher takes an active role in the life of an organization or community, observes and records interactions, and then analyzes those interactions

Path Analysis—*s*. A statistical technique that establishes relationships between variables with arrows between variables indicating the pattern of causal relationships usually in the form of a "path diagram"; typically used with "hard" or financial data; see also: Path Diagram

Path Diagram—*s*. A graphical representation of the causal relationships between variables showing both direction and strength of relationship; see also: Path Analysis, Structural Equation Modeling

Pearson Product Moment Coefficient (*r*)—*s*. A correlation statistic used with interval and ratio data; see also: Correlation, Data, Spearman-rho

Peer Index—*sm/s*. A statistic that indicates intermediary influencers; see also: Influencer

Percent of Change—*s/output/outtake*. A measure of increase or decrease of media coverage

Percentage—*s*. A descriptive statistic based on categorical data; defined as the frequency count for a particular category divided by the total frequency count; example: 10 males out of 100 people = 10 percent; see also: Descriptive Statistics

Percentage Point—*s/output/outtake/outcome*. The number that a percentage is increased or decreased

Performance—*m*. The act of carrying-out, doing, executing, or putting into effect; a deed, task, action, or activity as a unit of a program of performance

Performance Indicator—*m/s/outtake*. A sign or parameter that, if tracked over time, provides information about the ongoing results of a particular program of performance or campaign; *s*. an outcome measured during a public relations campaign that serves as a dependent variable; see also: Data, Dependent Variable, KPI

Performance Measure—*m/s/outtake/outcome*. A number that shows the exact extent to which a result was achieved; *s*. in a research campaign, an outcome of some sort serving as a dependent variable; see also: Data, Dependent Variable, Outcome

Performance Result (Key Performance)—*m/s/outcome*. The desired end effect or impact of a program of campaign performance

Performance Target—*m/s/outcome*. A time-bounded and measurable commitment toward achieving a desired result; a measurable objective

Periodicity—*s*. A bias found in sampling due to the way in which the items or respondents are chosen; example: newspapers may differ by being daily, weekly, weekday only, and so forth

Pie Graph—*s*. A representation of a frequency distribution by means of portions segment of a circle; the segments represent the percentages of the variable of interest; see also: Graph

Piggyback Survey—*m*. A survey that has questions from several clients or projects; see also: Omnibus Survey

Poll—*m*. A form of survey research that focuses more on immediate behavior than attitudes; a very short survey method whose questionnaire asks only very short and closed-ended questions; see also: In-Depth Survey, Survey Methodology

Position Papers—*m*. An output that serves to place a client or product or service in a particular light

Positioning—*m/s/outtake*. A process where a brand is identified by a target audience; a metric that examines where stakeholders are on key issues; a trend analysis factor that measures how a client or product or topic was positioned in the media (e.g., leader, follower)

PR Return on Investment—*m*. The impact of a public relations program on business results; *s*. the outcome (dependent) variable which demonstrates the impact of a public relations campaign or program investment on business program KPIs such as sales leads, customer retention, new customers, and so on; a causal indicator of public relations impact on business KPIs; see also: Causal Relationships, Return on Investment (ROI)

Predictive Analytics—*s*. Statistical programs that attempt to predict an outcome within a certain amount of allowed error; see also: Path Analysis, Regression, Structural Equation Model

Preference—*s/outtake*. A preference measure determines the choice of a single brand, product, or service to the exclusion of others

Probability Sample—*m*. A sample drawn at random from a population such that all possible respondents or objects have an equal chance of being selected for observation or measurement

Probe Question—*m*. A question used in a survey questionnaire or in-depth or focus group schedule that requires the participant to explain an earlier response, often in the form of "why do you think this?" or "could you be more specific?"

Product (Communication Product)—*m/output.* The end result of the communication product or process resulting in the production and dissemination of a brochure, media release, video news release, website, speech, and so forth; an output or outtake; see also: Output, Outtake

Program (Campaign)—*m.* The planning, execution, and evaluation of a public relations plan of action aimed at solving a problem or the taking advantage of an opportunity

Prominence of Mention—*m/s/outtake.* A metric of where in a story a client or issue is featured (e.g., headline, top of the fold, what part of a broadcast); *s.* an output unit of analysis used as a dependent variable; see also: Dependent Variable, Output

Proportion—*s.* A descriptive statistic based on categorical data; defined as the percentage as made part of one (1.0); example: 10 males out of 100 people are 10 hundredths of the sample

Protection of Proprietary Data—*m/*ethics. An ethical research value that keeps data confidential to those who paid for its collection

Psychographic Research—*m.* Research focusing on a population or sample's nondemographic traits and characteristics, such as personality type, life-style, social roles, values, attitudes, and beliefs

Psychometrics—*s.* A branch of psychology that deals with the design, administration, and interpretation of quantitative tests for the measurement of psychological variables such as intelligence, aptitude, and personality traits; also called psychometry, psychographics

Public—*m.* A group of people who have consequences on an organization or affected by the consequences of organizational decisions; a group of people from which the public relations campaign or program selects in an attempt to influence it regarding a company, product, issue, or individual; see also: Audience, Sample

Public Opinion Poll—*m*. A type of survey that collects basic opinions held by or facts about a specified population or sample; also known as a descriptive survey; see also: Poll, Survey Methodology

Public Relations Effectiveness—*s/outcome*. The degree to which the outcome of a public relations program is consonant with the overall objectives of the program as judged by some measure of causation; see also: Causal Relationship

Public Responsibility—*m/ethics*. A duty to communicate and act in the public interest

Purposive Sample—*m*. A nonprobability sample in which individuals are deliberately selected for inclusion based on their special knowledge, position, characteristics, or relevant dimensions of the population

Push Poll—*m*. An unethical survey technique in which an interviewer begins by acting as if the telephone call is a general survey to gain credibility, but then asks the respondent a question implying questionable behaviors or outcomes of a person or product; used by political and issues campaigns

-Q-

Q-Sort—*m*. A measurement instrument that focuses on respondent beliefs by asking them to sort through piles of opinion statement and sort them into piles on an 11-point continuum usually bounded by "most-like-me" to "most-unlike-me"; see also: Attitude Scale

Qualitative Research—*m*. Research that seeks in-depth understanding of particular cases and issues, rather than generalizable statistical information, through probing, open-ended methods such as depth interviews, focus groups and ethnographic observation

Quantitative Research—*m*. Research that produces generalizable findings by collecting and analyzing data in objective ways, such as experiments and closed-ended, forced-choice questionnaires of sufficiently large samples; research that relies heavily on statistics and numerical measures

Question—*m*. A statement or phrase used in a questionnaire or schedule that elicits either an open- or closed-ended response from a research participant; see also: Funnel and Probe Questions

Questionnaire—*m*. A measurement instrument that contains exact questions and measures an interviewer or survey researcher uses to survey through the mail, Internet, in person, or via the telephone; may be closed-ended and open-ended

Quota Sample—*m*. A type of nonprobability sample that draws its sample based on a percentage or quota from the population and stops sampling when that quota is met; a nonprobability sample that attempts to have the same general distribution of population characteristics as in the sample; see also: Poll, Survey Methodology

-R-

r^2 **Value**—*s*. The value calculated in a correlation between two variables; the amount of known relationship (explained variance) between two variables; $1-r^2$ provides an indication of how much is unknown; see also: Correlation, r-Value Score

Range—*s*. A descriptive central tendency statistics that expresses the difference between the highest and lowest scores in the dataset; example: responses to a question on a 1 to 5 Likert-type scale where all reaction categories were used would yield a range of 4 (5 minus 1)

Rankings—*s*. A metric of where an object is compared to other objects in the same class, industry, and so on

Ratio Data—*s*. Measurement data that are defined on a continuum and possess an absolute zero point; examples: number of children, a bank account, absolute lack of heat (0 Kelvin = −459.67°F or −273.15°C)

RDBMS—*m*. Relational Database Management System; see also: Relational Database, SQL, SQL Server

Reach—*m/sm/s/output/outtake*. A metric estimating the size of an audience exposed to a communication based on some audited system (traditional media); the number of unique social media mentions divided by the total mentions (social media)

Reader Engagement—*sm/s/output/engagement*. A metric of the number of comments and time spent on a website

Readership—*m*. Number of people who actually read each issue of a publication, on average, may be used as an at outcome variable at times; *s*. an output variable that often serves as a dependent variable; see also: Dependent Variable, Outcome

Refinement Stage—*m*. The portion of a campaign that starts with the initial baseline and continues through the evaluation stage; the portion of a campaign against which benchmarks are tested; see also: Developmental Stage, Evaluation Stage, Benchmark, Baseline

Reflexivity—*m/ethics*. The exercise of recognizing one's own position, viewpoints or influence in the process of data collection to reduce subjective interpretation and avoid bias; a secondary examination of data by those studied to test accuracy

Regression—*s*. A statistical tool that predicts outcomes based on one outcome (dependent) variable and one predictor (independent) variable; see also: Multiple Regression; *m*. a source of error or invalidity in experimental methodology that may impact on the validity of the experiment; see also: Experimental Methodology, Validity, Inferential Statistics

Relational Database (RDBMS)—*m*. A data management system that stores and retrieves data for use with other analytical programs

Relationship Engagement—*sm/s/outtake/engagement*. The state of engagement between an individual and other individuals, or between and among groups, and so on; a metric that analyzes the connection between individuals, groups, and so on

Reliability—*m*. The extent to which results would be consistent, or replicable, if the research were conducted a number of times; *s*. a statistical measure accessing consistency of a measure, usually through the Coefficient Alpha or KR-20 statistic in measurement or Cohen's Kappa, Hosti's reliability coefficient, Krippendorf's alpha, or Scott's pi; see also:

Measurement Reliability, Cohen's Kappa, Holsti's Reliability Coefficient, Scott's Pi

Reputation—*s*. An outcome variable often used as a dependent variable in research dealing with the public's perception of an organization's credibility, trustworthiness, or image based on the organization's behavior; see also: Dependent Variable

Research—*m*. The systematic effort before (formative research) or during or after (summative or evaluative research) a communication activity aimed at discovering and collecting the facts or opinions pertaining to an identified issue, need, or question; may be formal or informal

Research Bias—*m*. Unknown or unacknowledged error created during the design, measurement, sampling, procedure, or choice of problem studied; see also: Experimental Methodology, Validity, Regression

Research Instrument—*m*. A tool used to collect data; see also: Questionnaire, Interview Schedule, Semistructured Interview, Structured Interview

Respondent—*m*. The individual from whom data is collected through participation in a research campaign; sometimes called participant or, in psychological study, subject

Respondent Right—*m/ethics*. Ethical values in research that protect respondents from exploitation or abuse, such as that reported in Zimbardo's Stanford prison experiment

Response Rate—*m/s/outtake*. From survey methodology, the number of respondents who actually completed an interview; *s*. the percentage of completed surveys (often adjusted for mailing errors)

Results—*m/s/outtake/outcome*. The outtake or outcome impacted upon by a public relations campaign; *m*. that which is measured in a campaign as dependent variables; see also: Dependent Variable, Outcome, Output, Outtake, Outgrowth

Return on Expectations (ROE)—*m/s/outcome*. A metric that analyzes the combination of financial and nonfinancial outcomes that leads to public relations ROI

Return on Investment (ROI)—*s*. An outcome variable that equates profit from investment; see also: Public Relations Return on Investment, Dependent Variable

ROI (%)—*s*. Net Financial Return (net return: gross financial return minus the financial investment) divided by the Financial Investment × 100. A ROI metric is expressed as a percentage and the calculation is made after the actual returns, all actual returns, are realized

Retweet—*sm/s/output/outtake*. A tweet that one Twitter user decides to reshare with his or her own followers; see also: Tweet, Twitter

Retweet Efficiency—*sm/s/outtake*. A metric of how many retweets a Tweet gets per 100 or 1,000 or more followers

Retweet Velocity—*sm/s/outtake*. A metric that analyzes the likelihood of a Tweet to be retweeted

RSS Subscribers—*sm/s/outtake*. The number of people who have subscribed to a blog or other social media platform

r-Value Score—*s*. The calculated correlation between two variables; see also: Correlation

-S-

Sample—*m*. A group of people or objects chosen from a larger population; see also: Probability Sample, Nonprobability Sample, Convenience Sample, Panel Survey, Longitudinal Survey, Snapshot Survey

Sample Frame—*m*. How a population is generated by selecting some relevant group to sample

Sample Size—*m/s*. The number of participants in a study that have been drawn for observation

Sampling Error—*m/s*. The amount of error expected or observed in surveys that may be attributed to problems in random selection of respondents; *s*. the amount of error that a researcher finds acceptable or expected based on the sample size and expressed as confidence in sampling from a population; see also: Confidence Level

Scale—*m*. A measurement instrument consisting of attitude or belief items that reflect an underlying structure toward some attitude or belief object; see also: Attitude Scale

Scalogram (Guttman Scale or Cumulative Scale)—*m*. A measurement scale that assumes (a) unidimensionality and (b) that people, when faced with a choice will also choose items less intense than the one chosen; see also: Attitude Scale, Likert Scale, Semantic Differential Scale

Scattergram—*s*. A data visualization based on continuous data that graphically demonstrates how data are distributed between two variables, one variable on the *x*-axis and one on the *y*-axis; also known as a scatter diagram or scatterplot

Schedule—*m*. The timeline on which a public relations program or campaign is conducted; a list of questions, usually open-ended, used in focus group and in-depth interviews to gather data; see also: Survey Methodology, In-Depth Interview

Scott's Pi—*s*. A coding reliability measure employed in content analysis that reduces the impact of chance agreement among intercoder or intracoder coding; see also: Reliability, Content Analysis, Holsti's Reliability Coefficient, Krippendorf's Alpha, Cohen's Kappa

Screener Question—*m*. A type of question asked at the beginning of an interview or survey to determine if the potential respondent is eligible or qualified to participate in the study; see also: Funnel Question

Search Engine Optimization (SEO)—*m*. A method that allows outputs on the social media to be optimized such that they appear frequently when key word searches are conducted

Search Ranking—*sm/s/output*. A metric comparing paid versus earned media coverage; see also: Paid Media, Earned Media

Secondary Methodology—*m*. An informal research methodology that examines extant data in order to draw conclusions; a systematic reanalysis of a vast array of existing data; often used in benchmarking and benchmark studies

Semantic Differential Scale—*m*. An attitude measure that asks respondents to evaluate an attitude object based on bipolar adjectives or phrases separated by a continuum represented as consisting of an odd number of intervals; developed by Osgood, Suci, and Tannenbaum; see also: Attitude Scale, Guttman Scalogram, Likert-Type Scale

Semantic Space—*m*. The idea that people can evaluate attitude objects along some spatial continuum; often associated with attitude researchers Osgood, Suci, and Tannenbaum

Semistructured Interview—*m*. An interview conducted with a fairly flexible list of questions which allows for focused, conversational, two-way communication; it can be used both to give and receive information

Sentiment—*m/s/outtake/outcome*. A metric that assesses and determines the tone of a public relations output; a ratio of positive to negative; typically evaluated as positive, neutral, or negative

Sequential Equation Model—*s*. A statistical methodology similar to path analysis but that uses as measures that are created such as attitude, intelligence, reputation rather than actual indicators (e.g., sales, revenue) to test a hypothesized causal relationship between predictor (independent) and outcome (dependent) variables; see also: Dependent Variable, Independent Variable, Path Analysis, Regression, Multiple Regression

Share of Ink (SOI)—*s/output*. Measurement of the total press or magazine coverage found in articles or mentions devoted to a particular industry or topic as analyzed to determine what percent of outputs or Opportunities to See (OTS) is devoted to a client or product; an outcome often used as a dependent variable; see also: Dependent Variable, Outcome

Share of Voice (SOV)—*s/output/outtake/outcome*. A measurement of total coverage devoted to radio or television coverage to a particular industry or topic as analyzed to determine what percent of outputs or Opportunities to See (OTS) is devoted to a client or product; also known as *share of coverage;* an outcome often used as a dependent variable; see also: Dependent Variable, Outcome

Shared-Cost Survey—A survey method where the costs of conducting the survey are paid by several companies or researchers to reduce costs; typically provide fewer questions per company or researcher due to number of different clients in the survey; see also: Omnibus Survey

Simple Random Sample—*m*. A type of probability sample in which numbers are assigned to each member of a population, a random set of numbers is generated, and then only those members having the random numbers are included in the sample

Site Content—*sm/s/outtake*. The type of content found on a social media site type

Site Type—*sm/s*. The type of site used to communicate; mainstream media, online media, blogs, tweets, and so on

Site—*sm*. A social media platform either owned or earned. See also: Owned Site, Earned Site, Facebook, Twitter, YouTube

Situation Analysis—*m*. An impartial, often third-party assessment of the public relations or public affairs problems, or opportunities, that an organization may be facing at a given point in time

Skip Interval—*m*. The distance in a sample list between people selected from a population based on systematic sampling; usually defined as the total population divided by the number of people to be sampled (e.g., for a sample of 100 people to be drawn from a population of 10,000 people, the skip interval would be 100/10,000 = 100 individuals skipped between selected participants)

Snapshot Survey—*m*. A type of survey that consists of individuals or objects that is observed or measured once over a relatively short time period; see also: Cross-Sample Survey

Snowball Sample—*m*. A type of nonprobability sample in which individuals who are interviewed are asked to suggest other individuals for further interviewing

Social Media—*m*. Open source (i.e., publicly accessible) media sites on the Internet that accept user-generated content and foster social interaction; including blogs, microblogging sites such as Twitter and Sina

Weibo, photosharing sites such as Flickr and videosharing sites such as YouTube (see also: Social Networks)

Social Mention—*sm/s/outtake*. A metric that analyzes how many times someone or something has been mentioned in the social media

Social Network—*m*. Open source (i.e., publicly accessible) websites that facilitate social interaction and networking, such as Facebook, LinkedIn, Google+, and Renren in China

Social Return on Investment (SROI)—*sm/s/outcome*. A metric that analyzes the expected return on investment (ROI) by the social media in terms of cost-benefit and social accounting; a combination of ROI and BCR; see also: Return on Investment, Benefit-Cost Ratio

Sociogram—*s*. A pictorial representation of the actual relationships of individuals within a specified unit such as a public, target audience, or work unit

Source Strength—*sm/s/outtake*. A quantitative measure of earned-media sites

Sources Mentioned—*m*. A trend analysis factor that measures who was quoted in media coverage; also known as "quoteds"

Speaking Engagements—*s*. Print or broadcast or Internet communication product output; see also: Output

Spearman-rho—*s*. A correlation statistic used with nominal or ordinal data; see also: Correlation, Data, Pearson Product Moment Coefficient

Split-Half Reliability—*s*. A test for a measure's reliability where a sample is randomly split and one segment receives a part of the measure and the second segment receives the rest

SQL server—*m*. A specific Structured Query Language aimed at targeted audiences; see also: Structured Query Language, SQL, RDBMS

Standard Deviation (σ)—*s*. A descriptive statistic of central tendency which indexes the variability of a distribution; the range from the mean within which approximately 34 percent of the cases fall, provided the values are distributed in a normal curve

Standardized Score (Z-Score)—*s*. A descriptive statistic based on continuous data that expresses individual scores based on their standard deviations from the group mean; range of scores is usually −3.00 to +3.00; see also: Z-Score

Standard—*m*. A level of performance that establishes a measure against which comparative evaluations can be made; see also: Statistical Significance

Statistical power—*s*. The power of a statistical test based on the number of observations made; calculated as 1–β

Statistical Significance—*s*. The amount of confidence (as opposed to acceptable error) a researcher has in the outcome of a statistical test; the standard accepted error against which statements of difference can be made (α = 0.05 or 95 percent confidence in the findings are due to tested variables and not extraneous variables); see also: Analysis of Variance, F-Value Score, *t*-Value Score, *t*-Test, Correlation

Stratified Sample—*m*. A type of probability sample that involves first breaking the total population into homogenous subsets (or strata), and then selecting the potential sample at random from the individual strata; example: stratify on race would require breaking the population into racial strata and then randomly sampling within each strata

Structural Equation Model (SEM)—*s*. An advanced statistical procedure that produces estimated paths as coefficients of relationship; typically used with nonfinancial data or data that are attitudinal in nature; see also: Path Analysis, Regression

Structured Data—*m*. Data organized according to a well-defined structure, usually information stored in databases that index according to rows and columns

Structured Interview—*m*. An interview with a predefined set of questions and responses which may provide more reliable, quantifiable data than an open-ended interview and can be designed rigorously to avoid biases in the line of questioning; see also: Filter Question, Funnel Question

Structured Query Language (SQL)—*m*. A programming language used to manage relational database systems; see also: Content Analysis, SQL Server, RDBMS

Sum Basis—*sm/s/outtake*. A metric that adds up unique visitors to a social media platform as compared to mainstream media

Summary Measure—*s*. A measure that combines information of different types and from different sources which together permit a rapid appraisal of a specific phenomenon to identify differences (e.g., between groups, countries), observed changes over time or expected changes (e.g., as a consequence of policy measures); there are four key elements to summary measures: the selection of relevant parameters to be included, the reliable measurement or collection of these parameters, the unit in which the summary measure will be expressed and the relative weight of each of the constituents in the total summary measure

Summative Evaluation—*m/outcome*. A method of evaluating the end of a research program; the basis of establishing the dependent measures; see also: Dependent Variable

Survey Methodology—*m*. A formal research methodology that seeks to gather data and analyze a population's or sample's attitudes, beliefs, and opinions; data are gathered in-person or by telephone (face-to-face), or self-administered via the mail or e-mail; see also: Survey Methodology, Longitudinal Survey, Panel Survey, Cohort Survey, Snapshot Survey

Symbols/Words—*s*. A manifest unit of analysis used in content analysis consisting of specific words (e.g., pronouns, client name, logotypes) that are counted; see also: Content Analysis

Systematic Sample—*m*. A type of probability sample in which units in a population are selected from an available list at a fixed interval after a random start; see also: Skip Interval

-T-

Target Audience—*m*. A very specific audience differentiated from "audience" by some measurable characteristic or attribute (e.g., sports fishermen)

Targeted Gross Rating Points (TGRP)—*s/outcome*. Gross Rating Points (GRP) targeted to a particular group or target audience; an outcome often used as a dependent variable; see also: Dependent Variable, Gross Rating Points, Outtake, Outcome

Task Completion Rate—*sm/s/outtake*. A metric measuring the percent of visitors to a website who were able to complete the task they came to that website for

Technorati—*sm/s*. A program that analyzes how many links a blog has and evaluates that blog on its authority; see also: Blog

Test-Retest Reliability—*s*. A test for a measure's reliability by testing the same sample with the same measure over time

Themes—*s*. A latent unit of analysis used in content analysis that measures an underlying theme or thesis (e.g., sexuality, violence, credibility); see also: Content Analysis

Throughputs—*m*. The development, creative, and production activities (writing, editing, creative design, printing, fabrication, etc.) as part of the throughput stage of a communication product production process

Time on Site—*sm/s/outtake*. A metric that calculates the amount of time an individual spends on specific social media sites or platforms

Time/space Measures—*s*. A manifest unit of analysis used in content analysis consisting of physically measurable units (e.g., column inches, size of photographs, broadcast time for a story); see also: Content Analysis

Tone—*s*. Trend and latent content analysis factor that measures how a target audience feels about the client or product or topic; typically defined as positive, neutral or balanced, or negative; often used as an outcome and dependent variable; see also: Dependent Variable, Outcome, Content Analysis

Transparency—*m/ethics*. Allowing external publics and stakeholders to see inside the organization, so that others can know how it makes decisions

Transformation—*m*. The necessary conversion of data formats or structures to be consumed by a destination database; see also: ETL, Extraction, Loading

Trend Analysis—*m*. Tracking of performance over the course of a PR campaign or program; survey method whereby a topic or subject is examined over a period of time through repeated surveys of independently selected samples (snapshot or cross-sectional survey)

t-**Test**—*s*. An inferential statistical test of significance for continuous measurement dependent variables against a bivariate independent variable; used when total number of observations are less than 100; see also: Paired *t*-Test; Independent *t*-Test; Known Group *t*-Test, Inferential Statistics

t-**Value Score**—*s*. The calculated score obtained from a *t*-Test that is compared against tabled values; see also: *t*-Test, Statistical Significance, Standard

Tweet—*sm/output*. A 140-character text-based post used to communicate on Twitter; see also: Twitter

Type of Article—*m*. Categories of an item in media analysis, such as "product review," "by-lined article," "editorial," "advertorial," "feature story"; *s*. trend analysis factor that measures the nature of client or product or topic coverage (e.g., column inches, broadcast time); often used as a dependent variable; see also: Dependent Variable

Twitter—*sm/outtake*. A microblog website where 140-character messages are sent to those who chose to follow a person or organization; see also, Tweet

-U-

Unaided Awareness—*m/s*. Measurement of how much people know of an object without providing hints, descriptions, and so forth

Unfollowers—*sm/s/outtake*. A metric indicating how many people have stopped following a Facebook or other social media platform user

Unit of Analysis—*m*. The specification of what is to be counted in content analysis methodology; consist of symbols or words, time or space measures, characters, themes, and items; may be manifest (observable) or latent (attitudinal)

Univariate Analysis—*s*. The examination of only one variable at a time

Universe—*m*. The set of all the units from which a sample is drawn; also called the population

Unstructured Data—*m*. Data with no organized structure where an entity may contain its own structure or format; for example, textual documents, audio, video files

Utilitarianism—*ethics*. A paradigm that seeks to maximize the good consequences of a decision and minimize the harms or negative consequences, defining happiness or public interest as the good to be maximized

-V-

Validity—*m*. The extent to which a research project actually measures what it is intended, or purports to measure; see also: Measurement Validity

Value—*m*. An underlying cultural expectation, usually directs an individual's beliefs

Variance (σ^2)—*s*. A descriptive statistic of central tendency that measures the extent to which individual scores in a dataset differ from each other; the sum of the squared standard deviations from the mean (σ)

Verbatim—*m/s*. A reporting of data using the actual words of respondents and direct quotes from the transcript of the actual comments participants make in a focus group, individual interviews, or open-ended questions on surveys; many researchers include verbatims in their final reports to support their interpretation of the finding; *s*. data which may be used in content analysis; see also: Interview Schedule, Semistructured Interview, Structured Interview, Content Analysis

Video Views—*sm/s/outtake*. A metric that analyzes the number of times a video has been viewed on a website

Views Per Photo—*sm/s/outtake*. A metric that analyzes how many people have viewed a photograph in the traditional media; a metric that analyzes the number of times a photo has been viewed on a social media website

Visitor Loyalty—*sm/s/s/outtake*. A metric that analyzes how often a visitor comes to a website

Visitor Recency—*sm/s/outtake*. A metric that analyzes the length of time visitors have last been to a website

Visitor—*sm/outtake*. A unique individual looking at a website

Visits—*sm/s/s/outtake*. A metric that indicates the number of times a visitor comes to a website; see also: Visitor

-W-

Web Analytics—*m/s/outtake/outcome*. The measurement, collection, analysis, and reporting of Internet data for purposes of understanding and optimizing web usage; see also: Analytics

Weighted Average—*s*. An average that takes into account the proportional relevance of each component, rather than treating each component equally

Weighting—*s*. The assignment of a numerical coefficient to an item to express its relative importance in a frequency distribution; as used in survey research to reduce the bias found in a sample or generalize to the target population

Word Cloud—*sm/s/outtake*. A visual representation of text used for quickly perceiving the most prominent terms and determining their relative importance

Word/symbol—*s*. From content analysis, a unit of analysis consisting of the actual word or symbol communicated in the media; see also: Content Analysis

-Y-

YouTube Insights—*sm/s/outtake*. A website that provides metrics for number of video views, users, and subscribers; see also: YouTube

YouTube—*sm/output.* A video-sharing website on which users can upload, share, and view videos

-Z-

Z-Score (Standardized Score)—*s.* A descriptive statistic of central tendency that takes data from different types of scales and standardizes them as areas under the normal curve for comparison purposes; see also: Standardized Score

References

Allison, P.D. 1999. *Multiple Regression: A Primer*. Thousand Oaks, CA: Pine Forge Press.

AMEC. n.d. International Association for the Measurement and Evaluation of Communication. Retrieved from www.amecorg.com

Arthur W. Page Society. 2009. *The Authentic Enterprise*. New York, NY: Arthur W. Page Society. Retrieved from www.awpagesociety.com/site/members/page_society_releases_ the_authentic_enterprise/

Assessing the Representativeness of Public Opinion Surveys. 2012. *Pew Research Center for the People and the Press*. Retrieved from www.people-press.org/2012/05/15/assessing-the-representativeness-of-public-opinion-surveys/ (accessed May 15, 2012).

Backstrom, H., and G. Hirsch-Cesar. 1981. *Survey Research* 2nd ed. New York, NY: Macmillan.

Berger, B.K., and B.H. Reber. 2006. *Gaining Influence in Public Relations: The Role of Resistance in Practice*. Mahwah, NJ: Lawrence Erlbaum Associates.

Blalock, H.J. 1972. *Social Statistics*. New York, NY: McGraw-Hill.

Botan, C., and V. Hazelton. 2006. *Public Relations Theory II*. Mahwah, NJ: Lawrence Erlbaum Publishers.

Bowen, S.A. 2008. "A State of Neglect: Public Relations as Corporate Conscience or Ethics Counsel." *Journal of Public Relations Research* 20, no. 3, pp. 271–96.

Bowen, S.A., B. Rawlins, and T. Martin. 2010. *An Overview of the Public Relations Function*. New York, NY: Business Expert Press.

Bowen, S.A., and D.W. Stacks. 2013a. "Understanding the Ethical and Research Implications of the Social Media." In *Ethics of Social Media in Public Relations Practice*, ed. M.W. DiStaso and D.S. Bortree. New York, NY: Routledge.

Bowen, S.A., and D.W. Stacks. 2013b. "Toward the Establishment of Ethical Standardization in Public Relations Research, Measurement and Evaluation." *Public Relations Journal* 7, no. 3, pp. 1–25.

Brody, E.W., and G.C. Stone. 1989. *Public Relations Research*. New York, NY: Prager.

Broom, G.M., and D. Dozier. 1990. *Using Research in Public Relations: Applications to Program Management*. Englewood Cliffs, NY: Prentice-Hall.

Campbell, D.T., and J.C. Stanley. 1963. *Experimental and Quasi-Experimental Designs for Research*. Chicago, IL: Rand McNally.

Carroll, T.B. 2006. *Does Familiarity Breed Contempt? Analyses of the Relationship Among Company Familiarity, Company Reputation, Company Citizenship, and Company Personality on Corporate Equity.* Unpublished dissertation, University of Miami.

CASRO. n.d. CASRO Code of Standards and Ethics. Retrieved from www.casro.org/?page=TheCASROCode

Caywood, C.L., ed. 1997. *The Handbook of Strategic Public Relations and Integrated Communications.* New York, NY: McGraw-Hill.

Commission on Public Relations Measurement and Evaluation. 2009. Meeting Minutes, October 16.

Curtin, P., and L. Boynton. 2001. "Ethics in Public Relations: Theory and Practice." In *Handbook of Public Relations*, ed. R.L. Heath, 411–22. Thousand Oaks, CA: Sage.

Dillard, J.P., and M. Pfau. 2002. *The Persuasion Handbook.* Newbury, CA: Sage.

Dillman, D.A. 2007. *Mail and Internet Surveys: A Tailored Design Method.* 2nd ed. New York, NY: Wiley.

DiStaso, M.W. 2013. "Perceptions of Wikipedia by Public Relations Professionals: A Comparison of 2012 and 2013 Surveys." *Public Relations Journal 7*, no. 3, pp. 1–23. www.prsa.org/Intelligence/PRJournal/Documents/2013_DiStaso.pdf

Dozier, D., L. Grunig, and J.E. Grunig. 1995. *Manager's Guide to Excellence in Public Relations and Communication Management.* Hillsdale, NJ: Lawrence Erlbaum.

Geertz, C. 1976. "From the Native Point of View: On the Nature of Anthropological Understanding." In *Meaning in Anthropology*, eds. K.H. Basso and H.A. Selby, 221–37. Albuquerque: University of New Mexico Press.

Grunig, J.E. 1992. *Excellence in Public Relations and Communication Management.* Hillsdale, NJ: Lawrence Erlbaum.

Grunig, J.E., and T. Hunt. 1984. *Managing Public Relations.* Orlando, FL: Harcourt Brace Jovanovich.

Grunig, L.A., J.E. Grunig, and D.M. Dozier. 2002. *Excellent Public Relations and Effective Organizations: A Study of Communication Management in Three Countries.* Mahwah, NJ: Lawrence Erlbaum.

Grunig, J.E., and L.A. Grunig. 2006. "Characteristics of Excellent Communication." In *The IABC Handbook of Organizational Communication*, ed. T.A. Gillis, 3–18. San Francisco, CA: Jossey-Bass.

Harris, T.L. 1993. *The Marketer's Guide to Public Relations.* New York, NY: John Wiley & Sons.

Harris, T.L. 1998. *Value-Added Public Relations: The Secret Weapon on Integrated Marketing.* Lincolnwood, IL: NTC Business Books.

Herzberg, F. 1966. *Work and the Nature of Man.* New York, NY: Collins.

Herzberg, F. 1968. "One More Time: How Do You Motivate Employees?" *Harvard Business Review* 46, no. 1, pp. 53–62.

Herzberg, F., B. Mausner, and D.B. Snydermann. 1959. *The Motivation of Work*. New York, NY: Wiley.

Hickson, M.L. 2003. "Qualitative Research." In *Communication Research,* eds. J.E. Hocking, D.W. Stacks, and S.T. McDermott, 193–215. 3rd ed. Boston, MA: Allyn & Bacon.

Hocking, J.E., D.W. Stacks, and S.T. McDermott. 2003. *Communication Research*. 3rd ed. Boston, MA: Allyn & Bacon.

Holsti, O.R. 1969. *Content Analysis for the Social Sciences and Humanities*. Reading, MA: Addison-Wesley.

Institute for Public Relations Commission on Measurement and Evaluation. 2012. *Ethical Standards and Guidelines for Public Relations Research and Measurement, Version 10*. www.instituteforpr.org/topics/ethical-standards-and-guidelines-for-public-relations-research-and-measurement/

Institute for Public Relations. 2011. The Science Beneath the Art of Public Relations. Retrieved from www.instituteforpr.org

Jeffries, A. 2006. "Great Budget Tips for the Budget-Strapped." *PR News*, April 3.

Jeffries-Fox, B. 2003. *Advertising Value Equivalency*. Gainesville, FL: Institute for Public Relations. www.instituteforpr.org/topics/advertising-value-equivalency/

Legacy Tobacco Document Library. n.d. University of California, San Francisco, CA. www.industrydocumentslibrary.ucsf.edu/tobacco/

Li, C., and D.W. Stacks. 2015. *Measuring the Impact of Social Media on Business Profit and Success: A Fortune 500 Perspective*. New York: Peter Lang.

Likert, R. 1932. "A Technique for the Measurement of Attitudes." *Archives of Psychology* 40, no. 140, pp. 1–55.

Lindenmann, W.K. 2001. *Research Does Not Have to Put You in the Poorhouse*. Gainesville, FL: Institute for Public Relations. Retrieved from www.instituteforpr.org/topics/research-savings/

Maslow, A.H. 1970. *A Theory of Human Motivation*. New York, NY: Harper & Row.

McCormick, M. 1985. *The New York Times Guide to Reference Materials*. Rev. ed. 87–96. New York, NY: Praeger.

McCroskey, J.C., V.P. Richmond, and J.A. Daly. 1975. "The Development of a Measure of Perceived Homophily in Interpersonal Communication." *Human Communication Research* 1, no. 4, pp. 323–32.

McGrath, J. 2015. You Can Still Call About 40 Percent of US Households on a Landline. Retrieved from www.digitaltrends.com/home/you-can-still-call-about-40-percent-of-u-s-households-on-a-landline/

Michaelson, D. 2007. "Best Practices of Public Relations Research." Paper presented at the InterAmerican Public Relations Summit, Barranquilla, Colombia.

Michaelson, D. 1979. *From Ethnography to Ethnology: A Study of the Conflict of Interpretations of the Southern Kwakiutl Potlach*, 140. Ann Arbor, MI: University Microforms.

Michaelson, D., and D.W. Stacks. 2011. "Standardization in Public Relations Measurement and Evaluation." *Public Relations Journal* 5, no. 2, pp. 1–25.

Michaelson, D., and D.W. Stacks. 2007. *Exploring the Comparative Communications Effectiveness of Advertising and Public Relations: An Experimental Study of Initial Branding Advantage*. Gainesville, FL: Institute for Public Relations, Retrieved from www.instituteforpr.org/topics/advertising-media-placement-effectiveness/

Michaelson, D., and S. Macleod. 2007. "The Application of "Best Practices" in Public Relations Measurement and Evaluation Systems." *Public Relations Journal* 1, no. 1. Retrieved from www.prsa.org/prjournal/fall07.html

Michaelson, D., and T. Griffin. 2005. *A New Model for Media Content Analysis*. Gainesville, FL: Institute for Public Relations. Retrieved from www.instituteforpr.org/topics/new-model-for-media-content-analysis/

Michaelson, D., and T. Griffin. 2009. *The Media Reality Check: A New Approach to Content Analysis*. Gainesville, FL: Institute for Public Relations, www.instituteforpr.org/research/awards/golden-ruler/winners/2009-golden-ruler/

Michaelson, D., D.K. Wright, and D.W. Stacks. 2012. "Evaluating Efficacy in Public Relations/Corporate Communication Programming: Towards Establishing Standards of Campaign Performance." *Public Relations Journal* 6, no. 5, pp. 1–22.

Miller, D. 2002. *Handbook of Research Design and Social Measurement* 6th ed. Newbury Park, CA: Sage.

Miller, G.R., and M. Burgoon. 1974. *New Techniques of Persuasion*. New York, NY: Holt, Rinehart & Winston.

Miller, M.D., and T. Levine. 2009. "Persuasion." In *An Integrated Approach to Communication Theory and Research*, eds. D.W. Stacks and M.B. Salwen, 245–259. 2nd ed. New York, NY: Routledge.

Nefuri.com. n.d. "What Percent of the Country Has an Unlisted Phone Number?" Retrieved from www.nefuri.com/What_percent_of_the_country_has_an_unlisted_phone_number_702571.html

The New York Times. Group Attitudes Corporation Was Founded by John and Jane Mapes in 1950 and acquired by Hill & Knowlton in 1956. September 11, 1990.

Osgood, C., G. Suci, and P. Tannenbaum. 1957. *The Measurement of Meaning*. Urbana, IL: University of Illinois Press.

Oxford English Dictionary. n.d. Retrieved from www.oxforddictionaries.com/us/definition/american_english/standard?q=standards

Pew Research Center. 2015. "The Challenges of Polling When Fewer People Are Available to Be Polled." Retrieved from www.pewresearch.org/fact-tank/2015/07/21/the-challenges-of-polling-when-fewer-people-are-available-to-be-polled/

Pew Research Center. 2013. "Social Networking Fact Sheet." www.pewinternet.org/fact-sheets/social-networking-fact-sheet/

Pritchard, B., and S. Smith. 2015. *The Public Relations Firm*. New York: Business Expert Press.

PR Week. 2009. *Study: Recession Didn't Slow Consumers' Appetite for Cause-Fueled Products*. Retrieved from www.prweekus.com/Study-Recession-didnt-slow-consumers-appetite-for-cause-fueled products/article/155871/

Rawlins, B. 2007. Corporate and Governmental Transparency (openness). Paper presented at the International Congress on Corporate Communication, Barranquilla, Colombia, SA.

Rubin, R., A. Rubin, and H. Haridakisk. 2010. *Communication Research Strategies and Resources* 10th ed. Boston, MA: Wadsworth.

Rubin, R.B., P. Palmgreen, and H.E. Sypher. 1994. *Communication Research Measures: A Sourcebook*. New York, NY: Guilford.

Schutz, D.E., S.I. Tannenbaum, and R.F. Lauterborn. 1998. *Integrated Marketing Communications: Putting It Together and Making It Work*. Lincolnwood, IL: NTC Business Books.

Scott, W. 1955. "Reliability of Content Analysis: The Case of Nominal Scale Coding." *Public Opinion Quarterly* 19, no. 3, pp. 321–25.

Stacks, D.W. 2002. *Primer of Public Relations Research*. New York, NY: Guilford.

Stacks, D.W. 2011. *Primer of Public Relations Research* 2nd ed. New York, NY: Guildford.

Stacks, D.W. 2013. *Second Thoughts on Secondary Research*. Retrieved from www.instituteforpr.org/2013/06/second-thoughts-on-secondary-research/

Stacks, D.W. 2016. Understanding Standards and Practices in Social Media Research and Evaluation. Proceedings of the 1st Annual Conference of the Public Relations Society of China/9th International Forum on Public Relations and Advertising, pp. VIII–XXIV.

Stacks, D.W. 2017. *Primer of Public Relations Research*, 3rd ed. New York: Guilford.

Stacks, D.W., and S.A. Bowen, eds. 2013. *Dictionary of Public Relations Research and Measurement*. Gainesville, FL: Institute for Public Relations. Retrieved from www.instituteforpr.org/topics/dictionary-of-public-relations-measurement-and-research/

Stacks, D.W., and T. Carroll. 2004. *Bibliography of Public Relations Measurement*. Gainesville, FL: Institute for Public Relations. Retrieved from www.instituteforpr.org/topics/bibliography-of-pr-measurement/

Stacks, D.W., and D. Michaelson. 2004. A Pilot Study of the "Multiplier Effect" Presented at the Summit on Measurement, Durham, NH.

Stacks, D.W., and D. Michaelson. 2009. "Exploring the Comparative Communications Effectiveness of Advertising and Public Relations: A Replication and Extension of Prior Experiments." *Public Relations Journal* 3, no. 3, pp. 1–22. Retrieved from www.measurementmatch.com/Michaelson_Adv_vs_PR.pdf

Stacks, D.W., and D. Michaelson. 2010. *A Practitioner's Guide to Public Relations Research, Measurement, and Evaluation.* New York, NY: Business Expert Press.

Stacks, D.W., and M.B. Salwen, eds. 2009. *An Integrated Approach to Communication Theory and Research* 2nd ed. New York, NY: Rutledge.

Stephen, J.B., N. Ganesh, J.V. Luke, and G. Gonzales. 2013. *Wireless Substitution: State-level Estimates From the National Health Interview Survey, January 2007– June 2010.* Retrieved from www.cdc.gov/nchs/data/ nhsr/nhsr039.pdf

Taylor, F. 1919. *The Principles of Scientific Management.* New York, NY: Harper & Brothers Publishers.

Thurstone, L.L., and E.J. Chave. 1929. *The Measurement of Attitude.* Chicago, IL: University of Chicago Press.

Tinsley, H.E.A., and D.J. Weiss. 2000. "Interrater Reliability and Agreement." In *Handbook of Applied Multivariate Statistics and Mathematical Modeling,* eds. H.E.A. Tinsley and S.D. Brown, 95–124. San Diego: Academic Press.

Toth, E.L. 2009. *The Future of Excellence in Public Relations and Communication Management: Challenges for the Next Generation.* Mahwah, NJ: Lawrence Erlbaum.

U.S. Department of Commerce. n.d. United States Census Bureau. Retrieved from www.census.gov

Waksberg, J. 1978. "Sampling Methods for Random Digit Dialing." *Journal of the American Statistical Association* 73, no. 361, pp. 40–46.

Weiner, M. 2007. *Unleashing the Power of PR: A Contrarian's Guide to Marketing and Communication.* San Francisco, CA: International Association of Business Communicators.

Wikipedia. n.d. Search Engine Optimization. http://en.wikipedia.org/wiki/Search_engine_optimization

Williams, F., and P. Monge. 2001. *Reasoning with Statistics: How to Read Quantitative Research,* 5th ed. Fort Worth, TX: Harcourt College Publishers.

Wright, D.W. 1990. *Presentation Made to the Jacksonville Chamber of Commerce.* Jacksonville, FL.

Index

OTHER TITLES IN OUR PUBLIC RELATIONS COLLECTION

Don W. Stacks and Donald K. Wright, Editors

- *Public Relations Ethics: How To Practice PR Without Losing Your Soul* by Dick Martin and Donald K. Wright
- *MetricsMan: It Doesn't Count Unless You Can Count It* by Don Bartholomew and Zifei Fay Chen
- *Public Relations for the Public Good: How PR Has Shaped America's Social Movements* by Shelley Spector and Louis Capozzit
- *Excellence in Internal Communication Management* by Rita Linjuan Men and Shannon A. Bowen

Announcing the Business Expert Press Digital Library

Concise e-books business students need for classroom and research

This book can also be purchased in an e-book collection by your library as

- a one-time purchase,
- that is owned forever,
- allows for simultaneous readers,
- has no restrictions on printing, and
- can be downloaded as PDFs from within the library community.

Our digital library collections are a great solution to beat the rising cost of textbooks. E-books can be loaded into their course management systems or onto students' e-book readers.
The **Business Expert Press** digital libraries are very affordable, with no obligation to buy in future years. For more information, please visit **www.businessexpertpress.com/librarians**. To set up a trial in the United States, please email **sales@businessexpertpress.com**.